BIRTH

By the same author:

In a Different Time: the inside story of the Delmas four

PETER HARRIS

BIRTH

The Conspiracy to Stop the '94 Election

UMUZI

for Caroline

Published in 2010 by Umuzi
an imprint of Random House Struik (Pty) Ltd
Company Reg No 1966/003153/07
80 McKenzie Street, Cape Town 8001, South Africa
P O Box 1144, Cape Town 8000, South Africa
umuzi@randomstruik.co.za
www.randomstruik.co.za

First edition, first printing 2010
9 8 7 6 5 4 3 2 1

ISBN 978-1-4152-0102-2

Cover design by publicide
Text design by 128Design
Set in Aldus
Printed and bound by Interpak Books,
Pietermaritzburg, South Africa

AUTHOR'S NOTE

When I look back at how we got through the years of hatred, oppression, violence and our potential implosion as a country, I shake my head in wonder. There are many stories of those times, from the personal to the national. This is my story of the final part of that journey. It is also the story of those forces which conspired to stop and steal our country's first democratic election.

I am indebted to all those who gave generously of their time in the interviews and discussions, they are too numerous to mention.

I must acknowledge the following works as valuable sources of information for this book: *Tomorrow is Another Country* by Allister Sparks; *Mandela: The Authorised Biography* by Anthony Sampson; *Election '94 South Africa* by Andrew Reynolds; *Long Walk to Freedom* by Nelson Mandela; *Days of the Generals* by Hilton Hamann; *A South African Story* (unpublished) by Dr Anthony Turton. The extensive documentation sourced from the hearings of the Truth and Reconciliation Commission, IEC source material and voluminous press reports are also acknowledged.

I must thank Ivan Vladislavić for his invaluable advice and Charles Nupen for his comments on the book. My special thanks goes to Mike Nicol who edited the book and did so marvellously. I am deeply grateful to the Resolve Group whose three-month sabbatical gave me the opportunity to make real inroads into the completion of this book.

Finally, to my family, whose abiding love is my true inspiration.

PETER HARRIS
September 2010

PROLOGUE

I wake to a beautiful morning. Soon the country's first democratic election will be over and I shall return to my law practice and work a reasonably normal day. For three months I have been buried in the anxieties, the tensions, the dangers, the tribulations that went with putting this election together. My life has not been my own. It has belonged to the Independent Electoral Commission.

But now that madness is finally over.

I have slept well, and with my wife, Caroline, and the children, we sit down to eat our varied breakfasts.

It is Tuesday, 3 May 1994.

Outside it is cold as winter settles in. The trees are empty, the grass brown.

I take a mouthful of cereal. I am truly enjoying this breakfast.

Then my bleeper goes.

I know I have to look at it; I don't want to look at it. But I can't help myself. It's a message from the operations centre at the IEC: 'You need to get here now. We have a real problem, we've found something.'

The ops centre is the heart of the IEC. When something goes wrong there my pulse races.

I phone the centre. 'What's the problem?'

'It's in the results control centre,' I'm told. 'Sorry Peter, we can't talk about this over the phone.'

A stillness descends on me. I shiver and gasp for breath, suddenly feeling more than the chill of the winter morning.

I don't finish my breakfast. I no longer have an appetite for it anyway.

As I drive into downtown Johannesburg to the headquarters of the IEC, the dread keeps me staring straight ahead, trying not to speculate, yet wondering if the system in the counting centre has inexplicably crashed. Have our worst fears come to pass?

I park in the basement and take the lift to the ground floor, and then another to the secure floor of the operations centre, cursing the time it's taking, envying the staff chatting cheerfully.

The lift stops at every floor. It is unbearable. I want to push people out. I want to tell them to get a move on. I do not. The doors of the lift play their game too, staying open long after people have stepped out, before they close nervously.

On the floor below the operations centre, the doors open and three large men get in. I can see that they are security policemen: the suits never fit and the haircuts are never quite civilian, like birds without their feathers. We wait for the doors to close. They don't. The lift alarm goes, we are overweight. We look at one another. I wonder if the large policemen will observe the unspoken rule that the last in is the first out. I want to shout, Get out, get out. I cannot afford this delay. One of the large men smiles, backs out. The lift doors close, it rises slowly upwards.

At the ops centre my troubleshooter, Fred Hayward, is waiting. His face is drawn with fatigue. He guides me to my office, closing the door.

I look at him expectantly.

'Someone has hacked into the counting program,' he blurts out. 'It has been compromised.'

Again the cold, the breathlessness.

'What's the result?'

'The votes of three of the political parties have been multi-plied.'

'My God!' I am trying to remain calm, avoiding the terrifying and unspeakable thought that if the count is compromised, there is no election. It will have to be run again. But before that the country might erupt in violence. 'By how much?'

'We don't know yet, but at least by a couple of per cent for each of the three parties. It could even be by as much as ten per cent of the national vote. We will have to run a detailed check. We are pulling everyone in.'

'Okay.' I ask the obvious question even though I know the answer. 'Which parties have had their votes multiplied?'

'The Freedom Front, the National Party and the Inkatha Freedom Party.'

I am partly right. I had thought that it might be all of the main opposition parties, any party that would reduce the votes of the African National Congress. The objective is clear: the changes will not stop an ANC victory but will ensure that they are well below the two-thirds majority that would give them the power to change the constitution. It is a figure on which certain groups have become fixated over recent months, despite the assurances of the ANC leadership that they won't touch the constitution.

'Can the counting continue?' I ask.

'You don't understand, Pete,' Hayward says. 'The whole system has been hacked into. It is not just compromised. It is finished, the count is over. Whoever did this has the keys to the kingdom. We don't know who this person is. It could be anyone, anywhere. It could be one of the staff who originally worked on the program and installed it. It could be one of the staff who currently works on those computers every day in that secure room. It could be a senior person or a junior. It could be anyone. It could be a group. It could be someone sitting in Bangkok.'

He's right. We've had it. This is the end. After the bombs, the killing, the temporary calm of the election, we could be facing riots within hours, dreadful strife within days. We are back in the dark times of seven years ago.

CHAPTER ONE

It is 1987. It is the year the conflict that started in Natal lights a fire which cannot be extinguished.

Aided by covert groupings in the South African Police Force, the Inkatha Freedom Party wage a war on the ANC and its supporters which threatens to reduce whole swathes of the country to a wasteland. In those early days of the violence outside Pietermaritzburg, my colleagues Halton Cheadle and Clive Plasket and I bring successive Supreme Court applications in an attempt to interdict Inkatha from carrying out acts of violence.

In this we are instructed by Jay Naidoo and Alec Erwin of Cosatu (the Congress of South African Trade Unions), the local churches and certain community associations. After eleven court interdicts are obtained, we hope that the violence will stop. It does not. It continues through 1988, 1989 into 1990. It continues through the unbanning of the political movements, the release of political prisoners, the release of Nelson Mandela. The death toll mounts.

It is Saturday, 14 July 1990. Chief Mangosuthu Buthelezi, the leader of Inkatha, formally launches the organisation as a national political party. The cultural organisation that had been Inkatha, with its heartland in Natal and KwaZulu, quickly moves into other regions of the country. Busloads of Zulus from KwaZulu invade the hostels in the townships around Johannesburg, evicting non-Zulus. The real objective of the expansion is, of course, to establish political bases in the Transvaal, the industrial engine of the country's economy.

Inkatha do not waste time and barely a week after its launch, fighting breaks out between them and ANC supporters in Sebokeng, a township in the Vaal Triangle. The result: more than thirty dead. It is the beginning of the nightmare.

Using the hostels as a springboard, attacks are launched into the nearby communities: massacres of innocent train commuters by gangs of men in balaclavas, drive-by shootings, bombs in bars, attacks on clubs and commuters at taxi ranks, assassinations and random murder, women and children included.

In 1990, there is a hundred and sixty-three per cent increase in political violence, a magnification of murder on an unprecedented scale. It is the worst year of political violence in modern South African history. Three thousand six hundred and ninety-three people die.

It is in this context of looming civil war, murder and social dislocation that trade unions, businesses and churches hold discussions to address the deteriorating situation. The initial discussions take place in an upstairs private room at the Turn and Tender Steakhouse in Braamfontein, Cosatu's meeting place of choice for highly confidential discussions. It is there that the debates go on long into the night. Jay and Jayendra Naidoo of Cosatu, Halton Cheadle and Fink Haysom from Cheadle Thompson & Haysom, and Andre Lamprecht from Barlow Rand lead the discourse. The deliberations are assisted by the liquid largesse of Mervyn, the likeable owner of the restaurant. As the hours tick by, he keeps the drinks coming.

The discussions are premised on the recognition that the Nationalist government is either unable or unwilling to provide the necessary security that will ensure a relatively stable transition to democracy. A peace accord is called for. The premise of such an accord is based on the principle that everyone will want to endorse peace or at least be seen to endorse it. Which leader will stand up and not want to pledge to reduce the violence? Once committed, it is reasoned, the rest will follow and the parties will be bound more tightly.

After the building blocks for a peace accord are agreed, the discussions will broaden to include the National Party, Democratic

Party, smaller political parties, security forces and other groupings in civil society. It is a club of which few can afford not to be members.

Intensive negotiations produce a National Peace Accord, which is signed on Saturday, 14 September 1991 by all the major parties except the white right-wing groupings, the Pan Africanist Congress and the Azanian People's Organisation.

The chairman of the political structure governing the Peace Accord at national level is John Hall, a former executive director of Barlow Rand. The structures of the Peace Accord operate at a national, regional and local level throughout the country and include a commission of enquiry into the violence headed by Judge Richard Goldstone as well as special courts to deal with the perpetrators of violence. The primary purpose of the Peace Accord is to end or curtail the political violence and to ensure enough stability for negotiations to take place. Its stated aims are to 'create peace in South Africa and help in the development of its people and the reconstruction of society'.

It is December 1991. Codesa – the Convention for a Democratic South Africa – gets under way at the World Trade Centre in Kempton Park, with two hundred and twenty-eight delegates representing nineteen political parties. Like many courtships, it is off to a rocky start, with Nelson Mandela taking offence at a speech by President F W de Klerk and launching a stinging personal attack on him. De Klerk had accused the ANC of breaching an agreement to disband its army. Notable parties absent from Codesa are the Pan Africanist Congress and the Inkatha Freedom Party.

At the request of the political parties, I have been seconded from my law firm Cheadle Thompson & Haysom to head up the Witwatersrand–Vaal region of the National Peace Accord. It is May 1992. We quickly establish a substantial functioning structure, supplementing the funds provided through the government-funded peace structures with money raised from business.

I am fortunate to have as my deputy a young man by the name of David Storey. Storey, a lawyer by qualification, has an exceptional ability to plan and organise. This capacity, combined with an inspiring energy, makes the difficult job of ensuring peace in a dangerous region more achievable. There are others: Mahlape Sello, also a lawyer, and Carlson Ndaba, a taxi owner from the East Rand, a formidable giant of a man who never seems to stress and who is always available to go into tough situations. He's a volunteer who had walked into our offices, saying that he was sick of the violence and wanted to help end it.

Supported by the United Nations, the European Union, the Commonwealth, and African Union observers, we and thousands of trained monitors try to make the parties adhere to the code of conduct which they promised to uphold when they signed the Peace Accord. The monitors are volunteers and come from all walks of life: poor black township residents, unemployed youth, whites from the suburbs, professionals, factory workers, and retired men and women. They read about the work of the Peace Accord in the press and they phone or simply walk in the door, offering to help.

The work is arduous, starting at five in the morning on the weekends and ending late at night, generally in tough areas. More than that, the work is extremely dangerous.

Because hardly anyone in this country is truly impartial, monitors are grouped in teams of three or four. There is safety in numbers. Each team ideally contains a mix of people as far as race, age and political affiliations are concerned. After rigorous training in their duties as well as first aid, basic aspects of the law and conflict resolution skills, they are deployed with radios and Peace Accord insignia. On occasions too numerous to mention, they intervene in violent confrontations, resolve conflict and save lives. Gradually, over months, the teams coalesce as they learn to trust one another in traumatic and often life-threatening situations. Each evening they arrive back in the offices at Braamfontein, exhausted but charged with adrenaline, full of stories of their day, arms on shoulders as they stand at the long bar installed by the previous tenant, drinking the dry dust of the township from their throats. Sometimes, they come back after a particularly traumatic and violent day on the East Rand or in Sebokeng and there is silence as they stand at the bar, unable to speak, staring straight ahead. Some cry silently like people bereft; others sob, a dam breaking.

Camaraderie develops among these volunteers. They watch each other's backs, care for each other, recognising that regardless of politics, colour or origins, they are bound by a common commitment to one another and to reducing the violence destroying the country.

The Peace Accord volunteers patrol and monitor the areas hardest hit by the violence, places like Katlehong, Thokoza, Vosloorus, Daveyton, Evaton, Sebokeng, Boipatong, Bophelong, Sharpeville, Alexandra, Tembisa and, of course, Soweto. There are eighteen local peace committees covering the region. Meeting weekly and consisting of the main political parties, security forces, churches and civil society groupings, they address key issues in their community that could cause or lead to violence. Mass gatherings, political party meetings, marches, and funerals, all potential battlegrounds are strictly monitored and controlled to reduce conflict.

It is Friday, 15 May 1992. Codesa Two gets under way but soon collapses in a heap of recriminations with the major issue being the percentage required for the constituent assembly to take certain decisions. The ANC proposes a two-thirds majority, saying it is the norm internationally to change ordinary clauses in the constitution, while the government wants seventy-five per cent. Despite the ANC moving to seventy per cent for ordinary clauses and to seventy-five per cent for clauses of the Bill of Fundamental Human Rights in the constitution, the government remains intractable and refuses to move. Deadlock.

On Tuesday, 16 June 1992, the ANC commences its campaign of rolling mass action as political violence intensifies. There are mass killings in the midst of a radical escalation of violence on the East Rand and in Natal.

It is September 1992: a summit meeting is convened in Johannesburg between FW de Klerk and Nelson Mandela after the leadership in their parties realises that something must be done to halt the slide into conflict and violence. The country is on a descent into hell. The summit is preceded by numerous meetings where critical issues and pre-conditions are thrashed out and agreed. The result of the summit is a record of understanding in terms of which the two sides agree to resume negotiations.

The adage 'my enemy's enemy is my friend' is given firm expression in the shifting sands of South African splinter politics when Inkatha sign a 'non aggression' pact with the AWB (Afrikaner Weerstandsbeweging or Afrikaner Resistance Movement). It is late in 1992. The leadership of both organisations hold a press conference, publicly shaking hands to seal the deal.

The white right-wing are a fractious lot. Ever since the release of Nelson Mandela and the other political prisoners and the un-banning of the banned political organisations, they have gathered in their opposition to an integrated non-racial South Africa. They see this as a betrayal of their heritage and their people. Certainly, any election that may result in whites losing power will not just be opposed; it will be resisted by force.

The official parliamentary mouthpiece of the white right is the Conservative Party, which in 1993 is the official opposition to the National Party. Outside parliament, there is a range of right-wing groupings, from the loud and dangerous to the plain loud. The difficulty is in telling them apart. They are, however, united on two issues: no negotiations with the ANC and definitely no election for all the citizens of South Africa.

It is for this reason that the Conservative Party and all the extra-paramilitary white right-wing bodies refuse to participate in the negotiation process, preferring rather to align themselves with other parties and entities that have also decided to boycott the talks.

Thus the white right bands together with Inkatha (which claims to speak for the Zulu people) and a range of homeland presidents from Chief Mangope of Bophuthatswana to Brigadier Oupa Gqozo of the Ciskei – suspect types whose interests would be threatened by a democratic and unitary South Africa.

The AWB is the largest of the extreme right-wing paramilitary groups in the country. It is led by a bull of a man called Eugène Ney Terre'Blanche. He is determined to live up to his name, meaning 'white earth'. Terre'Blanche's family arrived in South Africa in 1704 from Toulon in France as part of the French Huguenots. His grandfather fought for the Boer cause as a Cape rebel in the Second Boer War and his father was a lieutenant colonel in the defence force.

Born in Ventersdorp in 1944, he captained the Potchefstroom Hoër Volkskool rugby team and then joined the South African Police, later becoming a warrant officer in the Special Guard Unit whose duties included the protection of cabinet members and the prime minister. Terre'Blanche, increasingly disturbed by the liberal direction being taken by Prime Minister B J Vorster, formed the AWB with six like-minded souls in 1973 in a garage in Heidelberg, southeast of Johannesburg.

Terre'Blanche, now fifty, with his full strong beard and steely blue eyes, has a voice that is a mixture of gravel, brandy and tobacco. It is an orator's voice, rich and powerful, which he uses to excellent effect in his speeches. Terre'Blanche holding forth on a platform in camouflage uniform or his khaki jacket with the AWB swastika, fiery and impassioned, full of imagery on the heritage of the Afrikaner people, has a messianic quality to his followers.

This man, who promises to lead them to their homeland, has a devoted and fanatical following, and is not afraid to openly proclaim his defiance of the Nationalist government that he brands as 'verraaiers', traitors to their people and their God. Terre'Blanche is less subtle than his colleagues in the Conservative Party. He threatens the ANC with 'total war'.

While Terre'Blanche is a man who commands respect among the faithful, his actions at times detract from the seriousness of his cause. It is rumoured that he drinks and is inclined to fall about a bit. On one occasion at a large AWB rally in the middle of Pretoria, he fell from his horse, hitting the tarmac with a dull thud. Journalists unkindly implied that he was not sober and that he seemed to be 'in trouble' from the moment he mounted his charge. AWB spokesmen lamented his fall but blamed the horse, stating that the unlucky steed had stumbled. Whatever the truth, it didn't look good. Boer fighters in the South African War of 1898 – 1902 were regarded as the finest horsemen in the world. When the somewhat porky leader of a modern-day Boer commando, who claimed the mantle of the great Boer leaders of the past, fell off his horse, it made people chuckle, if not snigger. Worse still, some cruel journalists sympathised with the beast rather than its burden.

Regardless of the trials and tribulations of its charismatic leader, within the AWB there is such reverence and respect for Eugène Terre'Blanche that he is not referred to by name, but by the title of 'The Leader'. Terre'Blanche prefers it that way.

Beneath the Leader are the generals in staff or fighting generals, as they are known to the rank and file. (The AWB assigns conventional military titles to its office bearers.) They are also members of the Uitvoerende Raad or Executive Council. The secretary of the generals in staff is a man by the name of Nico Prinsloo. Nico Prinsloo has significant military experience and expertise from his time in the South African Defence Force. This includes operational and combat experience in the Namibian bush war against Swapo and the Angolans, having been stationed at one of the most northerly SADF military bases, Katima Mulilo, where he held the rank of warrant officer.

Prinsloo's rapid rise in the ranks of the AWB is the cause of speculation and envy. As he only joined the AWB in early 1992, his progress has been nothing short of meteoric. In November 1992, he is appointed a general, in addition to being the secretary. This post carries the responsibility of heading the administration as well as the coveted and critical gatekeeper role of being the liaison officer between the fighting generals and the Leader. He is also responsible for liaison with the police and the SADF, and he's the point man with right-wing organisations across the globe. Prinsloo has access not only to information but to the Leader. Outside the AWB, like most of the fighting generals, he is a farmer and also works as a part-time insurance salesman.

The AWB structure is largely based on that of the SADF, and strict military discipline is the order of the day. Within the AWB, there is the Wenkommando or Win Commando led by a kommandant-generaal appointed by the fighting generals. His name is General Dirk Ackerman. The Wenkommando is divided into groups and commando areas. The fighting generals comprise the commanders responsible for each province as well as a number of additional generals. They gather monthly in group meetings, closed affairs as their discussions are top secret. Sometimes they meet at AWB headquarters at Ventersdorp but they are as likely to gather at restaurants, where they come casually dressed in order not to attract attention. This is in stark contrast to the open meetings of the AWB, where it is mandatory to appear in the full uniform.

Beneath the generals are the colonels, although the commander of AWB special forces has the higher rank of brigadier. Thereafter, in descending order, are four chief commandants, each in charge of a region of the country, followed by the normal commandants, then the majors, captains, lieutenants, field cornets, corporals and lance corporals.

The AWB also has its own medical corps, a logistics corps and an 'air wing'. Ominously, there is a general who is placed in charge of explosives, more familiarly known to his colleagues as 'the explosives general'. His name is Andre Smit. Generals are also appointed to look after issues of culture and recreation.

The women of the AWB are also organised into a unit. They are known as the Rooivalke, or Red Falcons, and receive weapons and unarmed combat training.

As with many fighting organisations structured along military lines, there is an elite component, that special band of men who guard the principals and inner sanctum of the organisation, men whose devotion and commitment are beyond question and who will lay down their lives for the Leader and the AWB. They are the Ystergarde, or Iron Guards, a crack unit responsible for the protection of the Leader. They are also the strike force of the AWB. As is customary in such matters, the Ystergarde report directly to the Leader. They are led by Brigadier Leon van der Merwe. Aspirant Ystergarde are known as candidate officers, until they have received their training and qualify to wear the distinctive and prized black uniform of the Garde. On qualifying, the candidate officers jump to the rank of lieutenant or captain.

The Ystergarde wear the logo of the AWB, the three-legged swastika, as a shoulder flash. On each lapel of their black shirts is a silver eagle and on their heads they wear a black cap adorned with the organisation's badge. Rallies and horseback processions are a feature of the AWB, with Terre'Blanche in his uniform and shiny knee-length boots leading on his horse. He carries a flowing red flag with a large white circle, in the middle of which is the chilling bastard swastika. The Ystergarde follow, the commanders each carrying their own AWB flag. The pageantry of the Nazis in Germany in the 1930s has not been lost on the AWB.

Terre'Blanche's organisation has many affiliate or aligned organisations of varying strength and right-wing political potency. They include the Orde Boerevolk, led by Piet 'Skiet' Rudolph, which is well to the right of the AWB and which has its own oath.

Even further to the right are other groups like the Orde van die Dood.

It is March 1993 at the World Trade Centre. A new Negotiating Council convenes, comprising twenty-six parties. The real players are two men in their early forties whose ability to negotiate, combined with their vision for their country, are to make them household names in South Africa and abroad.

The ANC negotiating team is led by Cyril Ramaphosa, the former general secretary of the National Union of Mineworkers and the current secretary general of the ANC. I represented Ramaphosa through most of the 1980s and early 1990s as his lawyer and knew him as a man of immense personal charm. His skills honed by years of negotiations with many of the largest mining houses in the world, he is arguably the best negotiator in the country, possessing an uncanny ability to read the situation as well as the minds of his opponents. These attributes, combined with an impeccable sense of judgement and an acute intellect, make him a formidable adversary. Ramaphosa is a man who never has to shout to be heard, treading softly but leaving a massive print.

His opposite number is Roelf Meyer, the minister of constitutional development. Meyer, whose forefathers came to South Africa more than three hundred years ago, is Afrikaner aristocracy from a lineage born to inherit the country, as generations had before him. History has left it to him to negotiate the best deal possible for his people. They might have the strongest army in Africa, but they are bereft of moral authority, bankrupt, their backs to the wall. Clever, considered and charming, Meyer looks much younger than his forty-five years. Meyer, like Ramaphosa, is a man of vision and knows where the country has to go, realising that the future can only be a common one as we emerge from our terrible past.

The Negotiating Council has made real progress. A growing consensus is developing between the government and ANC negotiating teams, although it's tainted by an increasing sense of marginalisation from Inkatha and particularly its leader, Chief Buthelezi. He feels jilted by the government. Which is exactly what has happened, and no one likes to be jilted. Then, as with so much in this country, when all appears to be on course and a happy ending is in sight, the unthinkable happens.

It is Saturday morning, 10 April 1993. I am driving with Jayendra Naidoo to the home of Chris Hani. An hour earlier I'd received a call at home that he'd been shot. Hani was the general secretary of the Communist Party and a former commander in chief of Umkhonto we Sizwe (MK), the military wing of the ANC. He'd been shot in the driveway of his home at Dawn Park near Boksburg on the East Rand. His murder was a catastrophe. It pitched the country nearer to civil war.

Chris Hani was a legendary MK fighter and one of its most popular heroes. I had met him, a quietly spoken man, a number of times while he was in exile, when I represented ANC guerrillas who had been arrested and brought to trial. I had always found him impressive and considered, far from the satanic public enemy number one that the government considered him to be.

On his return to South Africa, I had assisted him on a number of issues. During one of our consultations in his office in downtown Johannesburg – in the same building that housed Cosatu – he told me that he had just survived what he thought was an assassination attempt. He had been walking in the street when a silver Toyota Cressida had pulled up next to him. Two men got out, headed in his direction. They had their hands in their jackets and appeared ready to draw weapons, surely guns, Chris thought. He had body-guards with him and they drew their own weapons and faced the men from the Cressida. For a moment there was a standoff, then the men turned and got back into the car, which drove off. Chris had taken down the registration number, but when I ran a check, the plates were false. The trail ended there.

Now he is dead and I am petrified that the youth of the country, who idolised him, will rebel and attack the cities, stripping them like locusts, angered at the murder of one of their most charismatic leaders.

Thankfully, due to the intervention of Hani's white neighbour, an Afrikaans woman called Retha Harmse, the killer's car is identified and the killer arrested thirty minutes later. He is a Polish immigrant and well-known right-winger, Janusz Waluś. A few hours later Clive Derby-Lewis, another right-wing leader, and his wife are arrested. Derby-Lewis is a leading member of the Conservative Party.

Things cannot be worse as the country braces itself for the funeral. I fear that it will be the spark that ignites the blaze that will burn the country.

Mandela goes on national television to make a speech that gives me gooseflesh. 'A white man, full of prejudice and hate, came to our country and committed a deed so foul that our whole nation now teeters on the brink of disaster. But a white woman, of Afrikaner origin, risked her life so that we may know, and bring to justice, the assassin.' He appeals to both black and white for calm, and that they should not let this event destroy their future.

Much of the night prior to the funeral is spent at our offices mediating a code of conduct between the ANC and the police. The agreement is finally signed by the commissioner of police for the province and Thabo Mbeki, representing the ANC. The agreement makes the leadership of both the police and the ANC responsible for its enforcement.

One hundred thousand people fill the First National Bank stadium in Soweto for the funeral. I am in one of the private boxes in the stands in which we have set up a joint operations centre to monitor the situation and avert conflict or violence. I know the country is on a knife-edge. I feel that it will take a miracle to survive this crisis.

Surprisingly, the murder of Chris Hani, far from derailing the transition and plunging the country into chaos, impels the lead negotiators on both sides to publicly commit themselves to negotiating a settlement as soon as possible. This is surely the opposite of what Waluś and Derby-Lewis intended.

The assassination of Chris Hani galvanises the right wing and results in the formation of the Afrikaner Volksfront. It is May 1993.

The AWB and right-wing groupings seize on the words of the Boer Nostradamus and folk hero, Nicolaas 'Siener' van Rensburg, who lived from 1862 to 1926. Siener van Rensburg had prophesied that a powerful black leader would die and that a white disciple in a brown suit would take power and lead the Volk to war. The AWB, perhaps thinking of Terre'Blanche's khaki outfit, is quick to point out that the Leader is qualified to fulfil the prophecy. It is his destiny. Whatever relevance is accorded to Siener van Rensburg, there is no doubt that the murder of Hani helps to coalesce the white right.

The Volksfront, led by Dr Ferdi Hartzenberg, the leader of the Conservative Party, consists of twenty-one right-wing groups and has as its objective the achievement of self-determination for the Afrikaner people. While there are disagreements as to how this should be achieved, the concept of a homeland or Volkstaat remains central to the different organisations that form the Volksfront. It is hard to estimate the extent of support for the right wing however, based on the 1992 whites-only referendum De Klerk called to get his negotiating mandate, it is estimated to be a third of the white electorate. This includes its parliamentary mouthpiece, the Conservative Party.

Constand Viljoen, a former chief of the South African Defence Force, is appointed to lead a team of retired generals who must form a Volksfront army. He's a highly decorated soldier with extensive combat experience, and carries the total respect of those he commanded. In him, the conservative forces know that they have a leader who enjoys the support of that critical constituency, the mighty South African military and security establishment.

While the AWB is part of the broad coalition of the Volksfront, it increasingly adopts a hard-line militaristic stance to the negotiations and the achievement of its goal of a Volkstaat for Afrikaners.

It is Saturday, 29 May 1993.

Eugène Terre'Blanche gives the multi-party negotiating forum six months to grant a Volkstaat or else the AWB will 'take other steps'. Dressed in his trademark khaki uniform and his South African Defence Force bush jacket, he cuts an imposing figure with a voice powerful enough to chisel through rock. He emphasises his point by smashing his fist into the lectern before him, thundering that this ultimatum will expire on Monday, 29 November 1993. To cheers and roars of approval, he bellows that after that date the AWB will accept no responsibility for preventing people from using whatever means to ensure their freedom. The statement is abruptly underlined by his stiff, open-palmed right hand slicing through the air above his shoulder.

The imponderable on everyone's minds is whether Terre'Blanche is bluffing. Does his AWB have the resources and capability to stop or derail the transition?

Just as the national political negotiations are starting to make progress, another massacre occurs, this time in Boipatong, south of Johannesburg. Zulus from the nearby hostel enter the township and, like a plague, move through the homes of the residents. It is a massacre of the weak, a bloodbath. Of the thirty-eight dead, twenty-four are women, one of whom is pregnant. There is also a dead baby. The attackers use AK47s and short stabbing spears, the kind carried by Zulu warriors. It is Thursday, 17 June 1993.

In the aftermath the police make few arrests. The investigation is botched. Incomprehensible? Perhaps not.

About three thousand white right-wingers descend on the World Trade Centre. They crowd the main entrance, pushing and shoving at the gates and flimsy fence. When a Codesa delegate arrives, the crowd surges through the open gates into the grounds. They start vandalising cars.

This is not a coherent force; rather, it is a disparate collection of right-wing elements. The men, dressed mainly in combat camouflage, wear the AWB swastika-like insignia and carry handguns, rifles, and sheathed hunting knives. Among them are the ominous black uniforms of the Ystergarde but also men in business suits and farming attire.

They are followed by women and children, carrying food and drink in packets and cooler bags. The younger men and women also have braai utensils, as if they are going on a picnic. They hive off to the extensive green lawns that frame the centre, unpacking their food and drink onto blankets.

At the doors to the centre, the few policemen present try to form a cordon around the entrance. The right-wingers in the front step aside to reveal a yellow armoured vehicle, a Viper, driving slowly towards the entrance. Once clear of the crowd, it accelerates and smashes into the thick glass doors, shattering them in a shower of brilliant shards. The vehicle comes to a halt in the foyer.

One of the men who leads the charge into the centre stands out above the others, literally. At two metres in his socks and weighing in at 115 kg, Alwyn Wolfaardt is a big man, his imposing flowing beard adding to the general impression of size. He cannot be missed in the melee. Later described by the press as 'massive, bearded and violent', he is in the forefront, marshalling his men and barking instructions. Wolfaardt is a colonel in the AWB, a rank that commands great respect in the organisation and in his hometown of Naboomspruit. The respect for Wolfaardt is also based on his track record. On that day, he does not disappoint, leading his commandos from the front.

Following closely behind the yellow Viper, and shouting to the crowd to hold back and behave, is Constand Viljoen. His pleas for restraint are totally ignored by the Ystergarde, who run into the rooms of the centre shouting that they are 'after the kaffirs in here'. They run amok. The Leader, Eugène Terre'Blanche, enters the centre, surrounded by a phalanx of bodyguards, all with firearms, their military-style boots crunching the broken glass.

Racing up the stairs the men shout, 'Kaffirs, we are going to shoot you dead today,' as they kick down doors and smash glass partitions. The delegates take refuge under tables and in rooms, fearing for their lives.

Like football hooligans, the AWB men head for the bars and slug back bottles of brandy, whisky and vodka, a drunken free-for-all as they spray-paint AWB slogans and their three-legged swastika on the walls. Delegates are harassed and pushed, one is punched in the face. In the negotiating chambers, the right-wingers urinate on the furniture to the uproarious laughter of their fellows.

The mayhem comes to an abrupt halt when a deep disembodied voice on the public address system announces an impromptu prayer meeting in the main negotiating chamber. The prayer is broadcast over the PA system and for a moment the right-wingers stop their rampage, remove their head gear and pray. Once the prayer is over, bedlam resumes.

It is Friday, 25 June 1993.

After occupying the building for some hours, the invaders agree to withdraw peacefully as long as no one is arrested. After exiting the ruined centre, some depart in their vehicles while the majority cluster around the fires of their braais with their women and snap open cold cans of beer. The belated arrival of Unit 19 of the internal stability division of the police causes much mirth in the crowd. The men hurl insults at the helmeted latecomers, raising their drinks to the puzzled police as their chops and wors sizzle on the hot coals and laughing and joking as they circle the braais, avoiding the curious silver smoke of the fires.

The arrests by police of those responsible for the invasion of the centre start on Sunday, 27 June 1993. By Monday afternoon twenty-one right-wingers have been arrested under Section 50 of the Criminal Procedure Act. To the fury of the AWB high command, they are held at police stations in Soweto, making any 'rescue' mission to release them difficult, if not impossible. The AWB leadership predicts big problems if the situation continues.

The talk of war is not confined to the AWB, with Conservative Party MP Piet Gouws saying that negotiations signing away the Afrikaner's right to self-determination will signal a declaration of war.

On Friday, 2 July 1993, government announces that a general election will be held on 27 April 1994.

The violence escalates. It is indubitable that free and fair elections cannot be held in a context of extreme violence and intimidation. An Inkatha leader in Thokoza, Gertrude Mzizi, knowingly scoffs, 'If it is too dangerous to go to the shops to buy food, people will not go out to vote!'

In this case, the elements instigating and perpetrating the violence quickly acquire a name, the 'third force'. While it is strongly suspected that they are covert police squads and we spend much time gathering evidence of their complicity, it is not easy to prove.

Despite the views of the different factions in its ranks, the Volksfront soldiers under Constand Viljoen's leadership decide to participate in the negotiating process. To this end, in July 1993 they submit a series of proposals for the creation of a Volkstaat to the technical committee of the multi-party negotiating forum. This proposal situates the Volkstaat predominantly in the Transvaal and Orange Free State. The proposed Volkstaat comprises almost seventeen per cent of the country.

The Volksfront proposal is rejected by the multi-party negotiating forum.

On the Friday night of the election announcement, the railway lines into Katlehong are sabotaged, allegedly by Inkatha hostel dwellers. The area erupts in an orgy of violence. By Monday morning, there are forty-four dead and hundreds of people have abandoned their homes and taken shelter at the Natalspruit Hospital. We organise shelter and food for them.

That night is a bloody one, twenty-nine people are killed. At 18:40, five people are murdered on Black Reef Road when the minibus in which they are travelling is fired on. Entry points to the townships are barricaded and the streets are littered with burning cars. Police declare all roads near Katlehong and Thokoza no-go areas. The fighting continues through the night, with pitched gun-battles taking place.

To add fuel to the fire, the PAC youth-wing Azanyu reiterates its call for the killing of whites as a means of curbing violence in the black townships. Azanyu president Molotlane Petlane says that although it is not policy to kill whites simply because they are white, the organisation supports the call because killing whites has the effect of bringing down the number of black deaths.

Returning from Natalspruit Hospital on Tuesday, we convene a meeting of representatives of the ANC, Inkatha, Cosatu, hostel dwellers and taxi associations in an urgent and high-level mediation. The objective is to get them to stop the fighting.

This is one of the most difficult mediations of my life, made more stressful by the certain knowledge that with each passing hour, the death toll mounts. Eventually, we get past the recriminations and accusations. The parties undertake to restore peace.

It is two-thirty in the morning. I spend some time writing up the agreement and discussing implementation with the signatories to the agreement. It is dawn when I get home, hoping to snatch a few hours' sleep. I hear on the radio that the death toll now stands at a hundred and thirty-one. Over the next few days, it slows as the peace agreement forged between the parties takes hold. The barricades are cleared, the train lines repaired, and services resumed. Until next time.

Isolated but horrific acts continue in other corners of the country. It is the night of Sunday, 25 July 1993. A thousand worshippers have gathered for the evening service at St James's Church in the suburb of Kenilworth in Cape Town. The congregation is all white and includes one hundred and fifty Russian sailors. The service is interrupted by five masked gunmen who burst into the church and shoot indiscriminately. It is a withering fire.

Eventually, they stop shooting and lob hand grenades into the worshippers trapped in the church. They leave, closing the doors behind them.

The toll is twelve dead and fifty-six injured.

The attack is believed to be the work of Apla, the armed wing of the Pan Africanist Congress. It is not the first time that white civilians have been attacked by the PAC who, unlike the ANC, has refused to suspend its armed struggle and attend the negotiations. In the past eight months, they have claimed responsibility for attacking a packed bar in Cape Town, leaving four dead, five injured. Also for hurling a hand grenade into a Christmas party at King William's Town Golf Club, and a bomb thrown into a steakhouse in Queenstown.

With some exceptions, volatile and deadly moments are avoided during the day. At night, it is different. In Thokoza a no-holds-barred war has broken out between Inkatha impis and the fighters of the self-defence units of the mainly ANC residents.

Each morning, the cars of the Wits–Vaal Peace Secretariat go out to assess the extent of the nocturnal carnage. The monitors are based at the joint operations communications centre located in a building at Natalspruit Hospital, Thokoza. The centre, conceived and set up by the Peace Secretariat, is jointly manned by the Secretariat, ANC, Inkatha, the police, and international observers. The sophisticated radio system which communicates with cars and monitors on the ground is manned by two senior policemen from Scotland Yard, seconded from the European Union. It is these early-morning Peace Accord patrols that alert the police to the bodies and the ruins, the fruit of the night.

Invariably a breakthrough in the negotiations triggers a series of shootings or a massacre. The weekends are the worst.

It is the weekend of 31 July 1993.

Thirty-one people are killed in Tembisa, including two policemen. In Thokoza, Katlehong and Phola Park another twenty-four die. Train services are suspended to the area and there is gunfire throughout the night in Twala Section in Katlehong.

At the communications centre at Natalspruit Hospital, the radios are jammed as the reports come in of attacks, killings and the wholesale burning of houses. It is too dangerous to have our cars operating in the area after dark. David Storey orders all cars to return to the centre by nightfall. It's a war zone. There is also a strong rumour that Inkatha is going to attack the communications centre as they no longer see the Peace Monitors as impartial.

It is Monday morning, 2 August 1993.

I leave the Peace Accord office in Braamfontein at six o'clock and drive to the communications centre. The volunteers manning it are busy setting up for the day. I take a car and head for Katlehong through Thokoza, weaving my way between burning tyres and the rocks that litter the road. Houses are smouldering. I don't stop. I know I am being watched.

I drive down the infamous Kumalo Street leading into Katlehong, assessing the damage ahead of the day's deployment. Suddenly a rock smashes into the side of the car, driver's side, the noise loud and shattering, frightening. I glance to the right and see a youth standing there, a bandana on his head. I slow down and stare at him. He stands in the morning light, tall, maybe fifteen or sixteen, glaring at me, challenging but not openly threatening. I accelerate away, avoiding a large boulder in the road.

A few blocks down there is a group of youths on the corner of an intersection; one has an AK47, not bothering to conceal it, the barrel pointing into the air, the posture of a child soldier. They watch me as I drive past in the white Peace Accord Honda. I wave, they gesture back and move out of sight between the houses, an ANC self-defence unit weaving through the area that has come to be known as Sarajevo Section.

I drive back along Kumalo Street, turning left into the Thokoza Police Station, wanting to speak to the commander, to get an idea of the night's casualties. Squads of young policemen from the internal stability division lounge near their Casspirs, smoking. Some with crisp clean uniforms, ready for their day's shift, others with dirty crumpled camouflage outfits, eyes bloodshot with exhaustion from the night's patrols. A group sits against the wheels of their armoured vehicles, their automatic rifles propped up next to them.

I park my car and walk to the police-station entrance. On the flaxen winter lawn is a row of bodies. All men, in civilian clothes, in the nonchalant posture of the dead, the morning sun giving them no warmth.

The duty station commander comes out from the building. I count eighteen bodies. The blood has dried on their fatal wounds, now almost orange in the spreading sun.

'You see how many of them have been shot in the head?' the commander asks, and I notice for the first time the entry holes and the chunks of missing skull on some of the bodies. In others, the exit wound is invisible, probably on the side facing the ground.

'Yes,' I say. 'Executions?'

'We don't know, we heard a story from a bystander of a man with a big handgun simply walking up to a man in the street and shooting him in the head, right there in the middle of the street in full view, last night. We keep hearing this story but no one can or wants to identify the man,' he says. 'Could be a serial killer out there, a maniac,' he mutters, walking away to the men next to the Casspirs.

Shit, I think, that's all we need, a psycho on the loose in the area, taking advantage of the slaughter to pursue his pathology. The irony of a serial killer plying his trade in this carnage stuns me. My mouth is dry, my tongue pressed hard against my palate, holding back the dread.

Later that morning, Mzulisi Mashobane from the Transkei tells a journalist that his parents burnt to death when their taxi was stopped at the entrance to Tembisa by a group of armed men. The men shot the twelve passengers before burning them in the vehicle. Mzulisi escaped when his mother threw him from the window. Looking back as he ran, he saw the men shoot his mother many times. The boy is five years old.

Another survivor of the night's carnage, Corinne, says she was chatting to a neighbour when she was accosted by a group of about fifty armed men. She pleaded with them not to shoot her as she was pregnant. Without uttering a word, one man opened fire, hitting her in the chest. Leaving her on the ground, the men walked away. She heard one of them say, 'I think the dog is dead, let's go, brothers.' Corinne and her baby miraculously survived.

A meeting of a burial society at the Scaw Metals Hostel is attacked by gunmen, killing twelve and injuring twenty. It is Sunday, 22 August 1993.

In the following days there is much talk of revenge and reprisal attacks. The fear that the violence can move onto the factory floor, thereby providing a new site for the conflict, prompts Jay Naidoo to address the workers of Scaw Metals. Moses Mayekiso, the leader of the metalworkers' union, is with him. Naidoo appeals to the workers for calm, saying that the shop floor should be a place where different political and union allegiances are respected. If there are revenge attacks now, the gunmen will try the same thing across the country and the killers will have succeeded in their objective.

It is Wednesday, 8 September 1993. I am in the nursing home with my wife Caroline, who has given birth to twin boys, Luke and Dominic. A moment's reprieve from the mayhem outside. It is hard placing this intensely personal and happy moment in the context of my daily experiences.

Two minibuses arrive at a packed taxi rank at the peak of the rush hour in Germiston. The doors open and ten attackers armed with AK47s emerge. The crowd at the taxi rank stampede in panic as the gunmen open fire and mow down the screaming commuters.

It is Wednesday, 8 September 1993.

Twenty-one people die and twenty-three are injured. The gunmen are professional killers, calmly reloading their magazines when they empty and opening fire again. Once the slaughter's over, they quickly, but without rushing, climb into their waiting transport and leave.

Two hours after the taxi-rank massacre, a minibus taxi approaching Katlehong is fired upon. Two dead and three injured.

It becomes too dangerous for our monitors to go into Katlehong and Thokoza when there are running gun battles in the streets. We have to find other ways of getting to the hotspots. Also, when the fighting starts, all ambulance and fire services into the townships are suspended. Recently there have been incidents of emergency vehicles arriving at a scene only to be fired on by the perpetrators. The Red Cross in their soft-shell vehicles perform miracles with the wounded, stabilising them, transferring them to the overflowing hospitals. One of the bravest things I have witnessed was two Red Cross medics tending a man who had been shot at an intersection. During the fire fight everyone was crouched against the low walls of the houses lining the street. Eventually, the two Red Cross medics in the middle of the road stabilised the man, got him onto a stretcher and loaded him into their vehicle. They slowly left the scene. The shooting stopped as they drove off, only to resume once they'd gone. The man survived.

Fortunately, we in the Peace Accord and the international observers generally don't get shot at. We all enjoy a strange immunity. We hope it will last.

I approach Andre Lamprecht and ask if Reunert, one of the Barlow Rand companies that makes armoured cars, could donate a few. These are the vehicles that they supply to the South African

Defence Force, but in this case we need them to save lives and protect our monitors when there is shooting. Lamprecht agrees.

A month later a press conference is held at the Newtown complex in downtown Johannesburg to announce and receive the armoured cars from Reunert. To much fanfare, the two armoured vehicles drive into a circle of media people who eagerly crowd around snapping pictures and tapping the heavy steel armour plate excitedly. Some knowledgably kick the great tyres of the armoured vehicles and then nod smugly, as if satisfied with the tyre pressure. Not being a tyre-pressure kind of guy, I stand back and simply admire these beasts that will make our work much easier. The vehicles are white and look incongruous among the high-rise buildings, gleaming and gawky alongside ordinary motor cars. A journalist standing next to Lamprecht says, 'Aren't those the Mambas that the defence force uses on the border?' referring to one of the army's preferred combat-troop carriers.

'No,' replies Lamprecht, wanting to avoid connotations of the defence force and bush wars. 'These are armoured Doves.'

The journalist wanders away, puzzled and shaking his head. 'They look a lot like Mambas to me.'

'Doves,' says Lamprecht firmly. 'They are Doves, see, there are doves painted on the doors.' He points to the symbol of the Peace Accord, a dove with an olive branch in its beak.

The confusion is compounded when the back of one of the vehicles slowly opens and out steps Mahlape Sello, the deputy director of the Peace Accord in the region. Impeccably dressed, she is followed by the massive Carlson Ndaba in Peace Accord regalia.

'My God,' says a reporter next to me, 'this is incredible. I never thought that I would see this.'

One of the iron Doves is rigged with ambulance and medical supplies as well as fire-fighting equipment. The remaining Dove has been left with its troop-carrying capacity so that it can ferry monitors and those in need. Importantly, it will give us the ability to patrol at night.

A few weeks before a meeting is due to take place between Apla and the government, at which the issue of Apla suspending its armed struggle is to be discussed, South African special forces conduct a pre-dawn raid on a house in Umtata.

It is Friday, 8 October 1993.

The justification for the attack is that the house is being used as a base for Apla, which has carried out attacks on unarmed white civilians.

In fact, the house is occupied by a number of schoolchildren home for the holidays. The raid is a disaster, with five of the children ranging in age from twelve to nineteen being shot in their beds. Apla cancel the meeting with the government.

The stark reality is that every major breakthrough in the negotiation process between the political parties is followed by an outbreak of terrible violence. When the negotiators reach an agreement on the composition of the transitional executive committee, the structure that will run South Africa in the months before the elections, we in the Wits–Vaal region of the Peace Accord are petrified that there will be another incident, another massacre of innocents. We place our monitors on full alert.

In September 1993, the Volksfront had presented a further proposal to the negotiators. This also failed to impress the main parties in the negotiations.

With each passing week, the tension mounts and Viljoen finds it increasingly difficult to reconcile the more moderate groupings in the Volksfront with the far right, made up of the Conservative Party under the leadership of Ferdi Hartzenberg and a plethora of more extreme organisations like the AWB.

With the Leader's six-month ultimatum to the multi-party negotiating forum due to expire in just over a month's time, a massive Volkskongres, or People's Congress, is held in Klerksdorp on Saturday, 9 October 1993.

The Volkskongres is preceded by a parade through the main

street of Klerksdorp by thousands of AWB soldiers, all dressed in the organisation's khaki uniform. They wear purple military berets, strikingly similar to the berets of the elite parachute battalions of the defence force and 1 Reconnaissance Commando, some of the most decorated and feared units in the entire SADF.

The procession is preceded by the Leader on his horse, a huge brown beast. In his right hand, he carries a lance to which is attached the large fluttering red flag of the AWB with the chilling three-legged swastika. Behind the Leader are his fighting generals, also on horseback. The horses have red saddle blankets with the AWB swastikas stamped on each side. And then the thousands of men marching military style, arms swinging to the regulation shoulder height, fists clenched. They march well, these men, their polished boots cracking down in unison onto the concrete.

If the troops of the AWB march well, the Ystergarde in their crisp black uniforms, their faces obscured by black balaclavas, march perfectly. They are led and flanked by their commanders on horses, also carrying the red AWB flag. It is a spectacular show of force, a giant military spectacle, chillingly reminiscent of Nuremburg.

The crowd lining the street cheers and claps as the men march past. In the crowd are children, some of whom are dressed in miniature khaki AWB uniforms.

After the parade, the meeting is addressed by Ferdi Hartzenberg and also by the Leader. It is attended by all of the AWB generals. The Leader gives a speech that has the huge crowd in a frenzy, his voice rich and deep, ringing out.

In the evening, I watch the footage of the rally at the ITN studio where Caroline works, the camera crew drinking whisky as they tell me how this man can whip up a crowd in seconds, relieved that they managed to get through another right-wing rally without being assaulted. Such rough-ups are a not infrequent occurrence at these rallies where the 'donnerse Engelse pers' is regarded as filth.

The AWB march is powerful stuff and, begrudgingly, I have to acknowledge that this man Terre'Blanche is an exceptional orator.

His silver beard jutting before him is reminiscent of the beards of his forefathers, who took on the greatest imperial power in the world. His stirring voice strikes to the very core of those present. With every sentence, it is clear to me that he is deeply aware of his power, clinically using the orator's pause and cadence to great effect. The camera pans to the faces of the audience, mostly men, watching him with intense concentration and then breaking into roars of support. It is clear that he has a primitive power over them, these men in search of a leader and a homeland. I can see their identity etched indelibly on their faces: they bear the stamp of their fate, poor in a land of racial privilege.

As these images flicker in the editing suite, I wonder, Can we stop these people? If they get the support of the army, it will be difficult. The question races through my mind: Will the army stay loyal to the government or will they turn and follow Viljoen and Terre'Blanche?

Strange, I have never thought that I would want the army to stay loyal to the National Party government. Whatever my thoughts, the Leader has no such doubts; the police and defence force will follow him. His speech is an unequivocal call to arms. To vigorously nodding heads, the Leader makes it clear that he will 'only negoti- ate over the barrel of a gun'. The irony of the Leader misquoting Chairman Mao Zedong is not lost on the foreign journalists in the editing suite, as they top up their glasses.

Driving home, I know that if the army does 'turn', the country will endure another ten years of war, except that this time it will not be a low-intensity war, it will be a protracted and savage guer- rilla conflict that will dwarf our previous strife.

Shortly after the Klerksdorp march, the high command of the right wing gathers in secret on a farm in the Ottosdal district west of Potchefstroom. The meeting is attended by the fighting generals of the AWB, the special forces of the AWB, members of the South African Police, and members of the defence force.

The meeting has been preceded by a visit to the Cape by senior AWB leaders, where they liaised with military officials and right-wing groups. During the tour, meetings took place at the air-force base at Ysterplaat and also at the major naval base in Simon's Town. On the way back from Cape Town, the army's elite school of infantry at Oudtshoorn was visited. Ominously, Constand Viljoen was a part of the delegation to the military bases.

The purpose of the meeting of the AWB high command is to discuss the details and logistics of a plan to take control by force of a significant area of the country and declare it their Volkstaat. After much discussion, the area designated is the Western Transvaal. This objective is regarded as achievable.

Already, most of the towns in the Western Transvaal are controlled by the right in terms of administration. This is no secret, with the AWB proudly announcing that they have been given the freedom of the town in twenty-one urban areas in the Western Transvaal. In each of these towns, there is a committee called Wesbou, which comprises city councillors, city secretaries, financial persons, representatives from the traffic department, the commanders of the civil protection services and members of the local army commando. These towns form the foundations for the establishment of the Volkstaat.

There is talk at the meeting of an uprising of the Afrikaner people, an insurrection that will be supported by massive sections of the defence force and police, making use of the weaponry that has been stockpiled for years on farms and in the bush.

FW de Klerk, the president and leader of the National Party, is spoken of with bitter hatred: a traitor to his people, a man who has entered into a pact with Satan in the form of the ANC and the communists. They have tried to speak to De Klerk, even sent a delegation to meet with him in parliament. He has treated them with contempt, sending a minister to talk to them instead.

De Klerk has long been identified as a target for assassination but there is a difficulty as his security is tight and, despite their excellent contacts, the right wing cannot gain access to him. Even the Leader, a former member of the presidential protection unit, a man who intimately knew the intricate, interwoven procedures for the protection of the country's first citizen, is unable to find a chink in the presidential armour.

There is discussion about individuals who should be targeted for assassination. In addition, National Party offices in the Western Transvaal are identified for bombing in the coming months, including the one in Ventersdorp.

The fighting generals order intensive training every weekend for all AWB members. The training should cover the use of weaponry, including handguns and shotguns, self-defence, patrols and infantry tactics as well as explosives. It is decided that the AWB should be joined in this training by the Boere Krisis Aksie, although a number of individuals belong to both organisations. The stockpiling of weapons, explosives and foodstuffs, mostly non-perishables like tinned food, should also increase apace.

After the Ottosdal meeting, the Leader and General Nico Prinsloo conduct a tour of the Western Transvaal to identify secret locations for the further stockpiling of weapons and supplies. These will form the armoury of the Volkstaat and sustain them in the coming war.

Under pressure from his own right wing and particularly the AWB, Constand Viljoen suspends talks with the ANC and the National Party in October 1993. There is rejoicing in the AWB.

The AWB does not wait for the Leader's ultimatum to expire on 29 November 1993.

In early October 1993, Andries Stefanus Kriel, deputy leader of the Volksfront in the Northern Free State and AWB brigadier, instructs Jan Cornelius Labuschagne to organise a covert cell that will be part of a coordinated bombing campaign set to commence on Monday, 8 November. In giving these instructions, Brigadier

Kriel emphasises that the targets should be power installations and railway lines and that there should be no loss of human life.

Brigadier Kriel has considerable experience with explosives, having masterminded the bombing campaigns that resulted in the bombing of Hillview High School, Cosatu House in Johannesburg, the Verwoerdburg Post Office and the Krugersdorp Post Office. The irony of right-wingers bombing a post office named after the primary architect of apartheid, Dr Verwoerd, did not go unnoticed in the media.

Labuschagne, who holds the rank of colonel in the AWB, is told that 'through these actions the ... government had to be forced to take the Afrikaner Volk's ideals of a Volkstaat seriously and send a message to the ANC as to the seriousness of the Afrikaner's ideal of the Volkstaat'. The order to Labuschagne is to 'hit as many targets as possible and to damage as many properties as possible'.

Brigadier Kriel does, however, give the cell a wide brief by adding, 'Do whatever your hands find to do, just go and do it.'

The explosives are obtained from the mines. Using these explosives as well as fertiliser, the men make their own bombs.

Labuschagne chooses two men, Johannes Jacobus Roos Botes from Bultfontein and Daniel Wilhelm van der Watt, to join him in his cell. The cell members receive training in the manufacture, handling and use of explosives. The training takes place in the Bothaville area.

On a Sunday in mid-October, Inkatha plan to hold a funeral for two of its members from the Thokoza Hostel who were killed in the fighting. We are informed by the Inkatha leaders Themba Khoza and his deputy Humphrey Ndhlovu in the weekly meetings with the political parties that there will be a march from the hostel through the township to the cemetery. We have an agreement with all the political parties that if they intend holding a rally, a march or a funeral, they will inform us so that we can plan and implement preventative measures to avoid or minimise violence.

This march will proceed through parts of Thokoza and Katlehong that are ANC controlled and would normally be no-go areas for the Inkatha hostel dwellers. We know that the Inkatha marchers will be well armed with spears and pangas and that within their ranks will be a number of men carrying AK47s and other assorted firearms under blankets and overcoats. It's a certainty that if the march is fired on, they will retaliate, leading to a pitched battle in the middle of a densely populated residential area.

If the Inkatha marchers decide to attack the residents of the area, the ANC's self-defence units will retaliate, and there will be a bloodbath.

The ANC leaders tell us that it's madness for Inkatha to march through those areas. It's deliberate provocation. All the same, the ANC undertakes to control its members.

We know that all it needs is one shot and we will have a catastrophe on our hands. Our planning is meticulous in terms of the deployment of monitors, cars and our iron Doves to put an effective shield between the marchers and the wary residents.

There is liaison with Brigadier Zirk Gouws, the police representative on the Peace Accord committee. He assures us that the police internal stability division will be out in force with their armoured vehicles and they will also have a helicopter in the air. Gouws knows that if violence erupts his own men will become targets. The Red Cross and the international observers from the UN, the Organisation of African Unity, the Commonwealth and the European Union, who will be deployed in significant numbers, are part of the joint planning. The casualty section at the Natalspruit Hospital has been placed on alert.

The Peace Accord monitors and international observers leave the Braamfontein office in a large convoy early in the morning after detailed briefing sessions and the handing out of equipment. We have been up preparing since four.

By the time we get to the designated assembly point in Thokoza, the Inkatha members are out in force, milling about. There are hordes of them, and as I move through the gathering crowd looking for the leaders, I smell the bitter-sweet stench of alcohol. Uncharacteristically, it makes me feel nauseous.

It's clear that many of the men had been bussed in from other areas, as buses and taxis arrive and disgorge occupants. I can see a lot of knives, pangas, sharpened steel pipes and spears, but no firearms. I know they are there. It strikes me that this is not a grouping of peaceful protesters, this is a march of warriors ready for war, an impi. I have seen it before, many times.

I talk to Gertrude Mzizi of Inkatha, who lives in a house opposite the Thokoza Hostel. She confirms the route. Mzizi is a slim woman, almost slight, of medium height and tough. She is totally respected by the men in the hostels and obeyed without question.

'Are we going to have trouble today, Gertrude?' I ask, the plea in my voice unmistakable.

'We will not cause it. We just want to bury our dead. But if we are attacked, you know we will fight. We have no choice. If that happens people will die.'

Earlier that morning I had spoken on the phone to Duma Nkosi, a key ANC leader in the area, and he had assured me that they would not start any violence, but they would defend themselves. I believed him. I believe Gertrude Mzizi too.

Carlson Ndaba calmly gives orders to the monitors, who fan out along the Inkatha procession, which is several hundred strong. We have a person every twenty metres or so. In their bright orange bibs and with Peace Accord flaps they are easy to spot.

Ndaba, a resident of Thokoza, is respected in his community and, more importantly, by both the ANC and Inkatha. Now, he climbs into his car clearly marked with Peace Accord insignia and drives slowly to the front of the marchers. He has an ANC and Inkatha leader with him, as well as an observer from the UN. This formula is replicated in many of the Peace Accord vehicles. I decide to walk with the marchers and position myself about midway on the left.

The police Casspirs move into place on the sides of the march

43

and at the front and back. The troop carriers, like great armoured beetles, stalk the procession, the heads of the police and the barrels of their combat rifles piercing the sealed blue dome of sky. Casspirs and internal stability division police are also stationed at key intersections and potential hotspots.

The singing and chanting start as the procession moves down the road, which is completely deserted, the houses silent and still, their curtains drawn, their small gardens devoid of life. Even the dogs are quiet. It is an eerie thing, an empty city. Desolate, as if swept by a poisonous wind.

Hopefully no one here will die today, I say to myself.

The pace of the Inkatha marchers picks up. This is unquestionably a show of force, and a formidable one at that. It would take a well-organised group with real firepower to confront on an armed Inkatha impi of this magnitude. And they know it. The marchers shout at the houses, daring the occupants to come out, but there is no response. The sun is high by now and we are only a few blocks from the cemetery.

I check my watch, it is 11:30. It's hot, the fine township dust adding to the parched dryness in the air. The chanting and stamping of the marchers drum in my head. I wish it was over and I was home with Caroline and the children for Sunday lunch.

Suddenly a man bolts from the house on my left just ahead of me, tall and dressed in threadbare clothes. He runs towards the marchers, his eyes wide with panic, a rabbit flushed from hiding. He carries no weapon. I see the men in the procession face him as he gets closer. He realises he is too close to them, and turns away quickly. But he's too late. The short stabbing spear of a marcher strikes him in the throat, a jab really, a blur of motion, and the man goes down, falling on his back, his hands clutching at his throat, blood spurting.

The marchers do not stop; it is not even a diversion. I look for the man with the spear but he has gone, probably been shuffled to the middle of the pack where the men with the overcoats and AK47s are positioned, and then recycled to a different position in the throng.

I get on the radio and call in police and medics. The march moves on, leaving me and some of the monitors with the wounded man. The Red Cross are there almost immediately. Two medics jump from their van and run to the man. The pool of blood around his upper body glistens in the midday sun, the flow pulsing from the gash in his neck. The medics pull on their surgical gloves. One grabs a compress and puts it over the wound, pressing hard while his colleague settles the man's body, arranging his legs and arms. But the blood pumps out and cannot be stopped. The medic frantically pushes on the wound, the compress now a red rag, the blood washing through his gloved fingers, bright and slippery. The man on the ground says nothing; his eyes look into the face of the man bending over him, beseeching.

I glance up at the house from which the man came. There is a slight movement of the lace curtain, then nothing. I hear the bah bah bah of automatic fire. It comes from down the road close to the cemetery. A few shots at first, then a steady crackle. I'm glad I'm not there.

It is early evening when I drive home from Thokoza, the sun huge and orange on the western rim. I listen to the news but there is nothing about the march.

At home, Caroline asks how it went and I want to tell her but I can't, the words sticking in the dust in my throat. I see the twins, Dominic and Luke, lying on the floor in the sitting room, absorbed in their fun. I kneel down, kiss them both on the forehead before going out into the garden. I stand with a whisky in my hand as the colour fades in the thickening dusk. Tears well but I can't cry. I see the blood pumping from the hole in the man's throat. I see the Red Cross paramedic trying to stop the flow. But he can't. I see again the man jerk and convulse until slowly his body goes still. Then the medic stands and looks at me, the desperation in his dark eyes strikes into my soul.

It's pitch black when Caroline calls me inside.

During October 1993 Inkatha, some of the homeland leaders and the right-wing groupings form the Freedom Alliance. Television viewers are amazed to see images of public protests with Zulu warriors and Afrikaner militias marching side by side to demand autonomy for their peoples.

In November 1993, the Volksfront, led by Constand Viljoen, revises its decision to end negotiations and submits a proposal to the multi-party negotiating forum for a Volkstaat with limited autonomy (not independence) for Afrikaners. This time their Volkstaat proposal constitutes fourteen per cent of the country. The proposal qualifies the rights of blacks in that they will only be allowed to vote for the national government and not for the Volkstaat or regional government.

The negotiators in the main talks accept that this is a move away from the original objectives of the Volksfront and the Conservative Party. Talks between the major political parties and the Volksfront resume. It is also agreed that research be conducted jointly by a Volksfront/ANC committee into forms of autonomy at local and regional government level.

The bombing campaign of the Free State cell of the AWB under the command of Colonel Jan Labuschagne commences.

It is Monday, 15 November 1993.

Together with Jacobus Botes and Daniel van der Watt, he drives into the black township of Monyakeng, near Wesselsbron. They stop the car, open the door and delicately place a large homemade bomb on the ground. They then drive away. Six houses are badly damaged when the bomb explodes. Maria Bayo and her one-and-a-half-year-old baby Seipati Mokodutlo are injured in the explosion.

The precise target locations have been left to the discretion of Labuschagne. In exercising this discretion, he takes a wide interpretation and decides not to confine himself to acts of sabotage, and, contrary to his instructions, to target civilians. His men follow his instructions, although Botes is not present during a number of the missions, having taken time off to go fishing in Namibia.

The three men in the cell are deeply religious and before each bombing sortie, they pray together. The men also carry two home-made shotguns on their missions.

On Wednesday, 8 December in Viljoenskroon's black township, it is just after 10 pm when Labuschagne stops his car on the tar road close to the township. Botes and Van der Watt climb out.

It is dark and raining. The two men walk to the nearest house. Van der Watt is carrying a bomb which is larger than the one they had prepared and used in Wesselbron. A fence separates the two men from the houses, which are only a few metres away. They decide against climbing through the fence as it would impede their getaway. Also, climbing through a fence carrying a homemade bomb is not a recommended activity. Van der Watt stretches through the fence and places the bomb as close to the nearest house as he can reach. The men quickly retreat.

The corrugated iron shack belongs to a man by the name of Ramorakane. He shares it with many others. When the bomb detonates, the force of the explosion shatters the eardrums of the wife of Mr Ramorakane, rendering her permanently deaf. Andries Semelo, fast asleep in an adjacent shack, has both legs snapped by the blast.

In the early hours of the morning, after years of negotiations in-cluding stalled talks, break offs, resumed talks and more break offs, walkouts, boycotts, massacres, murders and an armed invasion of the venue of the negotiations, the main parties agree the final clause of the interim constitution. Inkatha and the right-wing parties are not part of the agreement. It is Thursday, 18 November 1993.

The toenadering, or coming together, of the Volksfront under Constand Viljoen with the main negotiating parties is continually threatened by Ferdi Hartzenberg. Hartzenberg wants an independent

Afrikaner homeland. Despite this, Viljoen goes into talks with the ANC and National Party. On Monday, 20 December 1993, he announces that the parties have reached an agreement and that the Volksfront will formally enter negotiations. The agreement states that 'the aspirations of many Afrikaners to govern themselves in their own territory should be addressed'. While this agreement is never signed, a joint working group is set up with a deadline to report back to the multi-party negotiating forum by Monday, 24 January 1994.

Shortly afterwards, again under formidable pressure from the increasingly militant far right of the Volksfront led by Hartzenberg, Viljoen is forced to declare that the Volksfront is pulling out of negotiations.

After the Viljoenskroon bomb, the Free State AWB bombers change their tactics and target mostly railway lines and power installations. They place twenty-one bombs, nineteen explode. Eleven of the targets are railway lines, three are power installations, four are in black residential areas, two are business premises and one is at Regina Farm School near Orkney. The fact that no one is killed by the bombs is more a result of fortune than planning.

However, Jan Labuschagne is becoming increasingly disenchanted. Both he and his superior, Brigadier Kriel, will resign from the AWB in January 1994, on the grounds that the members have become too 'undisciplined'.

CHAPTER TWO

The muscles in my thin shoulders are taut. I am being interviewed for a job that fills me with foreboding. I can see that my interviewers are looking for a lawyer who has practised for some years and who has a good working knowledge of the constitutional negotiations and the process that has led to the negotiated transition. They want someone who is seen as politically aware but independent and able to act in an unbiased and objective manner. Someone acceptable to the main political parties. They want someone who has built a large organisation from scratch, quickly, in very stressful circumstances. They want a person who is prepared to work like a dog and, for a few months, live like a dog.

While I am not sure that I possess all or indeed any of these credentials, I know that my time heading up a region of the National Peace Accord is a key consideration. Surely this position will be as difficult. So what pathology is driving me now, as I head to a similar fate so soon after the last one?

Of course, I put on my best face, even though deep down I know that I am not just playing with fire, I am rushing headlong into the furnace. But what a place to be, in the heart of organising and ensuring the freeness and fairness of our first democratic election? As a human rights lawyer, this is something I have fought for and committed myself to a long time ago.

But then again, I selfishly ask myself, do I want to be part of something which has all the potential to be a monstrous mess?

And I do think that I am sufficiently politically acute to know a disaster when I see one and, more importantly, to know when to create measurable distance from that disaster. In fact, most of my clients, politicos mainly, come to me for that specific reason: I put distance between them and trouble. That's what lawyers do.

I have also made a New Year's resolution that I will spend more time with my family.

It is Thursday, 20 January 1994 and I am being interviewed by IEC commissioners Dikgang Moseneke, Helen Suzman and Frank Chikane. The election date is a shade over three months away.

An election of similar proportions in a developing country would normally take between eighteen months and two years to arrange. But in South Africa, we do it in our normal way, at the last minute and on a wing and a prayer. I think, as I sit there with my interviewers, that this election will require nothing less than divine intervention.

The IEC was constituted little more than a month ago and since then the country's been closed for its annual holiday. It faces an impossible task.

Caroline and I have discussed at length the pros and cons of my applying for this job. We know it will place huge pressure on the family and particularly on her. But then we also know that it will only be for three or four months. Together we will get through it. She has given up full-time work to look after our children, Simon, Isabella, Luke and Dominic.

Her work as a journalist for the British Independent Television News was demanding, stressful and difficult to combine with the raising of four children.

A few days later, I am appointed as head of the monitoring division of the IEC. I am excited but filled with trepidation.

The Volksfront once again resumes political negotiations before the working group's report-back deadline of Monday, 24 January 1994. The weeks have passed amidst threats of violence from the right wing and belligerent public meetings. Agreement has yet to be achieved. There is now a new tone to the Volksfront and its factions. Constand Viljoen in his speeches talks of the use of limited violence to establish a Volkstaat. The Conservative Party under Ferdi Hartzenberg declares that it will establish a transitional Afrikaner authority before the end of the month.

The January 24th deadline passes with no resolution. The Volksfront and Inkatha, the key partners in the Freedom Alliance, table their demand for two ballots in the election, one for national and one for the province. They also insist that each province be allowed to write its own constitution. Unless these demands are met they will not participate in the election.

The Afrikaans newspapers write about plans by the right-wing organisations to take over certain regions, which they will use as launching pads for guerrilla attacks. Such an insurrection will take us down a bloody road to all-out civil conflict.

The election clock is ticking. 12 February 1994 is the deadline for the registration of political parties to participate in the election.

My offices are at the indescribably awful World Trade Centre in Kempton Park. It bears no resemblance in any manner or form to its illustrious counterpart in New York, after which it has been pretentiously named. It rose to prominence as the venue for the Codesa negotiations.

Locating the IEC there is a big mistake. The centre is a series of connected, cavernous warehouse-type structures. Ugly on the outside and worse on the inside. Gossip suggests that its owner, a Neels Swart, had made an exceptional amount of money from leasing the virtually unused building to Codesa, and now stood to gain a similar amount from the ignorance of the IEC.

My office is a large hangar-like space partitioned by black hanging drapes drooping from the high ceiling. As I sit down at my desk, a gust of wind sweeps through the area and the black curtains billow around me. I wonder if the phantom of the opera might be lurking in the undulating cloth.

'Shit, what a terrible place to work,' I say out loud. I am surprised by a woman's voice replying from the curtains close by in a rich English accent.

'Not as bad as some of the places I have worked in.'

I start with surprise and embarrassment. To my relief it is Helen Suzman who appears from behind the curtains.

'Parliament for one,' she says. We laugh. 'I was passing by and heard that you had arrived. I thought that I would stop in to see you. Do you have everything you need?'

'I am fine here. Interesting place,' I lie.

'Yes,' she says, drily, elongating the word. Turning, she is gone, disappearing into the folds of cloth.

The Independent Electoral Commission is chaired by a judge of the Appellate Division of the Supreme Court, Johann Kriegler, and consists of a number of prominent South Africans. The primary duty of the commissioners is 'to offer the electorate a genuine opportunity to determine the composition of the new national and provincial legislatures in substantially free and fair elections'. Broad stuff, clearly. The commissioners are appointed on the basis of consensus between the political parties and subject to the requirement that they be manifestly impartial and independent.

Impartial and independent! In South Africa!

In truth, while not questioning the integrity of the commissioners and their ability to behave objectively, a number of them are broadly representative of most of the political parties that will contest the election. (The right wing being a notable exception.) Indeed, certain of them have in the past occupied leadership positions in some of the political parties.

I know a few of them and have no doubt that, regardless of their personal history or political allegiance, they will act in the best interests of the country, even though this is a land that for centuries has lacked people who will act in its best interests. I wonder how these men and women, so prominent in their differing arenas and not without egos, will manage to reconcile their diverse views for the greater good. An endeavour in which South Africans do not have an exemplary record. I promise myself that I will simply put my head down and look up only when the election is over. Let the commissioners deal with the politics of it all.

The politics of the election are a task for which many of the commissioners are well qualified. The deputy chairperson is Dikgang Moseneke. Arrested at the age of fifteen, Moseneke was sentenced to ten years on Robben Island for his anti-apartheid activities, earning him the distinction of being the youngest prisoner ever sent to that bleak rock. He served the full ten years, during which he passed his matric and obtained a BA, majoring in English and political science, a B Juris law degree and, later, an LLB, all through distance studies with the University of South Africa in Pretoria. On his release from the island, he went into legal practice, eventually joining the Bar and rising quickly to the position of senior counsel, the first African in the Transvaal to do so. He had also, in the past, served in a senior position in the Pan Africanist Congress and has an acute understanding of South African politics.

Moseneke is joined on the commission by Helen Suzman, the veteran politician from the Progressive Party and later the Progressive Federal Party. Suzman is a woman of impeccable integrity and reputation, having been a lone anti-apartheid voice in a parliament largely dominated by male Calvinist National Party members. She is known internationally for her scathing criticism of apartheid politicians and also for her biting wit, including the now-famous one-liner, 'How often have I sat in Parliament and watched a shiver go up and down those green benches looking for a spine to crawl up.' One of the few to have visited Nelson Mandela regularly while he was in prison, she is regarded by him as a true friend and is highly respected.

Other commissioners include Dr Oscar Dhlomo, formally of Inkatha and now chairman of the Institute for Multi-Party Democracy, Johan Heyns, the former deputy chairman of the President's Council and chairman of the President's Council Constitutional Committee, and Rosil Jager, a former National Party MP. Frank Chikane, the former general secretary of the South African Council of Churches, has also been appointed. Chikane is a client of mine. I represented him when he nearly died after being poisoned by the security branch. His clothes had been impregnated with lethal toxins when he was travelling to the United States. Thankfully, on his arrival there, he had been admitted to hospital, where specialists had managed to accurately diagnose his condition and identify the exact poison used in the attempt to kill him.

Zac Yacoob, a well-known human rights lawyer and senior counsel from the Durban Bar, is also there, as is Charles Nupen, another highly regarded human rights lawyer and the national director of the Independent Mediation Service of South Africa. Ben van der Ross, an executive director of the Independent Development Trust, and Dawn Mokhobo, a senior executive from ESKOM, complete the impressive list.

I know these people to be strong-willed individuals, and I wonder how they will gel and work together in accomplishing what must surely be the most important national endeavour they have ever undertaken. Importantly, these commissioners are here to give the IEC the one component that is critical to this election – credibility.

Due to the general lack of technical electoral expertise on the commission, the South African commissioners are supplemented by the appointment of a small number of international commissioners, all of whom have significant reputations and expertise in the area of elections and international relations. There is Dr Jorgen Elklit, an elections expert from Denmark, with specific expertise in proportional representation and mathematical models for seat allocation. Also appointed are Ron Gould, the assistant chief electoral officer for Canada, R K de Silva, the commissioner of elections in Sri Lanka, and Professor Walter Kamba, the former head of the electoral supervisory commission in Zimbabwe and former vice chancellor of the University of Zimbabwe.

Gay McDougal, from the Lawyers' Committee for Civil Rights under the Law in Washington, is an appointee who I welcome. McDougal is an African American who I got to know well as a result of her organisation having funded the defences in a number

54

of big treason trials run by my law firm. She is exceptionally well connected in Washington, and internationally, with an excellent sense of political judgement and strategy. She is joined on the IEC commission by Amare Tekle, who has just run the Eritrean referendum. A herculean feat, to run a referendum with zero resources in a desert with raging wind storms. Sand-blasted democracy.

All in all, a strong bunch, but then this is an election with its own unique challenges. Frankly, we need all the help we can get. Organising an election in three months in this country will make Eritrea and Sri Lanka look like a breeze. These commissioners will have their work cut out for them.

Apart from the tense political situation, there are other complicating factors. Whole swathes of the country are simply not in a position to run a bath, never mind an election. Many of the homeland areas are in a state of complete administrative and functional breakdown.

The Transkei has all but collapsed in terms of government and the delivery of basic services. The Ciskei, its poorer relation to the south, is no better off. Wild and destitute, its capital, Bisho, was host to a massacre on 7 September 1992, when Ciskei Defence Force troops under the command of officers from military intelligence opened fire on a crowd of eighty thousand protesters marching on Bisho. Twenty-eight people were killed and over two hundred injured. As the attorney for the ANC in the subsequent commission of enquiry, I got to know the conditions in the Ciskei. They can be described in one word: anarchic. Its ruler, Brigadier Oupa Gqozo, is a man more comfortable with the structure of military command than democratic institutions. I would also describe the Ciskei as dangerous. This was confirmed when in January 1994 groupings loyal to Brigadier Gqozo carried out random shootings and grenade attacks on ANC supporters.

Most of the homelands, including the governments of Transkei, Venda and Ciskei, have recently announced that they accept the revocation of their independence that will take place on the date of the elections. They have also said they support the electoral process. However, the administrations in Gazankulu, Venda, QwaQwa, Lebowa, Ciskei, and Transkei are close to inoperable, the territories riddled by civil-service strikes, widespread corruption, looting of government resources, student boycotts and protests. These areas, lurching towards ungovernability and chaos, are hardly in a position to run a democratic election.

But incapacity is not the only issue in these engineered ethnic enclaves. The entire KwaZulu administration, largely represented by Inkatha, steadfastly refuses to participate in the elections, as does Bophuthatswana, the fragmented homeland around Pretoria. The leaders of both these Bantustans have refused to give the IEC authority to operate in the territory under their control.

Overall, not a pretty picture, with large chunks of the country incapable of administering an election, and some actually hostile to the idea.

I sit at my desk, which is completely bare, no induction booklet or briefing file, no kindly mentor and certainly no job description, just a ragged piece of legislation. I put my head in my hands: How did I get here?

The negotiators have agreed on an IEC that has two main operating divisions, which are supplemented by an adjudication secretariat. The electoral administration division has the responsibility of administering and running the election. This task has certain key elements, including the distribution and identification of voting stations, the staffing and provisioning of voting stations, communications, the conduct of the election and, crucially, the counting of votes.

In essence, the administration division is responsible for the guts of the electoral process. However, because the division will be staffed largely by officials from the department of home affairs who have run the previous elections, the ANC and other parties have little faith that government staffers will organise a fair election. In fact, there is a strong belief in the team of ANC negotiators that they will be biased against the ANC and could rig the election to favour the people who have given them their jobs, the National Party bureaucracy. Frankly, I share their concern. The man heading this division is Piet Coleyn, the director general of the department of home affairs.

Why would anyone want to run a free and fair election that will remove them from power? My experience as a lawyer has exposed me to the sharp edge of the Nationalist Party knife: treason trials, interdicts and representation of tortured clients, bombed buildings, have taught me that there is little that is free or fair about the government, and those who represent it. Very cynical, you might say. Absolutely.

Enter the election-monitoring division whose primary job is to ensure that the election is free and fair. My initial instructions are that this division has to monitor the external implementation of the electoral process. This involves the appointment of monitors to observe and report on the electoral process, including political meetings, canvassing and the conduct of the election. The division also has to register and regulate the activities of all international and local election observers and investigate infringements of the electoral code of conduct and other electoral offences. The division is mandated to utilise the services of the National Peacekeeping Force, the police and the defence force. It also has to investigate complaints arising from the electoral process and either resolve them or refer them to adjudication. Finally, the division has to initiate and coordinate meetings between the registered political parties. This means resolving any disputes.

These responsibilities are enough to induce permanent panic and feelings of endemic inadequacy in anyone tasked with fulfilling them. As if I didn't suffer from those conditions already. My appointment is to head this division.

I hear a throat being cleared politely behind the curtains that delineate my office. A woman enters, introducing herself as the secretary to Judge Kriegler. 'The judge would like to see you in his office immediately,' she says.

I first came into contact with Johann Kriegler when I worked at the Legal Resources Centre under Arthur Chaskalson in 1981. Kriegler was a senior counsel then and had the reputation of being very bright and one of the more respected seniors at the Johannesburg Bar. An Afrikaner whose forebears had arrived in the Cape in the late 1700s and whose descendants fought against the British in the Boer War, Kriegler is a man known for breaking the mould, for placing integrity before allegiance. I first met him when he attended lunches at the Legal Resources Centre along with Ishmael Mohammed, Jules Browde, George Bizos and Sydney Kentridge, all eminent senior counsel. Later, while I was doing my articles at Webber Wentzel in Johannesburg, he was one of their counsel of choice in complex litigation. As a judge, he was similarly respected and gained much acclaim for his finding against Lieutenant General Lothar Neethling. Neethling was the head of the South African Police Forensic Laboratory and had sued *Vrye Weekblad* and the *Weekly Mail* for one and a half million rand after they alleged that he supplied poison to the former head of a police hit-squad stationed at Vlakplaas. Kriegler dismissed Neethling's claim and ordered him to pay the legal costs of both newspapers.

My first inane thought, one of many while sitting in Judge Kriegler's office, is that he is a lucky man: his office has walls. We exchange greetings and he offers me coffee. I see that his hand shakes when he raises the cup to his lips but remember that he has had that affliction for some time. The judge has no patience with small talk, asking me in his low voice how I intend building an entire multi-functional division in three months. I tell him that I need to study and confirm my mandate with him and the commission, and that I will then draft a detailed operational plan that

I will put to the commission for approval. In the meantime, I will recruit key staff from the network of contacts that I have built up in the Peace Accord and from my law practice. I have a good idea of what is needed. He listens, waiting for me to finish.

'Peter, we have had some discussion in the commission about the mandate of the monitoring division,' he says.

'Oh yes, Judge,' I say politely, wondering where this is going.

'Yes, the issue is whether your role is purely externally faced in terms of the activities and conditions affecting the electoral process outside the IEC or whether it is both external and internal in terms of which you would monitor the workings of the IEC itself and specifically election administration operations.'

'Yes, Judge,' I say, again. 'Most of the mandate refers to the external environment. I'm hoping to guide him to the conclusion I want.

'Well, we got an opinion from senior counsel on this matter and his strong view is that the monitoring should be internal as well as external,' he says.

'Really,' I say weakly. As if we haven't got enough on our plate, we now also have to watch Coleyn's division and ensure that they perform their duties efficiently, fairly and without favour.

'Yes, and that is the position which we as a commission considered and adopted on January 19th, so when you prepare your plan for us, please bear that in mind.'

Trying to keep the whine out of my voice, I tell the judge that there is so much to do that adding more tasks is surely going to complicate an already difficult mandate and perhaps even compromise it. He listens or, as is the wont of judges, gives the appearance of listening, and then says that the decision has already been taken. There is no going back.

Leaving the judge's office, I bump into Dikgang Moseneke. He asks me with a wry smile if Kriegler has given me the news.

'Yes,' I say, 'he has just told me.'

'How do you feel about it?' There's a hint of mirth in the curl of his lips. Laughter is an understandable response to a situation which is already bordering on 'out of control' and which, thanks to the judge, is now very definitely 'beyond control'. Hysteria is actually justified here, I think to myself resentfully.

'Well, firstly, I am not sure that it is logistically possible given the time frames.'

He nods in agreement, now smiling openly. 'If you want to swap with me let me know. Certain commissioners have been allocated to provinces and particular areas of operations to lend expertise. Charlie Nupen, Gay McDougal and myself drew the short straw and got Natal and KwaZulu, the province where no one can agree on anything and where being on the other side can and will draw fire, or a sharp spear.'

'No, I think that province needs someone like you, Dikgang,' I say drily, suddenly thinking that maybe my job isn't too bad.

'I thought you might say that.'

I leave him already feeling better about a very bad situation.

Dikgang Moseneke is a remarkable man who unfailingly sees the bigger picture and always, whatever the odds, manages to be positive. After what he has been through, even this election is manageable, I think.

Tall, good-looking and urbane, Moseneke dresses well and speaks in a voice that most aeroplane captains would kill for. His reputation is of being impeccably polite and compellingly attractive to women. In KwaZulu and Natal, he will certainly need all the charm that he can muster.

The KwaZulu and Natal team is a good one, certainly among the best the commission can put together. Charles Nupen is a highly experienced mediator. Over the last decade, he has handled most of the major labour, community and political disputes in the country. He will be a valuable addition to the team that is required to oversee an election in a war-torn province with a party that is vehemently opposed to the election taking place at all.

Chief Buthelezi, the leader of the Inkatha Freedom Party and chief minister of KwaZulu, is a man who holds strong proprietary views about his region. He and Inkatha insist that the Zulu people have the right to self-determination and that KwaZulu should be a sovereign state with autonomous institutions from the judiciary to its security apparatus. These powers should be defined in its own constitution. Until these demands are met, Inkatha, with the apparent support of the Zulu king Goodwill Zwelithini refuse to take part in any of the constitutional negotiations.

As for protecting IEC officials in the area, it is worth remembering that Judge Richard Goldstone, in his commissions of inquiry into the violence sweeping the country, implicated certain KwaZulu police and Inkatha officials in the 'third force' violence.

Inkatha, with the fire of Zulu nationalism coursing through its veins, speaks increasingly of war and blood should the election go ahead. Subjects which rest uneasily on the sensitive shoulders of the (mainly English) white population of the province. Many of them have uncomfortable and disturbing memories of the fate their forebears suffered at the hands of King Cetshwayo's victorious Zulu army at Isandhlwana on 22 January 1897. Guns against spears and one thousand three hundred British dead – at the time it was the single largest defeat ever suffered by the British army. Now with Chief Mangosuthu Gatsha Buthelezi, the great-grandson of the legendary King Cetshwayo talking of war, it is a threat which is taken very seriously. The ability of Inkatha to destabilise the election in the entire province and in parts of the Transvaal is indisputable.

At home that night, there is complete chaos. In fact, it reminds me of the IEC. Simon, now almost five, is a hard-hat area. He leaves mayhem in his wake, but with a charm that forbids sanction. This evening, dressed in his Bat Man outfit in which he virtually lives, he careens through the house, cape flowing dramatically behind him as he drags a cart of fluffy toys rescued from imminent danger shouting bee baap, bee baap, in a manner of an emergency-service-vehicle siren. My two-year-old daughter Isabella has, without mandate, fed the twins, both in their feeding hammocks. She has accomplished this feat largely by smearing quantities of pureed vegetables over their entire faces and torsos, their clear brown eyes blinking in wonder through the green sea of mash covering them, now starting to dry and crack like the thick mud of the Kgalagadi pans in the dry season.

Caroline is on the phone in earnest conversation, gesturing wildly to me to intervene, like someone stricken in a deadly mime. I am immobile with indecision; as with the IEC, I am not sure where to start.

When the children are asleep and calm has returned to the house, she tells me that she has been asked by ITN to work in the few weeks before the election and over the election itself.

This election is massive news. It will be a dogfight as journalists scrabble and tear at every piece of news. There will be no shortage of either. Since early January, South Africa's first democratic election has occupied the lead space in many national and international news bulletins.

As with my position in the IEC, we agree that she must take the job and that we will try to manage the work and the children. So beautiful and calm when they sleep, we say. Over a glass of wine with dinner, like the election, it even seems possible.

CHAPTER THREE

My first days at the IEC pass in a whirl of meetings and black curtains. Increasingly, I feel as if I am in a surreal play with the central characters moving in and out of the drapes onto the stage only to exit left and disappear into the dark void until the next act. Surely this is a bad dream from which I will wake and find that I am part of the audience in a great national drama. Surely I am not one of the central actors who will shortly be booed from the theatre.

It is Thursday, 27 January 1994. The election is in three months' time. To the day.

The head of the administration division, Piet Coleyn, has two deputies, Tsinga Madiba, the chief director in the department of foreign affairs of the Transkei, and Yunus Mahomed.

I know Mahomed reasonably well as one of the architects and leaders of the United Democratic Front and as a prominent human rights lawyer in Durban. A soft-spoken man, he was detained a number of times by the security police and suffered house arrest. He is highly regarded in resistance circles. I am grateful that he is among the home affairs management: a good guy in the nerve centre. We meet and have coffee in his office. We agree to keep in constant communication.

The chief operating officer of the IEC is Renosi Mokati, a small and dynamic woman who is always scrupulously polite. She has the unenviable task of trying to make the IEC clock tick. Actually, she first has to assemble the moving parts and make the clock before she can even consider setting it in motion.

It is still Thursday.

At the IEC, time becomes a rare commodity. So rare that I cling to every minute, every second, clutching desperately at moments as they slip past. Every second brings us closer to the day. Election day. Either we will pull this off, or the country will burn.

I find myself getting impatient in meetings that take any longer than an hour. There are only twenty-four of them in a day, so precious. I am driven to distraction by people speaking for too long in meetings. My God! Don't they realise that there are only ninety-one days and six hours left and we have just lost one more hour? We are sixty minutes closer and have achieved nothing.

I know that in the monitoring division we need two things fast, a top flight head of administration and a head of operations to assist with the planning and segmentation of our many functions. I need the kind of administrative head who is supremely efficient and totally ruthless, a person whose mind works at the speed of light and who is able to bring order where there is chaos, light where there is darkness, a person who never sleeps and who is afraid of no one, who with a single lash of their tongue will galvanise thousands. There is such a person: Solveigh Piper, an ex-union administrator who also has large-scale project management experience. I've never met anyone (and I include myself) who isn't scared of Solveigh Piper.

The head of information and operations is Phiroshaw Camay. He and I worked at the National Peace Accord. Camay, now in his late forties and a former general secretary of the National Council of Trade Unions, played a major role in planning and conducting operations aimed at stemming the violence on the East Rand and elsewhere in the Wits–Vaal region. I never saw Camay panic, ever, even when I felt that he should have. With unfailing precision and authority, he manned the joint operations centre of the Peace Accord on the East Rand in Thokoza. Quietly spoken, he got things done. He also headed the Thokoza peace committee of the National Peace Accord as well as the Johannesburg peace committee, two of the toughest, most violent areas. He was trusted by all parties. He also showed exceptional bravery.

The operation we need to mount in this election will not be dissimilar to those we instituted at the Peace Accord. The only difference is in scale. This thing is huge.

I am fortunate that both Piper and Camay need little persuasion and are able to start work on a few days' notice.

The team is further strengthened by the appointment of two deputy directors, Kgomotso Moroka, a well-known advocate from the Johannesburg Bar, and Jerome Ngwenya, an attorney from Durban and a highly experienced mediator. It is agreed that Moroka will head the investigations department. Her responsibilities include investigating and reporting on all infringements of the electoral code of conduct, as well as other electoral offences specified in the Electoral Act and the Independent Electoral Commission Act. This is a crucial part of our mandate and I am grateful she's in charge.

Jerome Ngwenya is perfect to lead the mediation department, which will coordinate meetings between the registered parties. It will be up to them to resolve any issues or disputes. Disagreements cannot be protracted affairs. They will require quick, efficient action. I am also fortunate in getting an excellent personal assistant, Ireen Avidan.

Planning sessions are held long into the night. This is the easy part: the real work is to get the right people to head the key areas of responsibility. All on a few days' notice.

This is not an easy task as good people are already in employment and it is necessary to approach their employers to release them for a period of at least four months. Again, this is difficult when such people may be central to their business or organisation. It is a desperate search. I contact CEOs of major companies and other institutions, court them, sometimes beg them to help us. This is not my forte, but desperation makes it seem less demeaning. Fortunately the people I talk to realise the urgency of the situation. I don't have to tell them that if we get this wrong the country will implode as people rise up and take what they have been denied for so long. They will burn the bakery.

It is Saturday, 29 January 1994. There is a Volksfront meeting at the Skilpad Hall in Pretoria at which the Leader and Constand Viljoen speak.

Viljoen says that although constitutional talks have failed them, instead of violence, they must consider their strategic options, including potential participation in the elections.

The Leader takes over the meeting, calling on Afrikaners to grab their freedom by force. He speaks of war. There will be no negotiation.

The moderate voice of Constand Viljoen is drowned and booed in the roar of approval for the Leader. The support for the right wing and their cause is estimated by the Leader as being in the region of a million men. Behind them are the women of the Rooivalke. If the army – or even a small part of it – joined them, they would be unstoppable.

As we go into February we set up fortnightly meetings of the political party liaison committee. It is a meeting I have to attend. It is a meeting Dikgang Moseneke chairs.

These are difficult meetings in which former adversaries, who dislike one another intensely, have to discuss their concerns around the electoral process. We hope this will build consensus about how the election will be conducted. The members have information supplied by their intelligence units, material which they release sparingly into the process like misers, warily watching their opponents and their reactions, testing, floating kites, fishing, feinting, whispering ghost reports and dummy theories. All this gameplaying in the hope of eliciting further facts which they can carry back triumphantly to their respective organisations for dissection, analysis and response.

The first meetings commence with a feigned politeness and then, in the manner of politicians, quickly degenerate into low-intensity warfare. The ammunition of choice: sarcasm, sniggers, accusations, derisory laughter and scorn.

A major issue relates to campaigning in certain areas. The National Party and Democratic Party accuse the ANC and its supporters of intolerance when they attempt to canvass votes in Soweto. They feel at risk and can go in only under police guard.

The ANC says the same thing about parts of Natal. There is little we can do about this particular complaint as Inkatha is against the election. Occasionally, there are allegations of violence and assault on party campaigners, but thankfully these are few and far between. Other complaints are minor: the tearing down of campaign posters, defamatory speeches. The allegation by the ANC that the National Party is abusing state resources in its campaign is taken seriously and they are asked to lodge evidence to prove their assertion.

Of course, these gatherings are not helped by having Adriaan Vlok, the former minister of police during the brutal and repressive 1980s, on the National Party's team. He is anathema to those representing the ANC team – Popo Molefe, a former UDF leader and highly respected, Essop Pahad, a senior member of the ANC and the SACP recently returned from exile, and Azhar Cachalia, the former treasurer of the United Democratic Front. I know Cachalia well, both as a friend and as a partner in our firm. Detained numerous times in solitary confinement and constantly harassed by the security police, Cachalia is a fine lawyer. He brings a measure of rational discussion to these early meetings, showing his honed negotiating skills and sense of strategy. I admire his maturity as he interacts with Adriaan Vlok, especially as Vlok had sanctioned his detention on a number of occasions and later signed his banning order.

The Democratic Party is represented by Rex Gibson, a polite and clever man who sincerely tries to keep the major players to the issues. The other parties say little, deferring to the National Party and the ANC. Although they argue back and forth, I nonetheless marvel that these people are in the same room.

It is difficult keeping the meetings focused on the big picture. Each party has a tendency to concentrate on its own priorities. While this is understandable, the bickering and point scoring is sometimes relentless and draining. On these occasions, Moseneke displays the patience of Job as he softly massages the parties into resolution. For my part, I curse my misfortune at having to waste precious time.

As the weeks go by, as the election gets closer, the meetings settle and achieve their own equilibrium. Everyone realises the obstacles facing the election. Whether they like it or not, they are inextricably bound by their common future. They start to consider the issues and each other's concerns, often sharing their information without restriction and making suggestions that address the problems.

Sometimes Adriaan Vlok gives new details about the security threats. Minutes are not kept of these discussions, they are too sensitive. Mostly they are held between the ANC and the National Party, excluding some of the smaller parties.

To solve the problem of access to the no-go areas, the committee agrees that on a regular basis, buses of campaigners from the political parties will drive into these areas. Through loudspeakers, each party will have equal time in speaking to the crowds. The initiative is called 'Operation Access'. It is scheduled to start on Wednesday, 23 February 1994, two months before election day.

Throughout February there is growing consensus that the right wing poses a major threat. Intelligence sources report a mobilisation of all of the major right-wing groupings. Mo Shaik, a highly effective ANC intelligence operative who has established informer networks in the police and right-wing groupings, also feeds us information on the subversive activities of elements in the police and military. These include clandestine meetings of officers at certain military bases and also in some of the elite special forces battalions. It is agreed that every attempt must be made to counter the real possibility that the police and army, or significant portions of these forces, will not remain loyal to the process. Intense discussion is held on the potential of right-wing elements in the defence force to spoil the election or, equally damaging, to simply not do their duty, and fail to assist and protect the process.

As always, there is speculation and rumour. The media adds fuel to the fire by reporting that people are stockpiling canned goods, torch batteries, candles, and fuel.

In the monitoring division, we are moving fast to set up the necessary departments to fulfil our mandate. These are established at national level at IEC headquarters and then replicated in each province and, where appropriate, in regions and districts. Our primary function, to monitor the freeness and fairness of the election, is allocated to the accreditation and logistics department, which will be responsible for the task of hiring, accrediting and deploying the estimated nine thousand IEC monitors.

In addition, this department will also be responsible for the reception, accreditation and recommended deployment of the massive contingent of international observers who are expected to arrive to observe the election and to pass judgement on its freeness and fairness. Their number is expected to exceed ten thousand and will include observers from the UN, EU, OAU, Commonwealth, SADC, and also international NGOs like the Carter Centre and the various German foundations. As if this were not enough, there will also be the accreditation of thousands of domestic observers from local NGOs. Clearly, this is an election that will not go unnoticed. It will not just be watched, it will be surgically scrutinised. Not a bad thing in itself, but it does add to the pressure. A lot.

We are fortunate to get Professor Francis Wilson, a workaholic from the University of Cape Town with extensive experience in large-scale project management, to head this key department.

The various support departments are quickly identified and people with the requisite skills found to lead them. The education and training department is critical. Hundreds of training staff will need to be recruited or contracted. Training courses need to be designed. There need to be training materials and handbooks for monitors in the field, codes of conduct, rules of observation, and guidelines for intervention in difficult situations. And then, of course, the training itself of the nine thousand monitors and the thousands of foreign observers. The list is endless. The job demands a very special person.

After much enquiry, I am referred to Dr Namane Magau, head of human resources at the Development Bank of South Africa. I phone her, she agrees to meet me at the IEC.

By the time we meet, I have done some reference checks on her. Clearly she is exceptionally capable and also has that essential quality found in all good leaders, the ability to delegate while keeping strict control of the crucial elements. She also has a doctorate in education from Harvard University.

Dr Magau is a small woman, softly spoken and well dressed. She listens carefully as I explain what is needed. She does not blink when I tell her that if she decides to take this job, it is seven days a week until the election and not much sleep. She asks all the right questions and it is all I can do to stop myself from going on my knees and beseeching her to take the job. I stress the national importance of what she will be doing, the fact that she will be playing a role in history.

'You don't need to go on, Peter,' she says, smiling sweetly. 'I will take the job but I will need to speak to my boss at the bank.'

Relief pours over me. 'Do you want me to make the call?' I say.

'No,' she says, 'let me do that. I also want to ask for some of my staff to come and help me.' She stands. I can't help myself and give her a huge hug as she leaves. She smiles and says she will phone me. Three hours later, she phones and says that she will start work in five days' time, on Monday, 7 February 1994.

Transport will be required for the monitors, lots of it and on a countrywide basis. They will have to get to every polling station in the country, some ten thousand of them. And they will have to be relieved as the days of voting and then counting take place. They will need sleep and food. Where there is no telephone system, they will need to travel to the nearest centre to send their reports, first to the province and then to national. Preliminary estimations are that we will need in the region of two thousand cars. Khosi Ndlovu is recruited to head this department. Forceful, dynamic and highly organised, she hits the ground running, working out ways to get cars donated free or at budget prices, and then working out transportation grids according to the initial home affairs plan for the siting of the voting stations. Particular attention is given to the safekeeping of vehicles, fuel and maintenance arrangements and control of vehicles, which includes a detailed code of conduct for users.

We realise that if we are to counter real or potential threats to the electoral process, we need to gather information and intelligence. This will also have to be analysed and directed to the appropriate body for action. The information and verification department, a less sinister name than 'intelligence', is established under the joint leadership of Thele Moema from the ANC, and Admiral Dries Putter. Moema is a former member of MK in exile for sixteen years and a senior operative in the ANC's department of intelligence and security. Putter is a former chief of the South African Navy with close links to military intelligence. He's a measured man, over fifty and with silver hair, a veteran of his craft.

The last member of the spook farm, as they come to be known, is Stef Snel who is based in Cape Town. It is odd and yet invigorating to see Thele Moema and Dries Putter, both of whom share a strong common interest in philosophy, discussing the quandaries of life over a cup of coffee. Moema, with an MA in sociology, an MBA, and a doctorate in philosophy, likes nothing better than to discuss the existential choices that we face as a country. This belies a sharp mind and an acute nose for getting to the heart of an issue. Somehow he plies his gritty trade with the air of a philosopher rather than slouching into thuggery, as is the wont of so many in that murky and cryptic craft.

Moema's brother Ace was an MK soldier who was executed by

a police hit squad based at Vlakplaas outside Pretoria. I was told this by Dirk Coetzee, a former commander of Vlakplaas who defected to the ANC. At the time, the late 1980s, and at the request of Jacob Zuma, head of ANC intelligence, I took Coetzee's statement in Lusaka. Coetzee said that after the murder in 1981 of Ace Moema in the Eastern Transvaal, his body was burnt to ashes over an open fire.

One evening, Moema and I share a whisky in my office and I ask him how he and Putter and Snel are managing.

'You know, Peter,' he says, 'we have to make this work. We have everything to lose. It is my business to make it work. Luckily, Dries has extended the hand of friendship to me. I trust this man, and maybe, maybe, when this is over we can be friends. He has told me that he would like that. It is a shock when you realise that your enemy does not have horns.'

I laugh.

He goes on, 'We have a different approach. Dries starts with a worst-case scenario and then works backwards and I start at the beginning and end up at worst case. We come from contrasting backgrounds and start from different places when we analyse data, but we end up with the best solution or conclusion. Funny, I never thought I would ever say this, but for me it is no longer about sides, it is about what is in the national interest and right now we have to deliver an election.'

I nod, unsure of how they work but knowing that when I walk past their office at eleven o'clock at night, they are there working through papers, arguing and sometimes laughing. And then they are back at six the next morning.

The information from this team is fed into the political party liaison committee. The meetings with the spooks take place late into the night and involve a process of identification and prioritisation of threats. The counter measures to the threats are also pinpointed and the necessary forces and groupings placed on alert for urgent deployment. Again, not surprisingly, the right wing emerges as the most immediate and significant threat, with evidence pouring in of their increasing mobilisation. In KwaZulu and Natal there is mounting evidence of the establishment of military training camps and confirmation that large quantities of arms are being directed to the province by right-wing and rogue elements in the security forces. Putter and Moema are tasked to liaise with the state and ANC intelligence services to get us the information we need to address the menace. They are also asked to get any information relating to potential attacks on the IEC and its operations.

At a meeting at Lichtenburg in the Western Transvaal the AWB is given the freedom of the town. The meeting is addressed by the Leader as well as Constand Viljoen. The leader of the Conservative Party, Ferdi Hartzenberg, is also present.

The meeting starts in darkness as, coincidentally, the nearby power station has been bombed and is not functioning. The AWB brings its own generators to light the hall, but the machines are noisy, for which, with a wry smile, the Leader apologises. There is much grinning and knowing sniggers ripple through the men in khaki. This is just the beginning.

The message from the platform is stark, the Leader saying, '... there will be no negotiations with the ANC, bombs have already exploded and will be followed by even bigger explosions ... If the demands are not met, let there be more bombs.' The Leader is in fine form tonight as his fist smashes onto the table, his voice easily rising above the rhythmic throb of the generators. He finishes with a salute identical to that of the Nazi party. The crowd rises, reciprocating with a roar.

It is early February 1994.

The weekly planning meetings of the monitoring division take place at eight o'clock every Monday morning. On this Monday, 7 February 1994, we consider the reports from the departments we have set up and discuss the priorities for the week. It is tense and stressful as we work through the components of the operational plan that will take us through to election day. The ops plan is extremely detailed, listing each and every task that will need to be accomplished if we are to meet our mandate. It has been checked by UN electoral experts who have confirmed that it is correct and comprehensive.

We are disturbed by a banging in the passageway outside and raucous laughter. The meeting stops. We look at one another, puzzled. Down the corridor comes a procession of young men, some wearing football jerseys, kicking and dribbling an array of soccer balls. A few are bouncing the balls on their knees like true professionals. I look at them with envy. I wouldn't mind kicking a ball around on a day like this. They are followed by security personnel who are smiling. 'What are these soccer players doing here?' I ask. 'How did they get in? Are they mad? This is a serious place!' One of the security men replies, 'Haven't you heard, this is the Soccer Party and they have come to register as a political party for the election.'

'You are not being serious?' I say.

'Yes, I am, and so are they. They say they are the only people "fit" to govern this country.'

We all burst out laughing. The young men with their black-and-white patched soccer balls pass, enjoying the attention.

I tell everyone we should get back to our meeting. But before that I need a loo break. I'm standing at the urinal going about my business when another man steps in beside me. It is a small urinal and there is little room between us. I stare straight ahead, conscious of the unspoken etiquette that exists between men in such matters. Do not stare at the man next to you. Rather stare automaton-like, straight ahead at some fixed point on the wall or, alternatively, on the grey steel of the urinal in front of you. However, I do notice that this is a tall man next to me. He, too, politely stares straight ahead. As I finish, zip and turn, I see that the man standing next to me is Nelson Mandela.

'Oh, my goodness, hello, sir,' I say.

He politely turns and says in that deep voice, 'Aah, Peter, what a place to meet. And what is a lawyer like you doing here?'

I tell him, standing back to allow him access to the single basin in the toilet.

'Aah,' he says, washing his hands. 'So we are in your hands.'

'Not really, sir, there is a big team.'

He smiles and asks me if I remember the report I had given him a year earlier in which we had warned the police that at a particular gathering there would be violence from Inkatha. They had neglected the warning and people had died. At a meeting at his office at Shell House after the killings, Mandela had been incensed by the inactivity of the police, which had resulted in the deaths of innocent civilians. He had made much of this in the press and in a large public meeting in Port Elizabeth.

He steps back so that I can wash my hands. When we are both ready to leave, he stands, chatting, seemingly in no hurry. I ask him if he has come to register the ANC as a political party and he replies, 'No, I have merely come to wish you all at the IEC well. Registration will come later.'

The large shaved head of one of his security detail appears at the door, obviously wondering if his important charge has come to grief in the loo. He sees me, shakes his head perplexed and disappears, probably chastising himself or others for not first checking the toilet.

Mandela insists on my going out first, rebuffing my protestations, saying, 'Peter, you came in first and you should leave first.' I walk out into a barrage of security and press.

Back in the planning meeting, I say, 'Guess who stood next to me at the urinal?'

'The striker for the Soccer Party,' answers Solveigh Piper distractedly.

'No, Nelson Mandela.' We all laugh. 'The Soccer Party and Nelson Mandela in one day! How weird can this election get?' I ask.

Very weird, is the answer to that question. But right then I wasn't to know.

It is Tuesday, 8 February 1994. The Kiss (Keep It Straight and Simple) Party arrives to register. In an election in which the stakes are perilously high and the country teeters from crisis to crisis, the injection of light relief is welcomed by the media and a public desperately in need of levity. I love the Kiss Party with its logo of a pair of red lips in the form of a big smacking smooch. I wonder what it will look like on the ballot form. Most of the parties have pictures of their leader as their logo, so a kiss in bright scarlet lipstick will provide a pleasant change.

Each day brings a commotion and excitement to the IEC as parties come to register with their leaders and entourage. I am struck by the historic significance of Mandela arriving with senior ANC leaders and registering the party. This tall man walking with slow dignity greets all he meets along the corridor, sometimes stopping to shake hands and even to talk, listening, making a comment and then moving on.

The registration of the ANC by Mandela somehow makes the election certain, placing a seal on it. It will happen, whatever form it takes. It is irrevocable in intent.

The registration of the parties invigorates us. This formality is procedural yet has elements of high drama as the delegations arrive with their fanfare and hubbub, the press snapping away, the video cameras whirring as the teams retreat before the dignitaries.

The information we get from Thele Moema and Dries Putter is excellent and we are able to build a reasonable picture of the major areas of risk. On a daily basis Putter gathers critical information about the activities of the right wing from his various intelligence sources. Our objective is to find out where the groupings are situated, who leads them, what capacity they have, access to weaponry and, importantly, whether they should be taken seriously.

We are also buoyed by news that members of a right-wing cell in the Orange Free State, run by Colonel Labuschagne and his commander, Brigadier Kriel, have been arrested. It is Wednesday, 9 February 1994.

The information from our various departments requires analysis. Are there patterns? What is the strength of the various dissident organisations? What threat do they pose? If they strike, what will be the consequences? All this information has vital implications for the freeness and fairness of the election. We are also told that the commissioners will require a detailed final report after the election pronouncing on its freeness and fairness.

Steven Friedman is appointed to head the analysis department. Friedman is a highly esteemed political and social analyst. It takes some discussion and persuasion to get him to take the job. It's not that he is unwilling to help; rather, he has reservations that he will be able to do a professional job given the impossible deadlines. Since Friedman is only appointed in mid-February, with just over two months to go before the election, I can sympathise with him. But, in fact, nothing is ideal about this election. The only thing in its favour is that it is three hundred and fifty years overdue. It is an event whose time has come.

Friedman appoints Sam Makhubela as his deputy and together they set about establishing a network of experienced analysts at national and provincial level.

The Electoral Act provides for a two-phase election registration procedure.

The first requirement is that a political party has to lodge a formal application for registration, with a deposit of twenty-five thousand rand at the national level and five thousand rand for each provincial election. The registering party also has to commit to the electoral code of conduct.

The applications are then published in the *Government Gazette* and if there are no objections (or after a favourable hearing), the registration is accepted.

The second stage of the process is the submission by parties of their lists of candidates. If this list is not submitted in time, the registration of the party lapses.

The deadline for the registration of political parties to participate in the election is 12 February 1994.

The deadline arrives. By the end of the day, despite their protestations about the election, Inkatha have joined the election process. Many regard this as merely keeping their hand in, with no real intention of changing their non-participation stance.

Neither the Conservative Party nor the Afrikaner Volksfront register. This rings alarm bells all over the country, and with good reason. It is known that large elements of the defence force and police are close to the right wing. The role of the Afrikaner generals, the commanders of the strongest military force in Africa, is critical. The one grouping with the capacity to stop the election and the transition process have just voted with their feet.

It is 12 February 1994.

A shared vision has emerged between the two lead negotiators, Cyril Ramaphosa and Roelf Meyer, and a mutual agreement as to what must be done to defend it.

The ANC and the National Party negotiators know that if the right wing have the defence-force generals behind them, they have the ability to carry out the unthinkable, a military coup. It is entirely conceivable.

A message is conveyed to the Freedom Alliance – consisting mainly of the Afrikaner Volksfront, the Conservative Party, Inkatha, and Chief Mangope of Bophuthatswana – that every effort will be made to bring them into the electoral process even if registration deadlines have passed. If necessary, the IEC will propose amendments to the electoral legislation that will allow them to register. In order to accommodate this, a further deadline for political parties to register by Friday, 4 March 1994 is set by the IEC.

The ANC and National Party make an offer to the Freedom Alliance that involves significantly increased decentralisation of power to the nine provinces in the new dispensation. This includes greater control over their finances and legislative powers. Importantly, the principle of the right to self-determination will be enshrined in the constitution. A split ballot for national and provincial elections is also proposed.

The consequence of this concession is that parties that are strongly represented in the regions or provinces stand a chance of gaining reasonable representation, if not a majority. Thus, Inkatha, with a large support base in KwaZulu and Natal, could gain control of the province.

But these concessions are still not enough. The Conservative Party and the Volksfront reject the offer. Critically it does not address their demand for a Volkstaat *before* the election. Inkatha follows suit and also rejects the offer.

War talk from the right-wing groups escalates. In the midst of this, Constand Viljoen, desperate to avoid conflict and violence, continues to seek ways of reaching agreement with the ANC and National Party. The former commander of the South African Defence Force has seen much of war. And he knows what it brings. But the rank and file of the right wing show no such reticence.

I am under no illusions as to the extent of the threat posed by the right wing. The only issue is how much damage they will wreak on the electoral process and the transition. We all know what violence they are capable of inflicting.

It is mid-February. The election is two months away.

Fifteen ANC youths (twelve of them under eighteen years old) are killed in the village of Mahlele near Creighton in the southern Natal Midlands. They were sleeping at a derelict house after putting up posters advertising a voter education workshop. Four Inkatha officials are arrested and charged in connection with the incident.

It is Friday, 18 February 1994.

Heads are appointed to two more departments in the monitoring division.

Willem Ellis, a private-sector consultant and one of the most experienced communications specialists in the country, takes over the telecommunications department. This department must set up communications and radio links between the division's head office, provinces, sub-regions, monitors and observers. This includes links with voting stations and counting centres. That the process of the identification of voting stations is ongoing and not yet complete is a real problem.

Ellis moves so fast with his techies that other departments that have been around for weeks complain that he is putting them under too much pressure. Within a week he has established his entire team, mostly seconded from Siemens and Telkom. I like Ellis immensely, largely because he moves at pace and keeps to himself, presenting me with weekly progress reports that are so complicated they read like Russian, but which meet the deadlines prescribed in the division's operational plan for telecommunications.

Importantly, he has a great relationship with Telkom, who we desperately need to install telephones at operations centres and the voting stations that have already been identified. In one weekend, he gets Telkom to install telephones in every voting station in Soweto, an exceptional feat.

The final department is information technology. Getting the right person here is critical, especially as IT people are in short supply. Helmut Welte from the private sector is brought in to design, install and implement the systems. Special systems will need to be created to record each voting station using a special identifying code which will correspond with the geographic location. A complication here is that many polling stations have no specific physical address in the conventional sense. In addition, much of the software required is unique and cannot be bought off the shelf.

This doesn't prove an obstacle to Welte who, within a few days, has designed a software package to log and analyse election irregularities. This information will be fed through to the regional, provincial and national operations centres. More than one hundred types of incidents – from throwing stones, assault and verbal threats against speakers to tearing down election posters – are identified in the software. This is a vital component in the information flow which will later assist the commissioners in deciding whether there has been compliance with the twelve basic principles of a free and fair election.

The computer system will have to handle tens of thousands of reports filtering into forty-one operations centres. The system will need to be networked and will have to be totally secure so that reports and statistics cannot be manipulated.

It is Wednesday, 23 February 1994.

I walk into Welte's office and ask him how his planning is going and when he will be able to present his ops plan. He brightly tells me that the entire IT system for the division will take at least three months to set up before we can go live.

'Jesus, Helmut,' I explode, 'go live in three months! This election is happening in two months' time. We can't wait for three months. Go live!' My voice cracks. 'We will all be dead by then. I need this done in six weeks tops and I want to do a dry-run test in mid-April.'

Welte looks at me, his eyes narrowing like a man staring into a fierce sun, his lips purse and I fully expect him to spit on my shoes.

'Six weeks, are you serious?' he asks incredulously.

Only an IT propeller-head could be so calm when panic is the appropriate response. That is why they are a different species: they don't think like us. Maybe that's why they rule the world. They refuse to let things like dates and facts get in the way.

'Yes, Helmut,' I say softly, my teeth very close together. 'I am totally sure. Unless you feel that you can get a later date for this election. There are no choices here. Don't you think that I would like two years to plan for this election? Let me ask you a question. Were you watching TV on the day of Chris Hani's funeral?'

'Yes, I was,' he replies.

'And what were you thinking?'

'I was thinking that there would be a war, an apocalypse, and I was scared.'

'Well, that is why the politicians will not move the election date. Because they are even more scared because they know how close we came and this election is the one event that can usher in a new dispensation, a new country. Now can you do this in six weeks?'

'I have to, don't I?' he says quietly.

'Yes, Helmut,' I say, leaving his office.

By the time I get back to my office, I have cooled down, so I phone Welte and ask him to give me a mini ops-plan for his department as soon as possible. Trying to be a good manager, I give him encouragement and wish him well, stressing the national importance of his task.

I sit back in my chair thinking that it is now five o'clock and I still face at least another four hours of work. My phone rings. It is Betty Weltz, who runs the office of Judge Kriegler.

'Peter, the commissioners are in a meeting and would like to see you now if that is possible.'

I know Betty Weltz from her previous life as a political sociologist. I had used her as a witness to give evidence in mitigation in an ANC treason trial in Pretoria in which three white MK soldiers, Damian de Lange, Susan Westcott and Ian Robertson, were on trial for carrying out various military activities. They had been caught with enough arms and explosives to start a small war, which was exactly their intention. They had been betrayed by one of the members of their unit, one Hugh Lugg who had cracked under the pressure of operating underground. Early one morning, Lugg got up at the remote house at which they were staying in Broederstroom and went for a jog … to the local police station, where he trotted in and announced that he was part of an underground MK unit that was in the country to carry out acts of war. The half-asleep station commander, astonished by this gift from above, radioed the police task force, which hit the house within the hour and arrested the startled occupants, who later became known as the Broederstroom Three. Sadly, neither my role as a defence lawyer nor the evidence of Betty Weltz made any impression on Judge Kerlewis, who appeared to take some pleasure in sending them down for a lot of years, twenty-five of them to be exact.

'No problem, Betty,' I say, 'I'll be there in a minute,' wondering with some irritation what they want.

Outside the commissioners' meeting room, I bump into my opposite number, Piet Coleyn, and Mojanku Gumbi, the head of the adjudication secretariat of the IEC. We look at one another and shrug. We have no idea why we've been summoned. We enter the meeting room and a complete session of all the IEC commissioners. Judge Kriegler quickly cuts to the chase. He tells us that they have encountered a number of problems with Mr Neels Swart, the owner of the centre. Swart wants to charge the IEC extra for each telephone line installed. This led to an argument, and he has blocked the installation. Given the deadlines, this presents an obvious problem. In addition, the commission finds him difficult to deal with at all levels. It is clear from his attitude that his priority is not the election but the lucre he can make out of the IEC.

Gumbi, Coleyn and I nod in agreement. I am still nodding when I hear the judge say that they have decided that the IEC should move into town and that alternative premises are being sought.

I want to speak but find that I have trouble getting the words out. I am stupefied.

'You want to relocate the entire IEC or just parts of it to central Joburg?' I ask.

'All of it,' says Kriegler, 'we cannot stay here anymore.'

'We have two months before this election, with deadlines that are beyond tight. This will affect them further,' I say bleakly, looking at Coleyn and Gumbi for support. They nod vigorously.

'We have no choice, Peter. We cannot run the election from here. It will be impossible.' Kriegler's voice is tired. I glance around the room, realising that this has obviously been the subject of much discussion. Clearly the decision has been taken. Our job is to implement it.

'No problem, Judge,' I hear myself say hollowly, thinking of how I will have to go to IT and telecommunications and relay the news. Now Welte is definitely going to spit on my shoes.

We leave the room. Outside, we heave sighs that reflect our separate moods. We look at one another glumly and walk back to our offices. Seated at my desk, I look at the black curtains around me, thinking that they aren't so bad after all. It worries me that I have started to like them.

I can't work now so I resolve to head for the bar and a whisky. I feel some entitlement about that after the day I've had. I mean, having to move an entire election operation two months before due date is enough to drive most people to drink. Happily, I have never needed much driving on this issue.

I am relieved to find that I am not the only one in need of a stiff drink. Ben van der Ross, Charles Nupen and Zac Yacoob have also repaired for refreshments. Frankly, I'm surprised that the entire commission is not at the bar.

I had not met Ben van der Ross before I was seconded to the IEC, but his reputation is impressive. I have known Zac Yacoob for many years. He was blinded after contracting meningitis at the age of sixteen months but has adapted to this chronic disability and is legendary for his remarkable memory. I have seen him in court on a number of occasions quoting chapter and verse from cases and legislation without a single note or reference. It is both unnerving and inspiring to see him in action.

'Nice, guys,' I say sarcastically. 'As if we don't have enough on our plate already.'

'Pete,' says Nupen, 'it is impossible to run an election from this place. We should have realised it sooner and got out a lot earlier. We have no choice if we are to run this election.'

'But who leased this place for the IEC in the first place? Surely they must have realised that we could not run it from here. Was it deliberate or accidental?'

'We can only speculate on that – it was leased for the IEC before we were established. It was not our decision, but if they had remotely done their homework, they would have realised that the facilities are simply insufficient,' says Zacoob in his careful way.

Van der Ross adds, 'This guy Swart is doing everything possible to make our life here a nightmare. Just to get telephones is a huge mission.'

'So who was responsible for leasing this place?' I ask.

'The department of public works,' says Charles Nupen.

Typical. We look at each other as we raise our glasses.

It is my daughter Isabella's birthday. A momentous affair by any standards as she, with Caroline, meticulously plan every facet of the occasion. She describes the type of cake she wants, the entertainment – a miraculous magician she has seen at a friend's birthday party. Considerable time is spent ruminating over the not insubstantial guest list. The composition of the party pack, a small gift pack consisting of sweets and goodies given to departing guests – is also the subject of careful deliberation as is the order of events on the big day itself. She is turning two.

Preparations complete, we await the arrival of the first guests. The lawn has been mowed, the edges trimmed and picnic blankets have been laid on the grass under the large oak tree at the bottom of the garden. I look up at the cloudy blue sky wondering if the weather will hold or if a highveld thunderstorm will rudely interrupt her party.

It is Monday, 28 February 1994. The election is exactly two months away.

The first arrivals drift in, dressed in party mode and bearing their gifts, which Isabella accepts with a smile that lights up her face, her large brown eyes framed by her blonde hair. She is completely beautiful. I watch her deal with more guests as I stand a little aside, nervously greeting parents who stay for a cup of tea.

The party begins with the magician. He's a gangly man with long arms at the end of which are white gloves slipped over thin fingers that move constantly. They seemingly have a life of their own, like a pianist's, prehensile. The magician is really very good and has me, never mind the kids, completely foxed with his tricks, although there is one small boy who shouts out twice, 'I know how you did that.' This is very irritating, and I ponder whether I should wander across and give him a sharp cuff. I don't. His mother might be here.

As any good entertainer should, the magician makes a big fuss of the host, Isabella, who solemnly accepts the attention as her due. The show over, the children's minds quickly turn to food and drink. In anticipation, they tear around the garden in play. There is the occasional assault and battery as their exuberance moves beyond the boundaries of acceptable horseplay.

In all of this, I notice Isabella's absence. The food comes and goes and I search the garden, worried that something might have happened to her. I make my way inside and find her in the small TV room where she is intently watching the Peter Pan video, *Hook*. I go through the spiel: it's your birthday party, all your friends are here, you should be outside enjoying herself. She tells me that she *is* enjoying herself. I tell her that this is not a nice way to behave, that she should come outside. She tells me that it is *her* birthday party.

86

Nonplussed, I consult Caroline, who is busy putting the final touches to the cake on which two candles perch proudly. To much fanfare, the cake is carried into the garden and placed on a low table around which the kids crowd, eyeing the cake with naked hunger. The kids hold back, but I know this is only temporary.

Caroline looks at me as one would regard an incompetent assistant and crossly says, 'Go and get Isabella.'

'Look,' I say, pathetically, 'that is easier said than done.'

'Just go and do it.' The last two words stressed and linked: 'doo-it'.

I move fast to get Isabella. She has now sunk back into the armchair, oblivious to the world and completely absorbed in *Hook*. It is the version in which Robin Williams plays Peter Pan and, in my view, he is doing a fine job. I too lose track of time and watch the movie. In the middle of the first pirate scene, where they are carousing in the town and generally behaving badly, I jolt back to reality. 'Come on, Bella,' I cajole, 'you must join your own party. You can't be rude. Time to cut the cake.' She ignores me. I move to pick her up. She shouts, I back off, and she settles further into the chair. I try again, this time inching slowly forward, and again she shouts, but in a way that terrifies me. I stop instantly, now pleading piteously with her. She will not be moved.

I give up and rejoin the assembled masses in the garden who, driven by greed and hunger, are now making a lot of noise. I know from my own bad experiences of crowds that we are seconds away from a riot.

'She won't come,' I say to Caroline, who gives me a look that nearly turns me to stone. With a smile, she says she'll cut the cake for Isabella. I shuffle away.

Five minutes later, I see my daughter emerge from the house. Finally she's come to her senses. I believe that her joining the festivities salvages what little is left of my authority over both her and the general proceedings. It is, in my view, some small testament to the direction that I like to think I bring to the family.

Isabella stands on the patio examining her guests, who are now tucking into the birthday cake as if they will never see one again. Some smear cake as far afield as their eyes and ears. Isabella looks at them and then says loudly, 'Go away.' With that, she heads back inside to resume watching her video.

The party is a roaring success, with parents and their charges heaping praise on Caroline and Isabella for the food and the magician. Isabella is not there to receive the accolades. She emerges from the room only when *Peter Pan* is finished, reunited with Tinker Bell, the lucky fellow. It is about an hour after the last guest has departed.

'Did you enjoy your birthday, my darling?' I ask.

'I loved it, thank you,' she says, smiling sweetly.

CHAPTER FOUR

We are in the first week of March. The election is next month. The extended deadline for parties to register is this Friday. Rumours are rife about which political parties will not participate. Those who stand outside will not be bystanders. It is not in the nature of the right wing or Inkatha. These details gnaw at the country. And at my nerves. The security forces tell us they are prepared. Which is cold comfort.

The ground rules for the election are reasonably simple. The elections for the national assembly, or parliament, will be conducted at the same time as the elections for the nine provincial legislatures and there will be separate ballot papers for the two bodies. Half of the four hundred seats that will comprise the national assembly will be elected from a single national list while the other half will derive from nine provincial lists.

In contrast to the old system of constituency-based elections, this election will use a variant of the national list proportional representation (PR) system. According to this system, voters vote for a party and not for an individual who would represent their constituency. Each party list is compiled by the political party, giving the parties complete control over the candidates they choose to be on their list.

The smaller parties support PR as they know that they may never attract sufficient votes to win at a constituency level. In a winner-takes-all constituency system, their votes would probably be lost. Under the PR system, all the votes for a particular party count. Provided a certain minimum threshold of votes is met, the smaller parties will get the seats to which their vote total entitles them.

Thresholds vary internationally from five per cent in Germany to one per cent in Israel. In South Africa, in order to make parliament as representative as possible, the political negotiators have agreed that there will be no threshold. Except: there are no accurate population figures for the country so it is difficult to estimate the potential number of voters. Nevertheless, this has been put at twenty-two million. Of course, not all voters will go to the polls, so it is estimated that the actual turnout will be in the region of twenty million voters. That figure divided by four hundred seats means that it would take fifty thousand votes or point two five per cent of the total vote to get a seat in the national assembly. These are projections; the actual results in the election will accurately set the threshold and number of votes required to secure a seat.

In a new dispensation where minorities think that they will have no voice, this is critical. Besides, as the politicians like to righteously proclaim, it is more inclusive, and in a country with our past, that is important. Interestingly, the National Party, which has governed our beloved country with a racial iron fist for the last forty-six years, is a staunch proponent of inclusivity. A kind of ethnic damascene conversion has clearly occurred.

PR is a reasonably easy electoral system to run. The party compiles its list; the people vote for a party; the number of seats won are allocated as per the party list to equal the proportion of votes obtained by the party. The name and logo of the party as well as the face of its leader are printed on the ballot form and all the voter has to do is make a choice. X marks the spot. Could anything be simpler?

In this election, the franchise to vote extends to everyone over eighteen who is 'ordinarily resident' in South Africa. All they need to identify themselves is a valid identity document. Because many may not have identity documents, particularly in the rural areas, the IEC is vested with the authority to issue temporary voting cards. The Electoral Act also permits South Africans living abroad to vote.

That this election, for the first time, does not disqualify people from voting because of the colour of their skin brings its own challenge. Indubitably, it is a welcome one, but a challenge nonetheless. Previous elections, with the exception of the elections for the tricameral parliament which included Indian and coloured voters, had been for whites only. The problem is that the government has never really counted the exact number of black people in the country and its censuses were notoriously unreliable. Whatever the facts and figures of the matter, the bottom line is that whereas previous elections were for just over three million white people in areas where there were good roads, telephones, water and electricity, this election is for about twenty-two million people, many of them in regions that have little or no infrastructure. Put bluntly, this election is for an electorate at least seven times the size of the elections the department of home affairs used to conduct in the past.

Uncharted territory? Completely. This election is way beyond the realm of their experience. Even if they have the political will to organise this election, do they have the capacity? And even if they have the will and the capacity, can they do all this in what is now less than two months?

In the first week of March, Chief Lucas Mangope, the president of Bophuthatswana, announces that his homeland will not take part in the election. As far as he is concerned, Bophuthatswana gained 'independence' from the apartheid government in 1977.

Bophuthatswana is a replica of the other 'independent' Bantustans that the government has created around the country. This one is for the Tswana-speaking people. It is made up of a patchwork of, often, disconnected parcels of land.

Chief Lucas Mangope, an aristocratic-looking fellow, was appointed by Pretoria and was accountable to Pretoria, who also trained and supplied his army and police force. It is these security forces, generally commanded by former South African officers, that keep Mangope in power. They are greatly feared, and with good reason.

Mangope, as with many people placed in positions of power by others, has come to think that his position is self-achieved and deserved. Power, once sniffed, is a heady hallucinogenic. Apart from Sun City, the gambling Mecca of the sun king Sol Kerzner, there is little value to the soil of this sad place. The South African government, in allocating the land to the Tswana people, ensured that the borders excluded the world's richest platinum deposits.

Bophuthatswana does have significance, however. It is adjacent to much of the land in the Western Transvaal that the right wing is claiming as its Volkstaat.

Chief Mangope, at the age of three score and ten, is a man who does not enjoy the confidence of his people. In the homeland's last election in 1985, only fifteen thousand of the two and a half million eligible voters turned out. Less than point six per cent of the population.

The problem of the homelands was a vexing one for the political negotiators. What was now to be done with these rulers and their 'countries'?

The answer, as far as the negotiators were concerned, was that on Saturday, 1 January 1994, the citizens of all the homelands became South African citizens. With a stroke of a pen, residents of these poverty-stricken states, who had been deprived of South African citizenship, got it back. And the 'homelands' themselves? On the day of the election, they would be incorporated into South Africa.

It is the collapse of grand apartheid. It is also the collapse of the 'homeland' rulers, who find that they have been dumped and their land lost. And no ruler likes being dumped and losing his kingdom, particularly Chief Mangope, a proud man by all accounts. The consequence is that the ageing Mangope is now being recalcitrant and refusing to play electoral ball. The declaration by Mangope that his country will not participate in the elections sparks a fierce reaction from his subjects, who make their own announcement.

The response of public servants in Bophuthatswana is to strike, causing the collapse of the entire Bophuthatswanan public service. Their demand is a simple one. Since their homeland is due to disappear on 27 April 1994 into South Africa, they want their wages and pensions paid out in advance. While the demand is straightforward, its fulfilment is another matter in the land of Bophuthatswana, where there is no money in the fiscus to pay the strikers. With each day, the situation slides into violence and anarchy in the struggling homeland.

At the IEC we know that it will be impossible to organise an election in Bophuthatswana in such circumstances, even if Mangope were to allow us to do so.

A well-built man of medium height with silver hair and startling blue eyes arrives at IEC headquarters to register a political party. He is accompanied by a few supporters, not many, but enough to signify that he is not alone. The small delegation strides purposefully through the corridors of the cavernous World Trade Centre.

The man is greeted by Judge Kriegler, who has earlier been phoned and told that there will be one final registration before the clock strikes midnight.

The exchange between the two men is courteous and professional. The papers are quickly signed and the delegation leaves the offices, disappearing in their cars into the night. The whole process has taken about thirty minutes and has been briskly executed, almost with the efficiency of a military incursion. And so it should be.

The man is Constand Viljoen and he has just registered a new political party, the Freedom Front.

It is twenty minutes to twelve on the night of Friday, 4 March 1994.

There will be repercussions to Viljoen's action. Of that I am certain.

The entire IEC moves into downtown Johannesburg on the weekend of 5 and 6 March 1994.

Despite the fear that the relocation will be difficult and that we might lose up to a week of valuable time, the transfer, supervised by a committee led by Charles Nupen, goes smoothly and without incident, a significant accomplishment. The new building is at 41 Kruis Street opposite the Carlton Centre. It meets the requirements of the organisation and has the additional advantage of being close to the United Nations headquarters, the home base of many of the experts seconded to the IEC.

Immediately, one can sense a renewal in the IEC as people set about their tasks with new vigour and commitment, the dark cavernous spaces and drapes of the World Trade Centre receding thankfully into memory. The change in mood and spirit of the IEC is tangible.

My office is of reasonable size, with a view over roofs to a yellow mine dump. Not the best of aspects, but it doesn't depress me. At least I can see daylight.

Importantly, the monitoring division's national operations centre is now in a large secure area not far from my office. Phiroshaw Camay is particularly pleased. He is now being helped by two senior international advisors, Eddie Hendrickx and Jules Koninckx. Both men have been sent to us by the Belgian government after we requested senior police assistance in the establishment and running of the ops centre.

Hendrickx holds the rank of major in the Belgian gendarmerie and is the commanding officer of police operations in Brussels. This includes being the officer in charge of the meetings of heads of state of members of the European Union. He's disarmingly friendly and understated, a tall, well-built man who appears relaxed, if not languid at times, exuding an air of total competence and authority. His colleague Colonel Jules Koninckx is a serious man. Prior to his secondment to the IEC, he was the commander of the National Reserve Unit of the Belgian Police.

The purpose of the operations centres at national, provincial and sub-provincial level is to receive information on the progress of electioneering and voting, verify the information and direct it to the appropriate departments in monitoring for decision making and analysis. The ops centre has three components. All information will flow into it via the filter room, which will screen and route calls to the relevant desk where the information will be assessed, decided upon and executed. The third part of the centre is the information room where all data will be captured and from which status reports will be generated.

In addition, the operations centres will be responsible for the deployment and control of monitors and observers in the field. Also, they will be linked to the national police operations centre as well as to army intelligence.

The structure of the ops centres was derived from those utilised by the Wits–Vaal region of the National Peace Accord with great success during the funerals of Chris Hani and the former president of the ANC, Oliver Tambo. The original design drew on the experience of two senior policemen from Scotland Yard.

From early on Saturday morning Phiroshaw Camay, Eddie Hendrickx and Jules Koninckx are there to organise the national operations centre. Hendrickx takes charge of security regarding access precautions and perimeter control. Miraculously, within three days and three nights we have a functional ops centre complete with enlarged maps of each province, incident plotters, radio operators, tele-receptionists at banks of telephones, runners, typists, action evaluators and supervisors for each section.

Willem Ellis, head of our telecommunications department, solves the problem of getting Telkom to install lines by magically persuading them that it is in their interest to permanently move a team into an office on the floor above, complete with coffee machines and other office comforts that he has organised.

That evening Solveigh Piper organises a few drinks at our new offices to celebrate our move and also to welcome Hendrickx and Koninckx. Both men are friendly and at ease in their new surroundings, unlike, Hendrickx tells me, their host in Midrand. They are

95

housed with a Belgian chef who has been in the country for the last ten years. He is so concerned about the potential for South Africa to explode that he has sent his wife out of the country until after the election.

'Really,' I say, thinking that she is probably not the only one.

'You know, Peter,' he adds, 'there is a lot of concern in the international community that this thing may not work at all and that the country will lapse into violence and civil war. We were instructed to bring weaponry with us when we came here.'

'Shit, Eddie,' I say, my stomach suddenly hollow, anxious. 'Where are you keeping that stuff? You must be careful here.'

'It is no problem, Peter.' He laughs. 'It is kept locked up at the embassy in Pretoria and is only there for our use in an emergency.'

'Well, let's hope that we can avoid those,' I say cheerfully, taking a sip of my whisky.

'Yes, me too. Although my government will not be taking any chances.'

'What do you mean by that?'

'Jules and I have also been asked by our government to prepare a plan to evacuate all thirty-five thousand Belgian nationals living here.'

'You are kidding me, right?'

He stares at me. 'Peter, I never joke about things like that.'

I take a gulp of my drink. It bothers me that a lot of sane, rational people are planning for a disaster.

By Sunday night the new national ops centre has reached a point where Camay, Hendrickx and Koninckx can turn their attention to the provinces and regions. Together with their small team they fly out to help set up these centres, each a small-scale replica of the national centre. Nine provincial operations centres and thirty-two sub-provincial operations centres are planned. This team will work with the already appointed heads of monitoring in each province and region, who will take over the implementation of the centres once the initial establishment and training have taken place. According to our own planning, all operational centres must be operating and functional by Thursday, 24 March, about the time when the campaigns of the political parties will be in full swing.

We have been extremely fortunate in getting excellent people in place in the provinces. While most companies and institutions do not hesitate after receiving requests for their top managers to be seconded to help in the election, some move quicker than others.

Andre Lamprecht of Barlow Rand immediately answers the call. Within days, we have Ebby Mohamed, the general manager for Plascon, Western Cape, the giant paint and coating company, ready to assume duty as the head of monitoring in the Western Cape; Vuyo Ntshona from Barlow Rand head office to head up the Pretoria–Witwatersrand area; and Riel Pienaar, a senior manager at Barlow Rand Equipment Company to lead the Northern Transvaal province. South African Breweries seconds Bheki Sibiya to head up Natal.

The universities follow, with Professor Attie van der Merwe from the University of Pretoria to head the Eastern Transvaal, and Mark Anstey from the University of Port Elizabeth for the Eastern Cape. A lawyer from the Western Cape, Dines Gihwala, agrees to give up his practice and move to Kimberley to head up the Northern Cape Province. Each provincial head, with the assistance of headquarters in Johannesburg, has to find and appoint regional heads. Depending on the size of the province, there could be three or four sub-provincial regions.

In each of these provinces and sub-provinces, office space will have to be leased, equipped, staffed and the various national structures will need to be replicated. Thus operations, accreditation and logistics, training, transport, information and analysis, IT and telecommunications must all have a provincial and sub-provincial presence. The entire country has to be covered.

In making sure that all of this happens according to the tightest of operational plans, sleep is in short supply. Everyone operates on the brink of exhaustion, but somehow the importance of what has to be achieved provides the incentive, an intoxicant that cannot be resisted.

Men and women literally stop or interrupt their jobs and move to different parts of the country. In these places, some of them remote and rural, they work like Trojans and for little money in conditions that are often arduous and taxing.

Certain rural white communities are antagonistic to this election, so the managers and staff there have to be brought in. They work under hostile conditions. Sitting in my office at night, I feel humbled at the sacrifices being made. I am in a cushy post close to my home, and yet, so far, we have not received a single complaint. Solveigh Piper, who handles many of the provincial and regional offices with a style that is warm yet firm, constantly tells us that with few exceptions, everyone is committed to making their region work. People know the constraints, and yet everyone labours to overcome them.

Ebrahim Mohamed has 'agreed' to head up the Western Cape Province. He phones to tell me twenty-four hours after I made the call to Andre Lamprecht that he is at my disposal. When he comes to see me, he says that he had got a call from Lamprecht, who had asked him to fly to Johannesburg to discuss the election. He had done so, to be told by Lamprecht to clear his desk for three months and to contact me. When we meet, Ebby is electric with energy. Lamprecht had told him that working on the election was an opportunity of a lifetime.

'So what was your response?' I ask.

'I agreed with him, you always agree with Andre,' he jokes. Then adds, 'No seriously, he was right. This is history and I am now a part of it.'

The registration of General Constand Viljoen's Freedom Front is greeted with widespread acclaim and relief by the major political parties and the media. The euphoria accompanying Viljoen's registration is tempered by subsequent events. It is not all that cut and dried.

On Saturday, 5 March 1994, the Volksraad, or executive council of the Volksfront, rejects Viljoen's decision to register by seventy-three votes to twenty in a secret ballot. They vow not to submit their candidate lists to him by the required deadline, which means his registration will lapse.

The more vociferous members of the Volksfront and the far right label Viljoen a 'traitor' to his people. Ferdi Hartzenberg, the leader of the Conservative Party, is worried by the split and attempts to do some damage control. He thanks Viljoen for having the 'foresight' to register on a provisional basis. Cementing the impression of unity on the right, Viljoen accepts the decision of the Volksfront and remains a member.

Most editorials comment that Viljoen is keeping his options open and that not much should be read into his registration. The real speculation is whether this is a ploy to lull the ANC and National Party into a false sense of security around the issue of a Volkstaat and a military coup or whether he is genuine. And if he is genuine, will he carry his generals? That is the issue: the Afrikaner generals.

On Tuesday, 8 March 1994, Chief Mangope invites Constand Viljoen to a meeting of the Bophuthatswana Security Council where the heads of the Bophuthatswana Defence Force, police and national intelligence service and other ministers are present. Discussions centre on a report indicating that the ANC is sending MK cadres to infiltrate the territory and cause an insurrection. Isolated and scared, Mangope is reluctant to call on the services of his old ally, the South African Defence Force, fearing that they are under the thrall of the National Party and the ANC, and cannot be trusted. It is agreed that Viljoen will use the military capacity of the Volksfront to defend certain government locations if the situation deteriorates further, but only if called on to do so by the beleaguered chief.

I meet with an old friend on the UN team, Reg Austen. We had first met at a law conference in London and then again at a major anti-apartheid conference with the ANC in Harare in the late 1980s. Austen, a lawyer, has become an electoral expert for the electoral assistance division of the UN. A quiet man who prefers to listen rather than to speak, he has become a good friend. He has been involved in many elections over the years, particularly those known as 'first time elections' in countries which were previously one-party states. Austen was the chief electoral officer in the Cambodian election in 1993, an election which was run by the UN and regarded by many commentators as one of the most challenging to date.

Austen and I have lunch every fortnight or so and I assiduously pick his brain on electoral matters. On one occasion, he brings along his colleague Dong Nguyen, also from the UN. Nguyen is of slight build but steely resolve, from North Vietnam. He has run elections all over the world and has a sharp intellect. I later learnt that he had been one of the main advisors to Le Duc Tho, the key North Vietnamese negotiator in the peace negotiations that ended the Vietnam War. Nguyen is a formidable individual.

Our lunches are also joined by Michael Maley, an election operations expert from the Australian electoral commission. Maley has also worked on elections all over the world. He too is a quiet man. The lunches turn into meetings where I draw on their experience, endlessly putting problems to them.

'What are your reports telling you about the army and police? Will they cooperate and assist on the election days?' asks Nguyen.

I drink my coffee, the hot liquid scalding my tongue as I wonder where he's going with this question.

'At the moment, they are giving us information about the threat of the right wing and growing problems in KwaZulu and Natal.

All the indications are that they will be cooperative in the election, but we also need to have contingency plans.'

I see Nguyen shoot Austen a glance as he coolly sips his water. I move on. 'What should we be looking for in terms of warning signs re systems failure, communications options in rural polling stations? What about sabotage?'

The three of them are happy to share their knowledge, occasionally bringing in others from the UN to talk about monitoring systems, types of fraud and mechanisms that can be put in place to prevent it.

At one lunch in early March, Austen expresses some frustration and surprise that the administration division doesn't make use of their services. Never pushy, the three experts have found that instead of working at breakneck pace to help the division meet its almost impossible goals, they haven't been consulted at all and have much spare time on their hands.

My recurring nightmare is of an election that simply fails. Just doesn't work. What then? That's the part where I wake up sweating.

The administration of the election is the responsibility of the enigmatic Piet Coleyn. My terror is compounded by the attitude of the administration division, particularly Coleyn, who never sees anything as a problem. The news from Austen does nothing to still my unease. Nor does feedback from operations experts from my division delegated to sit in on administration planning committees. They are usually given short shrift when they raise concerns. Then, these meetings become less frequent, or maybe we are simply not being invited.

I raise this with Norman du Plessis, who has a senior position in the administration division. He responds, 'You don't understand, Peter, there are no meetings. They stopped a while back, and we are all just doing our own thing.'

'You're not being serious,' I say in horror.

'Oh yes, I am,' he says, walking away.

I try to get more information by inviting Coleyn for the occasional drink, an offer he seldom refuses.

'You know, Piet, you have a hell of a lot of experience in this area and you have been running elections for a while and have a hell of a reputation.' This is crude flattery but as it works on most people, especially me, I feel it's worth trying. 'But this election is for twenty-two million voters, not three million. This is a monster. There are serious elections experts from the UN that we can get to help us, people that ran the elections in Namibia and in Cambodia in very difficult circumstances. I have been talking to them and they are keen to help.'

Coleyn looks carefully over his shoulders around the bar of the Carlton Hotel, as if checking for eavesdroppers. He methodically lights up yet another cigarette. 'Peter, you have to trust us on this, the processes are not that complicated and are in fact simpler than in a normal election: we will just multiply the numbers and make sure we have the resources there. How bad can it be?' He takes a long pull on his smoke and follows it with a sucking sound as he lifts his glass to his lips.

'Jesus, Piet!' The room starts to spin, the muscles in my neck a fraction away from spasm. 'How bad can it be? How bad can it be? *How bad can it be?*' I say like a moron. 'Well, it can be a fucking disaster, and this place can go up in flames and then, frankly, you won't want to go to your home in Pretoria because you will be hunted down like a dog as the person responsible. This is not an all-white election in smart suburbs with electricity and running water. At least a third of these voting stations are in places that haven't got power or a telephone or decent roads, so what are you going to do when there is a problem there, when the ink runs out and voters get tired of waiting in the hot sun for twelve hours, and there is no water for them to drink. You know what? They will think it is a plot to rob them of the vote that they have been waiting centuries for, and they will burn down the polling station. The only issue is whether they burn it down with the staff inside it or not. The only thing that will be running will be the voting staff as they are chased by a mob wanting to hammer them. How are you going to get ballots to rural villages in the Transkei in a crisis when you can't even speak to them?'

Piet Coleyn looks at me with pity. A look which tells me in a single devastating moment that he sees me as being a young, interfering arsehole who does not know what he is talking about. While there may be a lot of truth to this, this is one of the few times when I do want to be taken seriously. And I mean it. Coleyn turns in his chair looking about the bar, bored with the conversation.

'Are you at least going to have a dry run before the election, to test your systems, Piet?' I ask, trying to keep my voice calm.

'We may, Peter, we may. There is lots to be done, you know.'

My teeth snap shut, crushing the ice cubes into tiny fragments in my mouth. There are seven weeks to the election.

The police join the public servants' strike in Bophuthatswana. Unrestrained, the strike disintegrates into a riot of lawlessness and looting. A starving and poverty-stricken population joyfully seizes this second 'Christmas' – looters and mobs storm stores and shopping centres in Mmabatho, smashing windows and leaping into the shops to seize the contents in a giant free for all. Entire furniture stores are cleaned out, with gangs carrying away everything from king-sized beds to fridges and stoves. Once emptied, the shops are torched.

The Mangope government, without a police force and reluctant to deploy the army, fearing that they may be sympathetic to the strikers and could mutiny, is powerless to stop the sacking of the capital.

In South Africa, the spectacle is covered by a voracious local and international media who show mobs rampaging through shops and government buildings. It is the worst nightmare of South Africans who fear that this portends their own fate. It is only a matter of time before the fire spreads to the rest of the country, scorched earth and bones.

By Wednesday, 9 March 1994, Mmabatho is in a state of anarchy, with bands of armed men ranging through the city. Students occupy the university. Television footage shows buildings being ransacked and burning. It is feared that the mobs will enter the adjacent white town of Mafikeng. The state broadcaster, the BOP Broadcasting Company, falls into the control of its own employees, who take the chairman, Eddie Mangope, one of the president's sons, hostage. In the Mmabatho Sun Hotel and Casino, guests barricade themselves in their rooms while the more relaxed camera crews and journalists drink cold beer with their lunch around the pool, resting after their exertions.

The carnage plays itself out on television for the entire world to see and for those in South Africa to fear. It is no longer about a strike for money, if it ever was. It is now about power and who wields it as the strikers and students demand the removal of Mangope and insist on participation in the election.

Desperate, Mangope makes the call to Constand Viljoen requesting the intervention and protection of the Volksfront. Viljoen flies to Mmabatho to meet with the beleaguered president, who makes it clear to Viljoen that there should be no forces from the AWB in the Volksfront group. Their presence would cause problems with his own forces. Viljoen understands this.

In the ops centre, we monitor the situation with growing horror. Dries Putter and Thele Moema feed us intelligence that the call has gone out for right-wing forces to gather on the borders of the territory with all the weaponry at their disposal. The ops centre moves onto a twenty-four hour operational footing. Eddie Hendrickx walks quietly between the offices as he receives reports from security, passing them to the right sections for analysis and action.

The pact of Mangope with Constand Viljoen is viewed with real concern, if not fear. We know that if the right wing, organised or not, go in and occupy Bophuthatswana, they will not leave. The only military group with the power to dislodge them will be the South African Defence Force. If they get sent in and are attacked there will be a major conflict which could spread to other homeland areas such as the Ciskei, which also has a ruler who has grown accustomed to power.

Wednesday, 9 March 1994. The hours are etched onto my nerves.

The big question is whether the South African army will confront a force with which it probably feels some sympathy and which is led by their former commander in chief, a man for whom they have total respect. It is common knowledge that the current commander in chief of the defence force, General George Meiring, is a protégé and former subordinate of Constand Viljoen.

To make matters worse, we receive reports that the Volksfront force entering Bophuthatswana will be led by one of South Africa's most decorated and experienced officers, Colonel Jan Breytenbach, the founder of 1 Reconnaissance Commando, the elite special forces unit, and later the first commander of the feared 32 Battalion composed of former Angolan FNLA fighters and South African officers. Three Two, or Buffalo Battalion, is the most decorated unit in the South African Defence Force since World War Two.

If the defence force refuses to act against Viljoen and Breytenbach, it will be mutiny, and then what of the rest of the country? Will the defence force follow the orders of the government? This could be exactly what the right wing wants: the opportunity to show that no member of the defence force will fire on their former compatriots and commanders. Is this the first domino that will fall? Is ordering in the defence force to clean up the mess a risk that the Transitional Executive Council is prepared to take? In my heart of hearts, I know that this army will not act against Viljoen and Breytenbach. In that milieu, those men are gods.

The concerns about the homelands imploding are well founded, as are the fears about the violence between the political parties, not to mention the dreaded right wing. But for me, the ever-present fear, no, let me say terror, is not putting in place the elementary basics on which all elections rely. There is no time to register voters. That means there is no register. This is going to be that rare electoral animal, an election without a voters' roll.

The consequence of not having a voters' roll is that people can vote at any polling station. This means that the number of voters at each polling station is unknown. It could be two hundred. It could be twenty thousand. Consequently, it is almost impossible to plan the proper distribution of polling officers and personnel and, more importantly, the proper distribution of electoral supplies from ballots to ink and stationery. Even an average number could turnout to be a radical under-estimation. No voters' roll makes proper planning a nightmare, if not impossible.

As if that were not enough, the small matter of issuing temporary voting cards is floundering.

In January the department of home affairs estimated that some two and a half million cards would have to be issued to citizens who did not have valid identification documents. The process of issuing temporary voting cards commenced in earnest early in February.

The problem is that home affairs has been moving too slowly and has issued slightly less than half a million cards.

It is Thursday, 10 March 1994. We have forty-eight days before the election. At this rate, it would take home affairs approximately eight months to clear the backlog.

It is depressingly clear to all of us at the IEC that while the politicians had given serious thought to ease of voting, they'd given little consideration to the ease of the administration of the election.

On Thursday, 10 March 1994 a formal request for assistance is received by the Volksfront executive from Rowan Cronje, the Bophuthatswana minister of defence. Eugène Terre'Blanche, a member of the Volksfront executive, takes it on himself to issue a call to all AWB commando units in the Zeerust and Lichtenburg region to 'head for Bop'. The call, made on Radio Pretoria, is also answered by AWB units in the Pretoria area. The AWB units organise vehicles and weapons for their mission. Their assembly area is designated as Rooigrond, on the border of Bophuthatswana.

Although the executive of the Volksfront gets wind of the mobilisation of the AWB and urgently orders Terre'Blanche to instruct his men to stand down, he tells them it is too late. The AWB forces are already gathering at Rooigrond.

It is apparent that the Leader believes that if Bophuthatswana can be seized and protected, this is separatist land. It may not be the Promised Land, but if they can hold it, it could be their homeland, or at least a part of it.

In Mmabatho, the situation has deteriorated. At two o'clock on Thursday afternoon, Chief Mangope is forced to flee the capital. He leaves in his personal helicopter, bound for his mansion at Motswedi.

Constand Viljoen contacts General George Meiring to inform him that Volksfront commandos are moving into Bophuthatswana and that they want to avoid any clashes with the South African Defence Force. General Meiring tells Viljoen that, as yet, the defence force has received no instructions to move into the homeland.

Viljoen then phones Douw Steyn and instructs him to gather a force of the Boere Krisis Aksie and move to the air-force base at Mmabatho. He tells them that they must go unarmed as it is important that they receive their weaponry from the Bop government. They are not armed invaders. It has previously been agreed with Chief Mangope that they will be armed from the government armoury when they reach the airport.

We have been getting reports of a build-up of weapons in KwaZulu and Natal, of massive arms caches that will be used to destabilise the election and potentially start a civil war. There are rumours of secret camps deep in the northern Zululand bush, where military training of Inkatha supporters is taking place. The training is alleg-edly being conducted by rogue right-wing elements in the police and defence force.

There is nothing new about these training camps. At my law firm, we had made submissions in 1992 and 1993 to the Goldstone Commission about the training of two hundred Inkatha fighters in 1986 in an army camp in the Caprivi Strip in Northern Namibia by instructors from military intelligence. We had also presented evidence to Goldstone about the role played by 'third force' elem-ents in the early 1990s in supplying weapons to Inkatha as well as joining them in killings. The objective was to escalate the conflict between Inkatha and the ANC.

Our evidence was based on reports from informers, defectors, ANC intelligence, and the ample evidence provided by circumstances of the killings and massacres. In December 1993, Judge Goldstone found that there was 'credible evidence' that a police death squad was operating in KwaZulu. The names of senior policemen in the KwaZulu police force were mentioned.

Now the reports coming in from Putter and Moema paint a disturbing picture of men preparing for war. In one instance, an informer speaks of truckloads of weapons being transported and hidden in the bush. The weapons include mortars, RPG-7 rocket launchers, grenades, AK47s, other assorted combat rifles and tons of ammunition. The weapons have been 'cleaned' and their serial numbers removed. The problem about reporting this to the police, which has already been done, is that the information implicates the police from top to bottom, including two senior South African Police generals at national level.

It is clear that we are headed for major problems in the province. I seek out Charles Nupen, one of the commissioners assigned to KwaZulu and Natal. As I step out of the lift, Zac Yacoob strides purposefully past me. It always amazes me how he walks with such confidence, neither feeling his way tentatively nor tapping cautiously with a white stick. I watch him as he walks, his tall frame almost loping down the passage, turning right into Nupen's office without hesitation.

'Charles, I need to chat to you,' I hear Yacoob call out. Nupen jumps, his concentration disturbed.

'Hello,' I say to Nupen, going on to express my incredulity that Zac Yacoob has walked down a wide corridor about sixty metres long and turned into Nupen's office with the confidence of a sighted person.

Nupen shakes his head, smiling. 'It's like that every day he comes into my office. The man is uncanny.'

Yacoob tilts his head in recognition of the compliment. He sits, again either by intuition or practice, knowing precisely where the chair is. 'I just follow Charles's cologne,' he says with a smile.

Zac Yacoob has become a legend at the IEC. Due to time constraints, it has not been possible to convert into Braille the extensive documentation of the IEC, including legislation. Instead, a reader has been provided. In the past few weeks, I have often gone into Yacoob's office to find him with his hands together, gazing at the ceiling as his reader brings him up to date by speed reading through the piles of paper. He memorises everything and will then quote lengthy clauses of law and other excerpts of documents to support his point of view when expressing himself before the commission.

We discuss KwaZulu. Nupen shakes his head. 'The place is a nightmare, I tell you. The word is that Inkatha will make it very difficult, if not impossible, to run the election there.'

Yacoob chips in, 'If we cannot get them to come into the election, which they clearly do not want to do, we must at least try to get an undertaking from the Inkatha leadership that they will not interfere in the election. You know, all we need is a few voters being killed on the big day or polling officials being attacked and *no one* will leave their homes to vote.'

'What is Oscar's view on this? Can he not use his influence to persuade them?' I ask, referring to one of the IEC commissioners,

Oscar Dhlomo, a former Inkatha heavyweight, and now retired from active politics.

'He has been involved,' says Yacoob, 'but he says they will not move on the election. When they're asked if they will stop the election in their areas, they say, "Of course we will not do anything against the law," but what else can they say? They said the same thing up here at the height of the violence and then went out from the hostels and people got killed. You know that, Pete.'

I nod. I know it too well.

The discussion continues, Yacoob speaking in that soft, infinitely reasonable way of his, reflecting the hope that something can be done while also acknowledging that the election will proceed with or without Inkatha.

Dikgang Moseneke joins us and after listening for a while says, 'You know, Johann and I have discussed this at our meetings with Mandela and De Klerk and their position is that every effort must be made to bring in Inkatha and the right wing, whatever it takes. If that means bending the rules and passing legislation that includes them in the process, we will do that. Cyril Ramaphosa and Roelf Meyer are continually trying to move them. On the Inkatha front, meetings at the highest level are scheduled between Chief Buthelezi, Mandela and De Klerk. They have even got the Zulu king Goodwill Zwelithini involved.' Nupen and Yacoob agree: this is an ark on which all must be aboard.

Deep down, though, we all know that only so much accommodation can be made. The main negotiators will not let anyone hold a gun to their heads. There are deadlines, and the next one is the artwork for the ballot paper. We need the name of the political party, its logo, and a picture of the party leader. This has to be couriered to the printer in England for printing by Sunday, 13 March 1994. In four days' time. That date cannot be moved. Anything later will mean that the ballot papers will not be ready by 27 April.

In the monitoring division, we have made it clear that no deadline will be missed. If this means working seven days a week for long hours or through the night, so be it. However, the sweat and grind at the IEC is occasionally interrupted by lighter moments as people find ways to inject humour and comic relief into what has become an exhausting and stressful cycle of deadlines and crises.

Vanessa Henry, Solveigh Piper's administrative fixer, is a Witwatersrand University law graduate. Blonde and blue eyed, she looks sixteen. She's efficient and hard working and popular, especially among the young finance men seconded on short notice from Price Waterhouse. She always carries a bag of sweets, which she offers to all and sundry, sometime leaving little piles on people's desks.

Vanessa has taken it upon herself to be the unofficial cheerleader for the division. She organises impromptu events, normally drinks, cakes for the odd morning tea and, when she gets wind of the dates, small birthday gatherings. She had asked me what she should do for Solveigh Piper's birthday. Knowing Piper to be a formidable woman and also a firm feminist who is not to be trifled with, I suggested that she should merely call together some of the head office admin people, and give her a card and a small present after a round of donations. Boring, I admit, but functional.

Late in the afternoon, Vanessa, ably assisted by the willing men from Price Waterhouse, calls everyone to a section of the open-plan office where she calmly announces that we are celebrating Solveigh's fiftieth birthday a week early, as she will be in Cape Town on her birthday assisting the Western Cape offices. She sits Piper down in a chair in the middle of the room and announces that the present is about to arrive. Everyone looks around quizzically. Loud music suddenly fills the office and a young, well-built man in the uniform of a Los Angeles traffic cop springs out from behind a partition and gyrates his way sensuously across the room to Piper, who has her eyes fixed on the man in alarm.

I can see what is coming and I shudder. She will resign on the spot, storm out, and I will have lost my head of administration.

111

I look at Vanessa, who is watching the proceedings with a big smile. It is too late to stop the inevitable. I sigh, and pour myself another drink.

With a wriggle of his hips, the young guy, who is very good-looking, whips off his shirt and, still with his peaked cap on, rips the tight silk T-shirt he's wearing, tearing it at the top to reveal a perfect tan and an abdomen so muscled it looks like wrestling snakes. The man's T-shirt is then whirled around his head, slipped over his body, passed between his thighs and across his taut stomach. He whisks it provocatively and softly around Solveigh Piper's open neck, brushing it lightly as he stands astride her, her face a whisper from the top of his belt. He blindfolds her gently, caressing her hair as the music slows. Piper sits unsmiling, facing straight ahead as if transfixed. The man moves around her, touching her faintly. Shit, I think, this is going too far, this is steamy stuff. But Piper does not get up from the chair – it's as if she's bound by an invisible cord.

The man, in one seamless movement, has his police pants off to reveal a skimpy set of jocks. Now, almost naked, right in front of her as the music increases in tempo, building to a crescendo, I see a small upturn of Piper's lips. He quickly slides off the silk blindfold, steps back and in a sensual, intimate way he puts both hands behind his head and throws his head back in abandon. The music slows and Piper, as if awaking from a dream, opens her eyes and stares, her mouth tipping into a wide smile as she laughs out loud amid the clapping.

Vanessa Henry walks into the circle bearing a large birthday cake on which are fifty sparklers, smoke curling from them. The stripper is still in his pose, lasciviously moving his hips slowly to the music. Who would believe this? Solveigh and the stripper, I think, as people raise their glasses and toast her.

Simultaneously, there is a loud squeak in the ceiling above us and a deafening alarm sounds. It has to be the fire alarm, set off by the smoke from the sparklers. There is a loud bang and the fire sprinklers in the ceiling come on, spraying water over the proceedings.

We are frozen, transfixed by the noise and the water showering down. Suddenly there is wild shouting and the two doors that lead into this section from the landing burst open and soldiers storm into the room, automatic rifles up and ready to fire. Involuntarily, we take a step back, as if captured. At least two of the secretaries raise their hands above their heads.

The soldiers stop dead at the sight of a middle-aged woman in a chair in the middle of a room, a half-naked male model suspended before her. Beside them, a young blonde woman with a big cake on which the spent sparklers are black smoking skeletons. Around them are a motley bunch of drenched men and women with glasses in their hands. All the while the music pumps, and the smoke siren screams.

The siren stops, thank God, releasing us. I apologise to the soldiers and congratulate them on their superb reaction time. 'Stay alert,' I tell them seriously, 'next time it could be the real thing.'

It has been a long day for Lawrence Lobotso, a resident of Lonely Park, Mafikeng. Together with a friend who has been helping him with a painting job at his local church, he is walking home along a road that cuts through the industrial area of the town. They have heard the shooting, and people along the way have told them to get off the streets, but they have no choice.

Lobotso hears a car pulling up behind him and, turning, sees a white Ford Cortina. There are white men in the car. He and his friend carry on walking, staring straight ahead, sensing trouble. He has avoided the troubles of the last few days, preferring to mind his own business.

'There are two kaffirs,' he hears a man saying in Afrikaans. Another voice says, 'Shoot them.'

Lobotso and his friend continue walking, faster now. He hears the car doors opening. He looks back. The men from the car are dressed in khaki. One of them is carrying a handgun. He raises it, points it straight at Lobotso. 'Today you are going to die,' he says.

113

Lobotso and his friend hold their hands above their heads, Lobotso pleading for mercy, both begging for their lives.

The man stares at them, saying nothing. He pulls the trigger, shooting Lobotso in the chest. Lobotso staggers and falls as the man shoots again, the second bullet hitting him in the neck. His companion falls to the ground. The men lie there, motionless, the friend whimpering, saying to Lobotso, 'We are dying.' Lobotso telling him 'keep quiet because those white people will come and finish us off'.

Lobotso prays to God to save him as he hears the man with the gun walk up to him, boots crunching the gravel. The footsteps stop, the man is standing over him. Lobotso stares into the ground, his face against the stones. He feels a hard boot on his neck, pressing his head into dirt.

'You must die in peace, bye bye.'

Lobotso waits for the bullet as the man lifts his boot. It doesn't come. An eternity. The car drives off. Lobotso passes out.

In the early hours of Friday, 11 March 1994, the Bophuthatswana Defence Force escorts one thousand five hundred members of the Boere Krisis Aksie under the command of Kommandant Douw Steyn to the Bophuthatswana Air Force base on the outskirts of Mmabatho. It is intended that retired Colonel Jan Breytenbach will take over command of the men later that morning. Colonel Breytenbach knows that his AVF force will require serious military hardware, including armoured cars, if they are to bring stability to the homeland. On arrival at the air-force base, the Volksfront forces are supplied with one hundred and fifty R4 rifles.

The responsibility for keeping stability in the territory now lies in the hands of these men. There are another three thousand Volksfront men on standby on the borders of the territory, who can be deployed within hours. The agreement is that the Volksfront men will guard vulnerable points for about four days.

Unfortunately, communication with the rank and file of the Bop army is virtually nonexistent. Largely unaware of the agreement to bring in the Volksfront, they are not expecting an invasion force of white right-wingers. The troops of the Bophuthatswana Defence Force are largely black, many of them economic conscripts, with white officers. Even before the call by Mangope to Viljoen, our intelligence was that these were not happy troopers.

A discussion on the final format of the ballot paper has been scheduled for this Friday. It is a topic that has generated considerable heat. It stands to reason that the ballot paper should be developed and printed with sufficient security measures to ensure that it cannot be forged and is also tamper proof. These ballots must be as safe as money. They are the currency that will buy a precious commodity unknown in South Africa: democracy. As in all things contentious in this country, everyone has an opinion and they are all correct and have to be defended to the death.

One argument goes: 'No printer in the country has the capacity to produce a ballot paper of such sophistication that it cannot be forged. Besides, the printers are all owned by whites and we know who they support. What is stopping them from producing many millions more than are needed and then "stuffing" the ballot boxes. Worse, the printers could take the order and then fail to deliver, thus stopping the election. We would be mad to place our future in the hands of such people.'

The counter to this is: 'According to Section 29 of the Electoral Act, the ballot paper counterfoils and books must be serially numbered so that they can be tracked to prevent fraud. This will prevent the production of extra, illegal ballots. Besides, the contract is of such a magnitude that it must go to a South African printer rather than a foreign outfit. Our economy needs the money.'

As it happens, the Government Printer is unable to handle the entire job without buying new equipment and this would take too long. Suspicion of the Government Printer by the ANC is another key factor. Consequently, Piet Coleyn advertises the tender and two local bids and two overseas bids are received, with the job being awarded to a British company, De La Rue, even though it is more expensive. There will also be the additional cost of transporting tons of ballots by plane from the UK, under tight security. On the plus side, De La Rue has extensive experience in printing ballots and has previously printed bank notes for the South African government. Eighty million ballot papers are ordered.

By the time Jan Breytenbach gets to the airfield and takes over command from Douw Steyn, there are already stories of AWB men running amok in Mmabatho, shooting at civilians. Breytenbach is under specific instructions from Constand Viljoen to get the AWB out of Bophuthatswana as soon as possible. Like all good commanders, he knows the importance of striking the correct military alliances, and an alliance with the AWB is the kiss of death. Terre'Blanche refuses to withdraw his men, saying that the AWB is there at the personal invitation of Chief Mangope.

After heated discussions between the Volksfront commanders and the AWB, agreement is reached that the AWB men can stay if they remove their insignia and place themselves under the command of Steyn and Breytenbach. The AWB men disobey on both counts. In desperation, Breytenbach holds a further meeting with an AWB commander, General Cruywagen. At first he agrees that the AWB will leave Bop, however, before they conclude their business they are joined by another AWB 'General', Nick Fourie. Fourie, hard-line and recalcitrant, overrules Cruywagen and refuses to withdraw the AWB contingent.

Both AWB generals are in uniform, armed for war, and Fourie is very aggressive. The meeting degenerates into an argument, Breytenbach telling the two 'generals' that the AWB is ill-disciplined and that they must leave the area. Furious, the AWB 'generals' storm off.

Meanwhile, the black Bophuthatswana army soldiers are outraged that white right-wingers have invaded their country. There is increasing talk of taking on the Volksfront men and the AWB. The Bophuthatswana army commanders have not told their men that Breytenbach's contingent is there at the request of the president to 'stabilise the country'. Those troops who have been informed doubt the Volksfront's intentions. Besides, they know that their president is safely ensconced in his luxury home.

The situation is exacerbated by AWB members careering around Mmabatho in their cars and bakkies, shooting randomly into houses and at civilians.

An AWB man, toting an automatic rifle, tells well-known photojournalist Greg Marinovich, 'We are going to shoot a little bit.' Other AWB invaders are more direct: 'Ons is op 'n kafferskiet-piekniek' (We are on a kaffir shooting picnic).

With each passing hour, more AWB men arrive in their bakkies and trucks. They are armed to the teeth and lusting for action. And what better place than a homeland government beyond the control of the South African Police and army, where the security forces appear unwilling or unable to take any action against them. It is the Wild West, and the sheriff is not in town. Matters are coming to a head.

A week after moving into the new offices, we are still battling to get our communication lines up and running. Fortunately, Willem Ellis has performed a miracle and all the lines in the national ops centre are functional. To add to our woes, not a day goes by without a call from Judge Kriegler or the commission requesting an urgent meeting on a matter of such urgency that if it is not urgently addressed, it will develop into an emergency. Invariably, such requests translate into more work for an already over-burdened team stretched to the limit.

This time the call is about voting stations. When the meeting is over, I completely agree that this is actually so urgent that it is a major crisis as it stands. It needs no further development or incubation, and it scares me witless.

The distribution of the electorate in an election will determine the number and location of voting stations. The administration division is relying on demographic data from the 1991 census figures provided by the central statistical service.

The date for the completion of this task was set as 11 February and the list of voting stations was to be published no later than 1 March. By law this list has to be made public at least forty-five days before the election to give parties sufficient time to canvass voters and to tell their supporters where to vote.

The identification of voting stations by the department of home affairs commenced in 1993 on the assumption that one station would be needed for every three thousand voters. This translated into seven thousand eight hundred voting stations. The process of siting these stations stalled when home affairs experienced difficulties in black and rural areas. In fact, the department was told to stop by the Negotiating Council. The expectation was that the IEC would take over the process when it came into existence in December 1993.

By mid-January 1994, the commission was under the impression that the administration division was identifying voting stations. According to their report-back: 'The computer system REGIS is being used to map voting stations. At present the technicians are working around the clock to ensure its efficient operation. The system should be operational by Friday, 28 January 1994.'

But through February we heard a radically different story. In essence, this told us that the administration division would miss the deadline of 11 February and that they were far behind. Worryingly, we could not get any clarity from the administration division. They were working flat out, we were told. The relationship between my division and Piet Coleyn's became increasingly strained.

Jan Breytenbach is a worried man. He has information that there is a real possibility of an attack on his men from the Bophuthatswana army. His concern is compounded by the fact that they have not been supplied with weapons from the armoury. Apart from the hundred and fifty R4 combat rifles, they have received nothing, and certainly no armoured cars. Indeed, the Bophuthatswana soldiers have refused to open the armoury at Molopo.

Breytenbach knows that in the terrain of the airfield, flat and with little cover, their R4s and assorted side arms will be little match against a force of armoured vehicles with proper weaponry and night-vision equipment. They also lack basic equipment such as spades in order to dig trenches. They are easy prey.

Breytenbach knows that he has to get his men out by nightfall. His reading of the situation is reinforced by an instruction from the head of the Bophuthatswana Defence Force, General Turner, that he is to withdraw the Volksfront men from their duties and leave the territory, as they are being equated with the AWB. Members of the Bophuthatswana army are threatening to attack them.

The time set for the withdrawal of the main Volksfront force is four o'clock in the afternoon.

The momentum for greater violence is mounting, with the strong possibility that the Bop army will rebel and attack the right-wingers. Were that to happen, it could cause a counter reaction from other right-wing groups waiting on the borders, at least three thousand in number. This could precipitate something we all dreaded, an Armageddon of the races.

While the men under Breytenbach's command are a disciplined force, the AWB continue to raid Mmabatho like pirates, shouting racial abuse at civilians and shooting randomly. Many civilians are dying. The anger in the Bophuthatswana army boils over, and the troops mutiny. Suddenly, there are soldiers riding armoured vehicles through the capital shouting ANC slogans and exchanging gunfire with the AWB men. Breytenbach deploys his men in defensive positions around the airfield, telling them to have nothing to do with the AWB mob.

Among the AWB vehicles driving round Mmabatho is a light-blue Mercedes-Benz. The driver is an AWB colonel, forty-five-year-old Alwyn Wolfaardt, a veteran of the invasion of the World Trade Centre. He's been living in the small town of Naboomspruit since 1986, when he moved there with his wife Ester. He lives on the outskirts of the town on a rented smallholding not far from the cemetery. Wolfaardt is well known in the nearby black township of Mokgophong, but for all the wrong reasons. His temper is legendary. He calls black people 'kaffir dog' and 'black monkey'. He assaults them for no reason.

In a sense, Wolfaardt is a product of his history. The wooden chest in the hallway of his modest home belonged to a forebear, Pieter Jordaan, who, with the famous Boer commando hero Piet Retief, was murdered by Dingaan. Years later, four of Wolfaardt's grandfather's siblings died in a British concentration camp during the Boer War, along with more than thirty thousand others, mostly women and children, who suffered a similar fate. His father, a general foreman at the government-owned steelworks, Iscor, went to jail rather than fight alongside the British in World War Two.

Wolfaardt grew up on a farm. But his early years were deeply scarred by the death of his mother when he was four years old. Although not an aggressive boy, his disposition changed after his national service spent in the war zone on the Angolan border.

In 1986 he and his wife joined the AWB. He rose quickly through the ranks, and became immersed in politics.

As far as he is concerned it's a 'sin' that South West Africa has been handed over to the blacks. He's determined that it's not going to happen in South Africa. He is not alone in his thinking.

The intelligence updates flow into the IEC. At eleven in the morning we learn that three civilians, Lawrence Seupe, Ernest Liekhobe and Johannes Makomo, have been shot. At twelve, that Joel Mokolong and his cousin Thulo have been shot. At one, it is Anna Nakedi and Sophia Mogale. Constance Kutoane, Sylvia Leinana and Leinie Moeng are also shot at approximately the same time. And so it goes on: the trucks chasing and herding the terrified fleeing people taking pot shots as if at a shooting gallery.

The few ambulances in the capital are working erratically. The massive civil service strike has put a halt to the delivery of most services, and those drivers who consider taking out their vehicles to attend to the dying and wounded are petrified that they too will be shot at by the rampant AWB. It is clear that these men respect nothing, shooting at men, women and children, assaulting journalists and smashing their equipment.

The plan is for the Volksfront force and the AWB to be escorted out of Mmabatho by a convoy of defence-force vehicles that have entered Bophuthatswana to protect the South African embassy. They are to leave with four Casspirs in the front and three bringing up the rear. The route is a series of detours to avoid the centre of the town and quickly take them to the periphery of the city and then out of the territory. Breytenbach and his men leave via the pre-determined route with the defence-force escort.

The AWB take a different tack; they do not wait to be escorted out, preferring to make their own way in a disorderly series of AWB cavalcades. They also decide to take their own route, one that goes through the centre of Mmabatho and Mafikeng. Along the way, they shoot at civilians from their cars and bakkies. Unlucky journalists who encounter the AWB convoys are brutally assaulted and have their cameras stolen.

The random shooting from the AWB cars escalates until they run into ambushes from members of the Bop Defence Force. Later, Colonel Hoskins of the Bophuthatswana army will describe the conflict as 'like World War Two, with the AWB convoys and the Bop army shooting at each other'. The AWB convoy approaches from the direction of the air-force base, along the Vryburg–Mafikeng road, past residential villages, police headquarters located at the Tswana Territorial Authority and over the railway bridge at the entrance to Mafikeng.

I meet with Piet Coleyn to try to defuse the tensions between our divisions. I also want information on their progress with the voting stations. Coleyn is exhausted. His skin has a greyish tinge. He is also stricken with a wrenching cough which makes me seriously worried that he might be very ill or close to breakdown.

We light up cigarettes in my office and he tells me that they do have serious problems. However, although the deadline has been missed, things are under control and they will have the voting station locations finalised soon.

In a voice that is low and strained, he tells me that one of the reasons that they are having problems is that the space criteria for the voting stations has changed. He was told in mid-February that there would now be separate ballots for the national and nine provincial legislatures. This meant a changed voting and queuing configuration and thus more space in the voting station.

I have sympathy for his position. Things change continually, instructions are simply given and there is the total expectation, as there often is by those issuing commands, that they will be obeyed. We part. I am not convinced that things are under control.

Lance Corporal De Koker is a member of the Bophuthatswana Defence Force conducting a patrol. He is with his commander Lieutenant Dikobe in a Mamba. They receive instructions to disperse a crowd that has gathered near the Tswana Territorial Authority and which may try to enter Mafikeng. As the Mamba approaches the crowd, a convoy of about ten vehicles with their headlights on moves towards them at speed. The vehicles are stoned by the crowd and the occupants open fire on them and the Mamba. The soldiers on the Mamba return fire. De Koker, seeing a woman fall to the ground, jumps from the Mamba and runs zig-zag to assist her. She has been shot in the back.

It is apparent that the original home affairs list paid scant attention to population densities when siting voting stations. The situation is exacerbated by the administration division's own finding that many of the identified voting stations are too small or too ill equipped to function as voting stations. Consequently every station on the current list will have to be inspected to ensure that it meets certain basic criteria, and new ones will have to be found.

This is why we now have an emergency. My division is being asked to send out over a thousand monitors to visit every voting station. Work in the division will come to a halt for four days while every available person is dispatched to check the voting stations. I have no problem with this; it is critical. Until the voting stations have been identified, they cannot be equipped with voting materials, nor can plans be made to move materials to the right places. Also, staff recruitment, training and deployment are problematic, communications cannot be set up, nor can security be arranged. Normally, counting stations cannot be located, as their placing is determined by the number of voting stations they serve. It is nothing short of a national crisis. And it is one that can stop the election.

Constable Menyatsoe of the Bophuthatswana police is in the kitchen inside police headquarters eating his lunch. On arrival at work that morning he had been issued with an R4 rifle and told that he should guard the Tswana Territorial Authority building from attack by right-wingers. Hearing shooting outside, he takes his rifle to investigate. He sees cars and trucks passing the barracks, full of white men dressed in khaki.

He jumps in fright as shots ring out, one of them hitting the ground close to his feet. He dives for cover, crawling to the perimeter wall. More shots are fired from the passing cars. A group of people, residents from the area, rush to the gates of the barracks, shouting that they are being attacked and that they want weapons. They enter the grounds of the Tswana Territorial Authority and ask Constable Menyatsoe for weapons to defend themselves. He refuses, but offers to defend them.

Menyatsoe crosses the tar road and takes cover in the bushes opposite. More cars pass by, the occupants firing at random as they burst through the barrier on the road. The soldiers yell obscenities and fire shots at the speeding convoy.

The last car in the convoy is an old, light-blue Mercedes-Benz. A man in the passenger's seat is shooting wildly through the open window. Menyatsoe opens fire on the Mercedes. A man close to him screams that he has been shot in the thigh.

Menyatsoe fires again at the Mercedes and sees it come to a shuddering stop, red dust swirling around the car. He glances around, sees a woman moaning as she lies on her back, blood seeping from her belly where she has been shot.

The driver's door of the car slowly opens and Alwyn Wolfaardt gets out, saying, 'Don't shoot.' General Nico Fourie is in the passenger seat, slumped forward against the dashboard. He has been shot. Fourie tumbles in slow motion from the car, blood pumping from his neck. The policemen, soldiers and crowd converge on the car.

What constitutes a free and fair election is a major issue for us. The high level of violence can have an adverse effect. In short, the tense situation in Bophuthatswana can jeopardise everything.

Declaring an election free and fair depends on a number of considerations, but chief among them is the 'freedom of voters to vote in secret, free from violence and coercion', and 'access to secure voting stations'.

Since his appointment, Steven Friedman and his information and analysis department have been monitoring the situation closely. Their final task will be to produce a report that will help the commissioners make a finding on whether the election was free and fair and a reflection of the will of the people.

I rather like the 'will of the people' bit; it reminds me of one of those classic legal catch-all clauses that provide an escape route if all else fails. It is a bit like 'sufficient consensus,' that famous methodology for reaching agreement at the constitutional negotiations.

124

In real terms this means that if the ANC and the National Party agree there was 'sufficient consensus', then bugger the rest. The real reason I like 'the will of the people' is because, as we hurtle closer to this election, it is clear to me that there is a lot that can, and probably will, go wrong.

I am also a bit worried about the people part. Our history is littered with wars and conflicts. I know the ANC will campaign as a non-racial 'broad church' of all South Africans. Then again, history has many stories of churches rent asunder. So, what 'people' are we talking about here? Can this thing, this 'people', come together? Can we become a nation? Can a national identity be forged?

I listen to the dire reports coming in from Bophuthatswana and know that there is one thing on which the vast majority is united: those who don't have freedom want it, and they want it now.

Alwyn Wolfaardt lies on his stomach in the red Bophuthatswana dust, his arms stretched out before him, one hand placed over the other as ordered by the soldiers surrounding the car. Nico Fourie is very badly injured. He lies prostrate next to the car, his head towards the rear, a pool of blood widening quickly in the soil around him.

Fanie Uys drags himself from the rear seat of the car to the rear left wheel and slumps against it. He is bleeding badly but manages to raise both his hands above his head in surrender.

The crowd of civilians, police and soldiers move closer to the wounded men, mocking and taunting them. The press are quickly there, cameras rolling. The panting silence is broken by Alwyn Wolfaardt, who begs the crowd, 'Please, God, help us. Get us some medical help.'

Peter de Ionno of the *Sunday Times* asks a Bop army colonel if he can get help. The colonel replies that an ambulance is on its way. De Ionno decides to wait at the scene. He talks to Uys but can get no coherent response. He turns to Wolfaardt, who answers some questions but then refuses to talk anymore.

Alwyn Wolfaardt is pressed against the earth, his massive back heaving as he begs for help. Time is passing, the sun harsh and baking.

Sergeant Mokgoko of the Bophuthatswana security branch arrives and instructs two policemen to disarm the men and search the car for weapons. The policemen find two pistols, a shotgun, ammunition and spent cartridges. Sergeant Mokgoko, taking charge of the scene, asks the men where they are from and what they want in Mmabatho. Wolfaardt replies that their officers sent them but that they do not know what their duties are. The talking is interrupted by the arrival of a lieutenant from the Bophuthatswana Defence Force, who assumes control. Sergeant Mokgoko takes the weapons of the AWB men to the nearby police barracks and locks the guns in a safe.

More journalists arrive and speak to the wounded men. They step back sharply when a Bophuthatswana policeman wearing a hard riot helmet approaches, his rifle pointed at the captured men. Standing over them, he shouts, 'Who do you think you are? What are you doing in my country? I can take your life in a second, do you know that?'

The men lie on the ground, breathing heavily. Flies crawl over the blood on their bodies and on the sticky earth.

The journalist Peter de Ionno walks slowly up to the policeman and puts his arm on the man's shoulder, speaking softly to him, telling him that the situation is under control and that he 'must stay calm, cool it'. The policeman, livid with rage, shouts, 'We want to shoot these fucking dogs. They have killed women. They are animals, not people.'

De Ionno keeps his hand on the policeman's shoulder, speaking gently to him, the words are indistinct, but gradually seem to affect the policeman, who turns and, with another policeman, walks away.

The man who lies prostrate next to the car has not moved for some time, his blood a thick pool around him. General Nico Fourie, the AWB commander of the Bophuthatswana operation, is dead.

Uys, propped up against the rear wheel of the Mercedes, is still alive, his hands raised in surrender but sagging, head lolling forward.

Wolfaardt lies close to Uys near the front door of the car, his short-sleeved khaki shirt and long khaki pants darkening from sweat, arms flat on the ground before him.

Everyone is waiting for the ambulance to arrive. It is now some fifteen minutes since it was called. Suddenly, another Bophuthatswana policeman arrives and strides purposefully to the three men on the ground. He stands above Wolfaardt and Uys. Pointing his R4 rifle at them, he says, 'These men nearly shot me.'

Constable Menyatsoe from the police barracks at the Tswana Territorial Authority looks at the men bleeding before him, but focuses on Uys. He glances up at the other policemen standing around the old bullet-riddled Mercedes, at the journalists poised with their cameras, hears the whirr of a movie camera gripped tightly by a large journalist. The man to the left of the cameraman is holding a long directional microphone covered in grey sponge towards the wounded men.

The building tension is unbearable. Blue heat waves rise in ripples from the red earth.

Menyatsoe turns to Uys and fires, shooting him in the head. Uys's left hand drops but his right hand remains up momentarily, palm open, and then slowly falls as his body topples to the left. Moving quickly, Menyatsoe puts a head shot into Fourie. He spins on Alwyn Wolfaardt, fires a bullet into the back of his head, the impact jerking the big man's body. Then Menyatsoe walks away, his R4 pointed upward to the clean sky. Flies buzz and settle on the bodies and the blood.

A journalist is overcome, saying, 'My God. Oh my Jesus,' reeling away from the scene, covering his eyes.

That night in Naboomspruit, Ester Wolfaardt and her eight-year-old daughter, Annalise, watch the news on television to see what is happening in Bophuthatswana. The AWB has neglected to inform them of Alwyn Wolfaardt's execution. They watch it in horror and grief.

It is a few hours before midnight. Political parties taking part in the election have to submit their list of candidates before twelve o'clock. Failure to comply will disqualify the party.

Tienie Groenewald, representing the Freedom Front, arrives at IEC headquarters. A retired major general and former chief of military intelligence, Groenewald is a man to be taken seriously. Norman du Plessis, who is in charge of the registration process, explains the procedures for the submission of lists. Groenewald informs him that he still has to meet with Constand Viljoen to discuss their options. There is no time for that, says Du Plessis. The deadline is irrevocable.

Groenewald picks up the phone and relays this message to Viljoen. A few minutes later, while Groenewald and Judge Kriegler are talking, Du Plessis stands outside his office chain smoking, aware of time passing.

Then there is a commotion at the lifts and Constand Viljoen turns the corner, escorted by IEC officials. The man looks calm and in control. It is a few minutes before midnight when he submits the list of candidates for the Freedom Front.

Viljoen's Freedom Front candidate list and public supporters include a number of highly influential former generals in the defence force as well as seven Conservative Party MPs and senior Volksfront officials. The response of the Leader is fast and furious, calling Viljoen a 'Brutus' and a 'political Judas goat'. He accuses Viljoen of betraying his people.

Inkatha misses the deadline and its registration for participation in the election lapses.

In the coming days, amidst serious security and secrecy, the format of the ballot is decided and delivered safely into the custody of the UK printers, De La Rue. They have to get the ballots back to South Africa by Sunday, 17 April at the very latest.

Once landed, these will be housed in secure regional locations for three to four days before the election. What qualifies as a 'secure regional location' is another argument.

It is Saturday, 12 March 1994.

In the gathering dusk, three helicopters land at the luxurious Motswedi residence of the president of Bophuthatswana, Chief Lucas Mangope. Pik Botha, the foreign minister of South Africa, and Mac Maharaj and Fanie van der Merwe representing, respectively, the ANC and the government on the transitional executive council, as well as General George Meiring, enter the elegant mansion of the chief. Mangope is seated on a small throne flanked by his two sons, Eddie and Kwena.

Pik Botha tells the chief apologetically that the South African army has moved into Bophuthatswana and stabilised the situation. The chief listens attentively as Botha tells him he has been deposed and is no longer in control and, furthermore, South Africa no longer recognises his government. Seeing that South Africa was the only country to recognise the Bantustan in the first place, this leaves President Mangope in a dark place.

The ageing despot pleads for time, at least until his parliament convenes in a few days. Maharaj intervenes abruptly, telling him that his administration has collapsed, his security forces have mutinied and it is over. Over. Eddie Mangope, the son who until recently had been the chairman of the national broadcaster, speaks softly to his father, who nods and sadly acknowledges that he will give up power.

The next day, emergency planning takes place in all IEC departments on how best to organise the election in the former Bophuthatswana. We have six weeks before the election to make it happen.

The rampage of the AWB in Bophuthatswana so appals Constand Viljoen that he states his outrage publicly and resigns from the Volksfront.

CHAPTER FIVE

In mid-March, I am in Cape Town, meeting with Ebrahim Mohamed, the head of the monitoring division in the Western Cape. It is very late at night, the work done for the day. I sip whisky while Ebby Mohamed tells me of his recent visit to sub-provincial offices. He looks at my whisky and, smiling, says that he nearly broke his vows as a Muslim. The flight back from George was the worst of his life.

I settle in as he tells me that Barlow let him use the company plane. He had flown to Vredendal, Beaufort West and George to establish, staff and equip offices. On this trip he was accompanied by Mary Burton, the head of the administration division in the Western Cape, the provincial chief of operations for the monitoring division, Peter Henstock, and our regional head of telecommunications, Tony Hoare, who had been seconded across from Plessey. They had arrived cold at each of the towns.

In Vredendal, they divided into two groups and agreed to walk down either side of the main street, looking for offices and equipment stores.

'Man, Peter, I am walking up and down the street that runs through the town,' says Mohamed. 'It's a very small town, you understand, but it serves a large geographic area. And people are just staring at me, this small Indian man and his handlangers. The fact that we had arrived in a private plane added to our mystery. They looked at us very curiously, I tell you.

'But there is bugger-all to rent there. So I walk into this law firm that has a big sign outside and I ask the receptionist if I can see the boss. She checks me out oddly, like I'm from Mars, and scuttles away. She comes back with this huge white guy. Enormous and very Afrikaans. Like they all are in that place. He introduces himself. I start to get worried that this thing is going to end very badly, so now I am talking very fast, because I want to get out of there before he bliksems me. You know, I am not a big guy.'

'Don't sell yourself short, Ebby,' I say poking fun at him while pulling on my cigarette and taking another sip of whisky. He doesn't get it.

'Ja, well … This okie just stares at me, not saying a word, checking me out. And I am shifting in my chair and checking the door, wondering if I can make it there before he klaps me. Man, I finish my spiel and look at him, just about to say thanks and run, when he suddenly sticks out this huge hand and shakes mine very hard. I tell you, the bones in my hand crunched together like matchsticks when he squeezed. Then he tells me we can use his office as a base until we can find or own offices, and that as he knows everyone in this town, he will help us get space and equipment. I was amazed, I tell you, speechless. And you know that never happens to me.'

I laugh out loud, imagining the scene.

'Then he says that he will second one of his staff to us until the end of the election. The next thing is, he wheels in this guy and I interview him on the spot, and he is just bloody great. He has all the qualifications that we need and will also have the backing of his boss. So I hire him there and then and now I get daily reports from this guy and he is fantastic and making real progress. How is that, hey?'

I grin at his good fortune.

'Ja, the team waiting outside were really worried that I was taking so long. They thought I had been kidnapped or taken prisoner.' He laughs. 'They couldn't believe it when I told them we had an office and also our first member of staff.'

'Incredible.'

'Ja, and somehow that set the tone for the trip. We flew out a few hours later and a similar thing happened in Beaufort West.'

It is now well past two in the morning, but I cannot stop him as he bubbles with the excitement of what he is doing. I am moved by his story, thinking that this is what this country should be about, everyone working together to pull off the impossible.

'Well, then we fly into George at 7 pm and set up in the Hurteria

Guest House,' he continues. 'By this time our contacts in Vredendal and Beaufort West have given us names of people we can see in George. We start the interviews for the position of manager for the area at the Hurteria, and on the second interview, with a guy called Frans Erasmus, an Afrikaner, hell of a nice guy and totally committed to the election, we hit it rich. Even though the interview ends at one o'clock in the morning, we hire Frans there and then and tell him to report for work at the Hurteria at eight the next morning.

'Frans is fantastic and helps us identify people and premises for most of the next day, but by now the weather has closed in and the pilots say it is too dangerous to fly. But I know those Barlow pilots, they are damned good, so I tell them that if there is the slightest break in the weather, they must phone us from the airfield and we will be there in a flash. I was desperate to get back to Cape Town. In this game, every hour is precious, never mind a day.

'So we're waiting at the hotel and it is raining and windy, really bad, stormy shit, and we're sitting in the lounge completely exhausted, looking at this moerse tree outside in the garden – a huge thing, looked like it had been there for three hundred years – when suddenly there is this hell of a crash of thunder, like right in the lounge. Shit! We all jump up and the lightning snakes down and strikes this fucking great tree right there in front of us, so help me God, lit it up like a Christmas tree, and there is electricity crackling in the room. Man, we almost shat ourselves. The tree was smoking like a bloody stick of dynamite.

'The next thing, the phone in the hotel rings and it is the pilot, calm as a cucumber, saying that there is a break in the storm. And I say to him, "Fuck, are you out of your mind, this place has just been struck by lightning and you want to fly in this?" The guy tells me that I'd asked them to phone if there was a break in the weather, and there was a break now. So if we want to fly we must get to the airport right now.

'I put it to the team, Mary Burton and the rest, and they look

133

at me in horror and then at the tree which is all fucked up now. They are speechless and I say to them, "Come on now, otherwise we could be here for days." They get up, looking at me strangely, and we get in the car and drive to the airport. I tell you, no one said a word.

'Well, we got out, but that was the worst flight. That plane bucked like a horse. It was the Wild West up there, except that we couldn't see a thing, there was such dense cloud. The moment we got on the plane the others started drinking, heavy stuff, spirits, just throwing it back as if there was no tomorrow. And I tell you, we thought there would be no tomorrow. After an hour, I looked at them drinking, with that plane heaving and dropping, and I thought, Maybe God will forgive me if I have a few drinks, just this once.

'We flew in dense cloud all the way from George to False Bay – that was only when it cleared. The others were poegaai by that time. I envied them.'

Ebby Mohamed and I part at two in the morning and I make my way to my hotel through the Cape Town rain. I am on an early flight to the Northern Cape in four hours' time.

It is Wednesday, 16 March 1994. Constand Viljoen withdraws his Freedom Front from the Freedom Alliance, leaving it to the other right-wing groupings and Inkatha.

The Goldstone Commission into third-force activities releases further findings on Friday, 18 March 1994. This report links Inkatha leaders on the East Rand, namely Themba Khoza and Humphrey Ndlovu as well as the deputy commissioner of the KwaZulu police force, General Sipho Mathe, to the fermenting of violence.

I knew Themba Khoza and Humphrey Ndlovu during my time with the Peace Accord. I need no convincing as to their complicity in the recurring massacres taking place in both the Transvaal and KwaZulu. Those two are hard men, capable of anything. Stories abound of their exploits. Themba Khoza travels with a loaded shotgun on the passenger seat of his car and has an armoury of weapons in his boot. He was arrested by police after they found unlicensed weapons in his car, but was then inexplicably released. Although a courteous man, Khoza's eyes are flinty black pebbles that never change. Eyes that could slit your throat.

Tension, excitement and exhaustion are the order of the day in the monitoring division. The mediation department, under the leadership of Jerome Ngwenya and his deputy Stax Masango, is swamped with issues needing resolution. Each night they work late into the early hours to sort out the numerous disputes referred to them by the political parties. Ngwenya has quickly established a panel of highly professional mediators throughout the country as well as an efficient case-management system. They are assisted by a Colombian electoral mediation expert, Eduardo Marino, seconded from the UN, an unassuming and highly effective mediator. In some ways, this department is a victim of its own success, with a settlement rate of more than ninety per cent. The political parties, realising that their disputes can be efficiently and quickly resolved, make increasing use of mediation.

Sixty-five per cent of the disputes relate to access issues. Access to areas to campaign, access to advertising, and access to facilities. Tolerance is a commodity in short supply. So in the Transkei, the government of that territory denies the National Party access to the entire region. The National Party lodges a complaint and after mediation it is agreed that the National Party may campaign there. Also, the Transkei government is instructed to provide them with twenty-four hour security. A bit of an about-face, but that's politics.

The local authority in Potchefstroom denies the Democratic Party the right to display posters on electricity poles. That privilege is conferred only on the political parties the municipality favours. After mediation, all parties are allowed to display their posters. A successful series of meetings are held with the mayors of certain

East Rand towns that are charging some political parties excessive deposits to put up posters. These municipalities also deny specific parties the use of town-hall facilities for public meetings.

In Port St Johns many residents are forced to flee their homes after conflict breaks out between the ANC and PAC. The ensuing mediation results in a peace agreement which enables people to return to their homes and reopen the schools.

Ngwenya, a large affable man, is unflappable in the face of urgent and constant pressure as the disputes stream in. By mid-March, more than one hundred and fifty separate mediations have been completed.

Like mediation, the telecommunications department is a victim of its own efficiency. In mid-March, the commission requests that the department provide telecommunications to the entire IEC. In so doing, Willem Ellis's department is provided with one of the greatest challenges the South African telecommunications industry has ever faced.

I am nervous about communicating this new instruction to Ellis. Everyone here is already operating beyond their limits. Just yesterday I had asked a head of department, a hugely capable and resourceful person, to address a crisis in the Eastern Cape. He had stared at me for a full minute, a wild look in his eyes, clutched his hair, then put his face in his hands and sobbed like a child. This didn't bother me too much; I knew exactly how he felt and it would probably have been my reaction had I been in his shoes.

Ellis's reaction to the news is totally impassive. He looks at me and merely nods. 'I will need more people,' he says.

'No problem,' I respond, relieved at his reaction. 'Where will you get them?'

'From Telkom,' he replies. 'And the private companies, Siemens perhaps. Wherever I can find them.'

He has to provide a system that will handle all the traffic between the head office and the different regions and sub-regions plus all contact with the general public. The biggest challenge will be to get communication with all the voting and counting stations.

I see a glint in his eyes which worries me: it is as if he relishes the challenge.

Our planning meeting for the monitoring division early the next day is a disturbing one. Very. The specialist monitoring department led by Imraan Haffagee reports that they are experiencing difficulty in getting information out of the administration division. Specialist monitoring is comprised of experts in the various technical phases of the electoral process, the majority of whom have been seconded at our request by the UN and various electoral commissions around the world. They are serious people who gain delicate pleasure from their intimate knowledge of polling procedures, ballot structuring, voting-station structure and streaming, the vagaries of tally sheets and counting procedures, information technology for electronic counts, and systems for the translation of votes into seats. It is their job to attend and observe the meetings and preparations of the administration division.

The meeting is a difficult one. Some of the department heads feel we should ignore the problems in admin and focus on our own tasks.

But, of course, part of our job is to monitor that division. If we are picking up problems, we can't just keep quiet and hope they will go away.

It appears that the admin division is far from ready. They haven't finalised the location of voting stations. Their training courses are still being compiled. They intend training massive numbers of polling officials in the rural areas by radio.

Our situation is better, I'm relieved to hear. Our deadline for the training of nine thousand monitors is 10 April. Due to the increase in the projected number of voting stations, that number has increased to fifteen thousand five hundred and ninety monitors. We compiled our training materials to meet a deadline by mid-February and our 'train the trainer' courses commenced on schedule on 22 February and finished in early March. We are now training thousands of monitors all over the country each week. It is anticipated that we will finish training the extra six thousand by 22 April.

That is the bright news.

Those in the monitoring division who have experience of the training procedures, Namane Magau, her deputy Syriana Maesela and Alan Brews, are adamant that the training of police officers cannot be done by radio. That's part of the bad news. As Magau puts it, 'Our people are just monitoring the people who are carrying out the actual procedures, a much easier task. I am telling you, Peter, this cannot be done by radio.'

The other part of the bad news comes in the form of stories about the general lack of preparation in the administration division.

'Okay, okay,' I say, irritated by the torrent. 'I will chat to Piet Coleyn. If there is no satisfactory explanation, I will go and speak to the judge. I will also speak to Yunus Mahomed. He will give us an accurate picture.'

I finish my coffee in my office, the fourth cup of the morning. Piet Coleyn is not in his office but his deputy Yunus Mahomed is. I find him at his desk, looking down at a piece of paper, dazed, as if someone has rabbit punched him on the back of his neck.

'Yunus,' I say. He looks up and smiles at me in a distracted way. 'Jeez, Yunus, are you okay? You look sick!'

'No, I am not okay,' he says simply. 'I just can't see our way out of this and now Piet is ill and has apparently been ordered by his doctor to stay at home for at least ten days.'

Aghast, I say, 'There are only six weeks to the election.'

'We are in real trouble, Pete,' he says.

I head for Zac Yacoob to voice my concerns, if not hysteria, about the state of things in admin. It is not the first time that he and I have had this discussion. Also, that Coleyn has been admitted to hospital with pneumonia speaks for itself. Yacoob tells me he will raise it in the commission and that I should also alert Judge Kriegler.

Later that morning, I meet with Judge Kriegler in his office. I wonder if there is any chance of delaying the election, if only for a month, although six weeks would be better.

He looks at me, the rings under his eyes furrows of black pencil. The date can't be shifted.

'I appreciate that, Judge,' I say, 'but if the IEC cannot put together this election and it is a disaster and fails, then the consequences will be far worse than a postponement. It is my duty to tell you that election administration is not ready. It is no one's fault, it is just a fact.'

He nods and says that he will raise it in an urgent meeting of the commission.

That evening I get a call from Zac Yacoob. 'Peter,' he says, 'there was a lot of discussion in our meeting and all the commissioners are reluctant to ask for a postponement. We also know the answer we will get, the words that have been used over and over: "This election date is set in stone."'

In stone, I think, bitterly. Our epitaphs will be written in stone if this election is a mess.

On Monday night, 21 March 1994, a powerful bomb wrecks the offices of the National Party in the right-wing dorp of Ventersdorp, Eugène Terre'Blanche's home town.

At a national meeting of the heads of provinces, Ebby Mohamed from the Western Cape has us all in stitches with a story of the new mobile phones that Motorola has lent to the IEC. While these phones are mobile, they are not easily so. They are bulky. But they're a vast improvement on the mobile phones we used in the Peace Accord, which stood three bricks high and weighed slightly less than a car battery. Whatever their size and weight, the new phones are highly prized.

Mohamed tells how, when they got their small allocation of phones, he gave one to Norman Arendse, a well-known advocate from Cape Town who had volunteered to work at the IEC, and told him it didn't need a landline. Arendse looked at the phone suspiciously, gingerly turning it over and weighing it in his hand.

'I told him, try it. Phone someone, phone your wife. He wanted to know how. I said, "Just dial the number and press the green phone sign on the face." So he phones and his wife answers. But Norman's holding it like a radio handset with one end in front of his mouth.

'"Darling," he says, "this is Norman, come in, come in, over."

'Her reply's muffled because he's got the one end of the phone against his chest.

'"Come in, come in, over," he keeps saying, when he hears his wife's voice.

'I tell him it's not a radio and to hold the damned thing like a telephone. Which he does. He puts it to his ear and his eyes light up. She wants to know why he's speaking as if he's on a radio. To which he says, "Roger." Then he explains that he's on a mobile phone, but he keeps saying "over" at the end of each sentence. She thinks he's playing the fool, so she rings off. He gives me the phone back, saying, "Over and out." Man, I was sore with laughter.'

Brigadier Oupa Gqozo, the military ruler of the Ciskei, has long made it clear that while his administration will not stop the election in the Ciskei, little will be done to make it a success. It is a grim place, this independent homeland, as armed militia ensure the silence of political opponents of the military strongman with assaults, abductions, murder and the torching of houses.

The military has served Gqozo's career well. After dropping out of school in 1972, he started work as a prison warder in Kroonstad, his home town. Then, he joined the South African Defence Force, where he became chief clerk for 21 Battalion, based in Lenasia outside Johannesburg. In 1982, he moved to the Ciskei Defence Force and in March 1990, while the chief minister of the Ciskei, Lennox Sebe, was visiting Hong Kong, Gqozo staged a military coup and seized power in the Ciskei.

Given his Machiavellian rise to power, the brigadier is clearly chary of a democratic election. Especially one that might dislodge him as ruler of the realm.

With the election a little more than a month away, this sprawling, starving, stricken territory lurches towards systemic breakdown as civil servants, following their colleagues in Bophuthatswana, go on strike. They too want their pensions paid out prior to their incorporation into South Africa.

On Tuesday, 22 March 1994, chief of the police, Commissioner Ngoya, is scheduled to address police officers at the Bisho Police College about their pension and other payment concerns. Ngoya does not arrive for the meeting. This provokes the policemen, whose numbers quickly swell. Not surprisingly, the police officers' demands turn political. They demand the removal of their ruler, Brigadier Gqozo.

Frustrated by the lack of response from the police commissioner or the head of state, they descend on State House in a police Casspir. There they find Brigadier Gqozo, frightened and perplexed. His authority is unravelling while his erstwhile allies, the South African government, look on.

He informs the police officers that he has resigned as head of government. The officers don't believe him. They suspect treachery. Back at their college they erect barricades and arm themselves by breaking into the armoury, anticipating an attack. Their fears are exacerbated when troops from the Ciskei Defence Force gather outside the police college.

The next day brings with it more troops. The soldiers announce that they will join the police protest. Nonplussed, the police commanders consult together. They are deeply suspicious. They cannot believe that the brigadier, a ruthless man who has always shown little tolerance for dissent and much regard for the trappings of power, would give up without a fight. And now, his loyal defence force wants to mutiny. It cannot be true. It must be a trap. They instruct the soldiers to leave the area. The soldiers stay put. More troops arrive.

Later, the police dispatch a delegation to speak to the police commissioner. A trembling Commissioner Ngoya confirms that their ruler has indeed resigned.

The police now join forces with the soldiers and head for the Independence Stadium in Bisho, where twenty thousand striking civil servants have gathered.

Bisho is electric with rumours, including speculation that the South African Defence Force is about to invade the territory. The Ciskei Defence Force opens its armouries and distributes weapons to soldiers as well as groups of militia. These bands take to the streets. Tomorrow, there may be a war.

The night of Wednesday, 23 March 1994 is tense. Sporadic gunfire is heard across the capital.

Judge Kriegler leads a small group of IEC commissioners to Ulundi, the capital of KwaZulu, where they are to meet with King Goodwill Zwelithini, Chief Buthelezi and other senior figures in Inkatha. Kriegler is also to address the legislative assembly of the territory and attempt to persuade them that even if they choose not to participate in the election, they should at least cooperate to make a free and fair election in KwaZulu possible.

The composition of the delegation has been the subject of some debate. Clearly, the chairman will have to lead it. Anyone less may be seen as an insult by the KwaZulu legislature. Kriegler believes things can turn ugly at Ulundi and decides it would be wiser to leave deputy chairman Dikgang Moseneke in Johannesburg.

He asks for volunteers and the diminutive Helen Suzman quickly puts up her hand. The judge responds that his sense of chivalry will not allow him to include a woman on the trip.

Suzman bites back, telling the judge exactly the types of places her career has taken her, and alone at that. Her anger silences the meeting. It is quickly settled. Suzman will be part of the team that travels to Ulundi.

It is an apprehensive delegation that flies to Ulundi on Wednesday, 23 March 1994. They are headed for hostile territory where the IEC is viewed with real animosity.

Their expectations are met when they receive a reception from the Inkatha leadership that is cold and little short of antagonistic. After tea with King Goodwill Zwelithini, Chief Buthelezi and his cabinet, they're taken into the legislative assembly. The king is first to speak. His speech is a rousing one, greeted with applause and spontaneous outbursts of approval. He is forthright in his advice to his subjects, making it clear that he cannot recommend that they vote. The king returns slowly to his seat. He is followed by Chief Buthelezi, who reinforces the no-vote view. And then a succession of speakers loudly and aggressively make the king and the chief look like models of diplomacy. Finally it is Kriegler's turn.

Kriegler begins but is interrupted by loud jeers. He soldiers on, trying to make his point that at least the election should be allowed to happen. Again he is drowned out by the booing of the delegates. He tries in vain to make his point but is shouted down. The other commissioners shift uncomfortably in their seats as they feel the mocking anger from the floor. The Inkatha leadership does nothing to protect Kriegler as he struggles on. It is a calculated show of force, a blatant exhibition of contempt for the IEC and its leader. Kriegler is jeered from the podium and leads his delegation out of the assembly chamber. Before they depart, it is made clear to Kriegler and the commissioners that they will receive no cooperation from the KwaZulu administration.

The IEC delegation is dropped unceremoniously at the Ulundi airport. Their plane is parked at the far end of the runway. With no transport available, the IEC commissioners pick up their bags and begin the long lonely walk to their aircraft. The pilot anxiously watches them approach.

'Why are you parked down here?' the judge wants to know.

'I was told to,' replies the pilot.

Back in Johannesburg, a shaken Kriegler describes their reception in the KwaZulu assembly as 'choreographed humiliation'.

Under orders from the chief of the South African Defence Force, General Meiring, an armoured column enters Bisho. It is Thursday, 24 March 1994. Quickly and clinically, the South African soldiers take control of the city, including all major government installations. By nightfall, the defence force is patrolling the streets, the Ciskei police and defence force having surrendered and handed over their weapons. The Ciskei has fallen.

The IEC has exactly thirty-two days to organise an election in the vast Ciskei territory.

On Saturday, 26 March 1994, Charles Nupen heads for the Eastern Cape to assess the situation in Ciskei and Transkei. He has back-to-back meetings in Port Elizabeth, East London and Bisho.

At midday on the second day Nupen arrives at the East London airport to see a small single-engine plane perched on the runway. Aware of IEC policy that commissioners should fly only in planes that possess two engines and two pilots, Nupen asks at the information desk for news of the plane hired to fly him to Umtata.

There are two reasons Nupen sweats with tension as he waits for the answer. The first is that if his plane is delayed somewhere, he will be late and miss his appointments. The second, more serious, reason is that Nupen has a phobia about small planes. This phobia is not confined to small planes: it extends to all objects propelled by machinery, lifts included. He has been known to walk up the stairs of twenty-storey buildings.

'That is your plane, sir,' says the man at the information desk, gesturing out the window.

144

'That one?' says Nupen, pointing to the only plane on the tarmac.

'Yes,' he's told. 'Your pilot is over there.'

Nupen sees a very young man in his early twenties sitting on the other side of the room. He goes over and introduces himself.

Sweating profusely, Nupen asks, 'Where is your colleague?'

'Colleague?' says the pilot. 'No, it is just me, I'm afraid.'

Using his mobile phone, Nupen puts through a call to Glen Cowley, the man responsible for organising transport. Cowley doesn't get to say much as Nupen blasts him at length about breaking rules and arranging a small plane flown by a child pilot. There is a long silence from Cowley.

'What should I do now, Glen?' asks Nupen.

'Do you really want to know?'

'Yes,' says Nupen, 'I really want to know.'

'Pick up your briefcase, walk slowly to the plane, walk around it once, and place your briefcase down on the tarmac. Look carefully at the plane, walk up to it and kick it hard in the ribs. If the wings don't fall off, you pick up your briefcase, get in the plane and fucking fly to Umtata,' Cowley shouts into the phone.

'Yes, Glen,' says Nupen.

The tiny plane has a thin Perspex floor. Nupen, petrified, stares straight ahead until the plane lands in Umtata.

In five days' time, at the end of the month, the administration division is to brief us on their state of readiness. I have a lot of sympathy for them. Not only are their tasks enormous and their timelines deadly, but they also have staffing problems. Fortunately, the man who has de facto taken over the running of election administration is very competent and probably knows more about elections than anyone else in the country. Norman du Plessis is affable, works tirelessly and always deals with his mounting challenges with great calm. Recently, however, they have had the good sense to bring in experts from the private sector to assist in critical areas.

One such area is the delivery of voting materials around the country. Voting materials are divided into two categories: sensitive materials such as ballots, marking ink and presiding officer's stamps and seals, and then other material. Sensitive materials will be delivered a few days before the election, under armed escorts, to strategically located secret warehouses, where they will be under twenty-four-hour guard. The 'other' materials are voting-station kits made up of two hundred and forty-eight individual items. The difficulty is getting all this material out on time across the entire country, including places where there are no roads. The administration division finds these problems almost insurmountable, until a bright soul mentions that the one commodity that can be found in virtually every corner of this country is, wait for it, beer! And in most cases can be found chilled – no small achievement.

Accordingly, South African Breweries, arguably the company with the largest and most efficient distribution network on the African continent, is consulted and, after some persuasion, agrees to second their senior planning and logistics executive to oversee the distribution of voting materials. This logic resonates with me, as I have long been an admirer of SAB and their products. If they could get their beer to a remote village in the Kalahari desert where I had arrived one lonely Christmas day in 1981 in search of liquid, then they had my vote.

The distribution of materials is to be entrusted to the green pantechnicons of that venerable company whose pedigree exceeds a hundred and thirty years, namely Stuttaford Van Lines. In general, we are happy that South Africa's brightest and best are being brought to bear on this election.

However, we are less happy about the arrangements being made for the electronic count. It has been decided that the boxes of ballots should be transported by the officials from each polling station to the six hundred and seventy counting centres. These counting centres will then be responsible for the transmission of the 'tallies' to a central collation point where verification will take place. To this end, election administration has established a results control centre. This is a secure location in head office that is sealed and under permanent guard.

On the one occasion we are allowed to view it, we see a large room with banks of computers and rows of fax machines.

'Are you sure you have enough fax machines?' I ask the techie showing us around. 'You don't want to have a jam when the results all start coming in at once.'

'We have made our calculations based on the plans developed by our experts,' the man replies stiffly.

There are flow charts on the walls detailing the steps to be taken as the results arrive.

The votes are to be counted in batches of three thousand at the counting centres. Then batch-tally forms that reflect the number of votes for each party are to be completed and sent to the results control centre. Once all votes at a station have been counted, another form detailing the final vote-count has to be completed, signed by officials and counter-signed by the political parties. Then it is dispatched to the control centre. We are talked through the process which, at face value, sounds impressive. Not too complicated.

'The computer program we have for the count is fantastic and very sophisticated,' says our guide proudly. 'It cost a fortune to develop but it is worth it, and it is completely secure.'

'Can we have our people look at it?' I want to know.

'I can check, but it is already complete and we do not want people interfering with it,' he replies.

'I understand that. But can we check its integrity?'

'Let us come back to you on that,' he says, leading us to the door of the room.

Back in my office, I ask Imraan Haffagee to find out more about the system that they will use for the electronic count, and how secure it is.

'That will not be as easy as you think,' says Haffagee. 'We have tried to get our people in there, but they are cagey and very protective. At our last meeting, there was a standoff when we asked for access to the control centre. They see us as interfering. I have been told by Norman du Plessis that even he is not allowed in. The only people allowed in, apart from those that work in the centre, are Piet Coleyn, Tsinga Madiba and Yunus Mahomed.'

I nod, and push my request. 'See if you can get a UN expert in there that can satisfy us on the integrity of the system.'

'I'll try,' says Haffagee wearily.

Two days later, he reports that the electronic vote count will run on a Windows NT Advanced Server-based network with Windows for Workgroups on the workstations. The administrative network is connected to the main IEC network. The computer software developed for vote counting and recording was written using Microsoft Access version 1.1 and the actual workstations that will enter the data are using Microsoft Access Distribution Kit.

'Shit, Imraan, what language are you speaking?' I ask. 'That means nothing to me. Is it secure? That is the issue.'

'We cannot get access to it because they do not want to compromise security. We're in a catch-22 situation,' he replies. 'No one is allowed access. But they have reassured us and all the commissioners that its security cannot be breached.'

In the accreditation and logistics department, the registration of thousands of international and domestic observers is well under way. Observers pour into the country in their thousands, inundating the IEC with requests and well-meaning advice.

Delegations of observers come from all over the world. Some are from large multilateral organisations like the United Nations, others from small NGOs in remote countries. By late March, Lucia Mtshali, who is in charge of this department, has accredited more than ninety international and some thirty domestic organisations.

Each group has to submit a list of their observers. They are given bibs identifying them and a basic kit that will assist them in their work. Every observer has a registration card with his or her photograph and particulars on it. After training and orientation, they are allocated recommended areas for deployment. While we cannot tell them where to go, we can make proposals. This is done to avoid an uneven spread of observers. We don't want ten thousand eager observers descending on Cape Town to 'observe' the electoral processes in that fair city. This is a popular spot for many observers, and they pointedly tell us that we should not attempt to limit their freedom of movement. They want to go to Cape Town. 'The restaurants in Camps Bay will be happy to be observed in this election,' I tell Lucia Mtshali sarcastically.

The closing date for receiving accreditation applications from delegations is Sunday, 27 March 1994 – date to date a month before the election. But this deadline means little to many observers, who continue to arrive well into April. They will phone and say, 'We are here in your beautiful country to observe your elections. We are one hundred observers, how do we get accreditation?'

'Thank you,' we say with a grimace, knowing the extra work involved. 'You are most welcome in South Africa.' We curse the commissioners who have given the instruction that no one should be turned away.

There is a lighter side as Mtshali regales us with wonderful stories of wide-eyed observers careering around the country. One phoned her team for advice after being bitten by a mosquito. Another wanted suggestions on what to eat in the Karoo. A third asked if the water was safe to drink in Venda. A fourth wanted the Zulu words for 'I am here to watch your election. I am lost, please help me.'

A group of five senior policemen from Scotland Yard, who are here to observe the conduct of our own police force during the election, telephone to say they wish to see me. They are in the Carlton Hotel, across the street. Can they see me immediately. I restrain a sigh and say yes.

An hour later they arrive, sporting bloody noses and bruises, their clothes tattered and torn.

'My God, what happened to you?' I ask in horror. These big men look as if they have been in a bad car accident.

'We got mugged crossing the road by a group of small boys,' one of the policemen tells me, wiping blood from his face with a white handkerchief. 'We didn't see them coming. They were so fast.'

'Please accept my apologies,' I say. 'And welcome to South Africa.'

By mid-March, some six hundred and twenty thousand temporary voting cards have been issued. It is not enough. Unless something drastic is done, millions of voters will be disenfranchised. This will not only detract from the freeness and fairness of the election but could lead to mass protests that could affect the running of the election. I would not want to be the chief polling officer in a rural village in Transkei when the entire area turns out to vote for the first time in their lives, only to be told that the piece of paper they have is invalid and that they will not be able to vote. Clearly, this is a very emotive issue.

The commissioners appoint a special task team consisting of engineering and management consultants in conjunction with home affairs people. More staff are put into the field and temporary voting cards are now available at the issuing stations seven days a week. Mobile units visit two hundred prisons, mine compounds as well as hostels in a few weeks. They are superbly organised and achieve exceptional results.

By Sunday, 27 March 1994 they are issuing an average of half a million temporary voting cards a week.

The right wing and Inkatha move in flickering shapes through my mind, dark shadows that wake me up in the early hours of the morning. I have nightmares of bombs and shrapnel slicing through the flesh of civilians. I wake, alarmed, wondering if the

IEC headquarters will be targeted by a right-wing bomb squad. As if that were not enough, I have visions of Zulu impis converging en masse – horns of the buffalo stuff.

The twins, my own personal warriors, wake up at 5 am and jolt me from my morbid reverie. Now more than six months old, they are beautiful and yet so vulnerable as they lie in their cots. I wonder what they dream about.

Caroline comes through and feeds them both at the same time, no easy feat, the gentle suckling noises somehow clean and pure, not yet besmirched by the contagion of the world into which they have been born. Isabella joins us, her eyes wide and big from sleep. She is carrying two dolls, one on each arm, in the fashion of Caroline with the twins. Simon wakes up later and starts dressing for nursery school, a lovely happy child. We each prepare for our separate days.

It is Monday, 28 March 1994.

I leave home early on that morning, driving fast through the empty streets. Leaving my bag in my office, I go straight to the ops centre. An Inkatha march and rally are scheduled to take place today in the centre of Johannesburg. I know about Inkatha marches from my time in the Peace Accord, and they still bring out a sweat. Quite simply, when that impi advances with spears and guns, anything can happen.

Even the police are careful about angering an Inkatha march; they know that in the centre of the marchers are the guys with guns. When it is deemed necessary, they will be shuffled to the edges and then the shooting will begin. Those marchers are fearless.

Generally the participants congregate early, preparing in the hostels with singing and rituals as they psyche themselves up. In full warrior dress with shields and spears, they move from the hostels and adjoining houses to their assembly points on foot. No one who is not Inkatha lives in a house adjoining an Inkatha hostel. From the assembly points they head for the train stations,

151

which by that stage are deserted, as are the trains. Only the fool-ish and the suicidal would climb onto the same train carriage as an Inkatha impi on their way to a rally.

When I get to the ops centre Eddie Hendrickx and Phiroshaw Camay are already there. The place is buzzing as telephone and radio reports come in of the gathering marchers. We have radio communication with the Peace Accord monitors patrolling the perimeters of the march. The number of marchers is estimated at between twenty and thirty thousand.

I turn to Captain Marina Rossouw of the SAP, now stationed permanently in the ops centre. 'Are your people in place? Do you have sufficient forces out there?' I ask her. 'We are less than a month from the election and we don't need anything to go wrong today.'

'We have reaction units all along the route of the march and at the final point of the rally, Library Gardens,' she replies. 'That area has also been cordoned off from the general public and we have choppers in the air monitoring the marchers as they emerge from the trains. They will follow the march. We also have people on the rooftops around Library Gardens and on standby.'

'Good stuff,' I say. I like this policewoman. She is professional and easy to work with. Whenever we have requested things from her, she has delivered. We were suspicious of her at first but she has won the respect of those in the centre, particularly Camay and Hendrickx.

Rupert Lorimer, who took over my job in the Peace Accord when I came to the IEC, had briefed us the previous afternoon on the arrangements that the Peace Accord, political parties and security forces would be making for the march. Lorimer, in his sixties and a former Progressive Federal Party politician, is a good man. I have seen him defuse highly volatile situations when lives were at stake on many occasions. In particular, I remember being with him in Phola Park on the East Rand when, as we were negotiat-ing with police and residents, someone shot at the meeting. The police internal stability unit got stuck in and the next thing, we were caught in a serious fire fight between residents and police. Eventually, Lorimer, who I had never heard swear before, stood up and shouted, 'Fuck you, fuck you, fuck you, stop firing, dammit!' And they did, just like that. Which was a good thing because it was getting dark. Had he not made them stop it would have escalated and gone through the night. Unconventional behaviour perhaps, but effective.

Thankfully, the march proceeds peacefully, although there is not much in their path to cause an incident. All the shops along the route and in the nearby streets are locked with strong metal shutters. There are a few confrontations where hawkers are chased away, their wares grabbed by the marchers.

I can hear the clack, clack of a chopper overhead and surmise that the marchers are approaching the centre of town. So far so good. We had been very worried about this march. The country is a tinderbox and anything can set it off. A march by thousands of armed Inkatha supporters through the centre of Johannesburg has the potential for serious conflict. It is a relief that the marchers are sticking to their route. I return to my office, light a cigarette and open the windows to let the smoke out. The familiar sounds of the city are comforting, nothing unusual.

There is a knock on the door and one of the people from the ops centre comes in. 'We think we may have a problem: thousands of marchers have peeled off from the main march and seem to be heading towards Hillbrow,' he says.

'Hillbrow? What do they want there?'

Back in the ops centre, the Peace Accord representatives are speaking to their people on the ground. Some have stayed with the breakaway contingent. Captain Rossouw says two police armoured cars are following the marchers headed towards Hillbrow. The room is alive with speculation. And then the penny drops. ANC headquarters is located in a building called Shell House close to the edge of Joubert Park, right next to Hillbrow.

'They're going to Shell House, not to Hillbrow,' I say.

'My God!' exclaims Camay. 'This is real trouble. The security guarding that building are all MK. They will shoot if they are threatened. Those guys are soldiers.'

I turn to the police representative: 'See if you can get those police Casspirs and vehicles following the march to speed to the front. We need a buffer between the marchers and Shell House. And they must be stopped.' She immediately gets on the radio to the police control-room.

It is too late. The Inkatha contingent arrives close to Shell House and fans out along the side of the building, facing its entrance. The security guards retreat into the ANC headquarters, locking the doors.

Next, shots are fired from the Inkatha contingent at the building, which is now under siege. Men with shotguns emerge from the crowd and open fire. The few police stationed in front of the building take cover behind pillars.

In the ops centre we're getting reports of gunfire all around Shell House. Hendrickx turns to the police captain and tells her to get police reinforcements down there immediately.

At first, ANC security fire warning shots. When these go unheeded, they fire directly at the marchers. The security personnel guarding Shell House are all former MK soldiers who have just returned to South Africa after years in the ANC camps in Angola. Many of them have been involved in combat with Unita in the protracted Angolan war. They are battle-hardened veterans unused to the strictures of civilian life and legal regulation, such as the ones that prohibit a gunfight in the middle of town. Right there in downtown Johannesburg, a pitched battle ensues.

Inexplicably, the two police vehicles following the breakaway marchers retreat around the corner, leaving the ANC and Inkatha to fight it out. Inkatha marchers take cover and aim at the people firing down on them from the building. MK soldiers move from window to window, firing selective shots. Classic fire and movement.

The men on the streets are exposed. They shelter at street corners, behind the pillars of buildings and parked cars, all the time engaging with those shooting at them from the building.

The fire fight lasts for thirty minutes before Inkatha starts to withdraw, trying to carry their dead and wounded with them. The streets are littered with bodies: the wounded quiet in their pain, not crying out, afraid that their cries will attract gunfire. The Peace Accord monitors in their bright orange bibs move among the wounded, calling in ambulances and trying to get the police there. The police are nowhere to be seen.

The retreating Inkatha marchers are joined by the others from Library Gardens. They move back to the stations and to their hostels. Along the way there are more casualties as they vent their anger. They are also shot at by unidentified gunmen from the rooftops overlooking the Library Gardens. Inevitably they return fire. It is chaos.

The police arrive much later. I look hard at Captain Rossouw in the ops centre. Visibly upset, she shakes her head saying, 'I'm sorry, I'm sorry.' By the end of the day, fifty-three people have died in the fighting and there are over four hundred wounded.

The ops centre is overcome by gloom and despondency; the worst has come to pass. The predictions by doomsayers of civil conflict in South Africa no longer seem exaggerated or inflammatory. How can we hold an election in conditions like this?

Internationally, the press are forthright. The London *Daily Mail* reports that 'Emergency plans are being made to airlift up to three hundred and fifty thousand Britons out of South Africa should the country slide into chaos after this month's elections'.

There is no lessening of the tension from Chief Buthelezi, who states publicly, 'We have now entered a final struggle to the finish between the ANC and the Zulu nation.' And we believe him. Implicitly.

The presentation by the administration division to address the concerns about their readiness takes place at the end of March, late one afternoon, before the full commission chaired by Judge Kriegler. It is a damned impressive performance. Slick and professional and chock-a-block with data, organograms, pie charts, and flowcharts with moving pieces jetting in from all angles, some with a smacking sound, others moving with the silence and stealth of assassins as they glide into their locked positions. Completely incompetent in the formulation of such sophistry, I am awed by the technological brillance of the presentation and definitely feel more at ease with each passing slide. The private sector types lend weight to the men from home affairs.

I wonder if maybe I've got it wrong. Perhaps we are simply prejudiced against the men from the ministry because of their background. Perhaps we are too suspicious or even over cautious and have done them an injustice. I feel that we are in the wrong and need to atone somehow. I feel more remorse when Zac Yacoob asks when the identification and location of voting stations will be complete. He is told, perfectly reasonably, that due to the changes in the voting procedures, the requirements for voting stations have altered, but that they should be complete in the next ten days.

While this is way beyond deadline, they are doing the best they can in a bad situation, surely. We should not be unreasonable. And then I think again. I list what is still to be accomplished. I go cold. I go cold because I still think that the election cannot be done on time.

Afterwards, I have dinner with Zac Yacoob, Charles Nupen and Ben van der Ross at the Squires Loft Steakhouse opposite our building. We drink whisky while we wait for our meals.

'So,' says Nupen, 'what did you think? It looked fairly impressive?'

'A lot better than we thought,' says Van der Ross.

I agree.

'I don't know what you saw and obviously I couldn't see the slide presentation,' says Yacoob. 'I could only hear what they were saying and I must tell you, it was crap. There was little of substance. Smoke and mirrors, guys. I think we are in shit. Pete, you and your folk need to start making contingency arrangements in case parts of the administration division go belly up.'

I feel sick to my stomach. I don't eat much. In fact, I don't even drink much.

It takes a blind man to see it as it is.

The troubled country and the worsening violence raise another question: the safety of those who have voted. In a land rife with schisms, every action carries consequences. Sadly, voting in this election could be one of them.

In many elections around the world, those who have voted have their thumbs marked with permanent ink. In this election, visible ink is not an option. In some areas a mark indicating that you have voted could get you killed. In order to obviate this possibility and to comply with Section 35(4) of the Electoral Act, invisible ink will be used. It will be invisible to the naked eye but will light up under the ultraviolet lights that will be supplied to each voting station. A brilliant solution, but not without its problems.

It is imperative that the ink cannot be replicated and mass produced. A local supplier is ruled out; instead, the contract goes to De La Rue in the United Kingdom.

Of course, the choice of invisible ink gives rise to a host of jokes. How can you tell if it has spilt? How do you know how much you are applying? How will you know when the ink pad needs replenishing?

Actually, the ink is needed not just to ensure the anonymity of voters. In a country where certain sections of the population are in possession of multiple identity documents, invisible ink is a necessity to stop them from voting more than once.

By early April the wide area network – WAN – is ready to service more voice and data users than any other network in the country. Willem Ellis proudly informs the commission that the network he is establishing will be one of the largest private networks if speed, traffic, users and geographical distribution are taken into account.

While I am not a WAN kind of guy, I know enough to realise that this network of five thousand extensions, three thousand four hundred trunk and tie lines, more than one thousand terminals, forty-three main network nodes (a word I now toss out stylishly) and forty-eight satellite dishes is an extraordinary feat.

Ellis marshals his staff like a general. For them there is little rest. He tells me that Telkom has laid one point five million kilometres of cable to support the infrastructure for the elections. We had been worried that Telkom, a conservative government parastatal, would be less than enthusiastic about providing assistance to the elections. Not so. They come to the party in a big way, generously giving us what we want and reacting expeditiously to the requests.

The major problem we have on the communication front is contact with voting stations in areas where there is no infrastructure at all. This is debated at length in the weekly meetings of the monitoring division. The reality is that we will not be able to use landlines at all. They simply cannot be laid and installed in the time available. Ellis refuses to be stymied by the facts. He solves the problem by setting up a series of networks in the remote rural areas using mobile radios. In order to extend the range of the radios, he incorporates commercial radio network repeaters. Base stations are set up at IEC headquarters and in all provincial and sub-provincial headquarters. In total, over three thousand mobile and hand-held radios are deployed.

I am in awe of his operation. I am not the only one. Major Eddie Hendrickx, now known as Eddie the Belgian, says of Ellis: 'Peter, this guy is seriously impressive. He is a total professional. I would work with him anywhere in the world. Do you know how long it normally takes to set up these kinds of networks? He is achieving the impossible. You know they have put beds into one of the offices on the floor above and they don't go home. They live here. They sleep in shifts and run a twenty-four hour operation.'

I shake my head, worried that I didn't know this.

The next night I leave the office at about two in the morning. Passing Ellis's office, I hear a lot of noise and excited chatter. I knock and open the door to find Ellis with a number of his staff, poring over charts, speaking in Afrikaans. My Afrikaans is reasonably good but they are talking WANs and LANs, nodes and connectors, a mystifying jargon that is way beyond me. More than that, they are speaking with animation and vigour, like a family planning a holiday. I look at them and smile, shaking my head. 'Don't you guys sleep?' I say.

They grin back. I can see they want me to leave so that they can get back to work.

Dikgang Moseneke has the unenviable task of keeping lines of communication open with Ulundi. Despite the obvious difficulties and danger, Moseneke's regular visits to Ulundi and contact with Chief Buthelezi pay off. A trust and mutual respect grow. He assures the Inkatha leadership that should they decide to participate in the election, they will be treated fairly.

On one of his trips in early April, Moseneke arranges a meeting with the American ambassador, who is in Durban at the same time. It is known that Chief Buthelezi has ties with groupings in the United States and it is hoped that the ambassador may be able to assist the IEC in its dealing with the chief.

Moseneke is due to be picked up at Durban airport by a young woman called Louise Oliver and driven directly to meet the ambassador. On arriving at the IEC offices in Durban, Oliver is told that the IEC car allocated to her has been taken by someone else. Oliver, a resourceful person, decides to use her own vehicle. She is, however, concerned that her car, which is old and in a state of some disrepair, may not be suitable transport for the deputy head of the IEC. That aside, there is a fair amount of rubbish, including some of her clothes, on the back seat.

Not one to be diverted by such issues, Oliver drives fast to the airport and waits for Moseneke, who coolly appraises this attractive woman.

They walk to her car, chatting amiably. When they reach her small car she self-consciously explains her predicament regarding the transport. Moseneke, realising that beggars can't be choosers, and that he remains in the company of a very appealing woman, climbs into the front seat, saying that it's not a problem. But, he adds, they should hurry so that he is not late for his appointment. Still apologising, Louise Oliver drives out of the airport onto the highway.

The light banter in the car puts her at ease and she relaxes. But moments later, her car engine dies with a tired sigh. The car glides to a slow halt on the side of the highway, with Louise frantically pumping the accelerator, simultaneously switching the ignition key on and off. To no avail.

Panic stricken, she looks at Moseneke, who returns her look with raised eyebrows, saying nothing. The impasse is broken when they both admit, almost simultaneously, that they know very little about cars.

Moseneke checks his watch. It is agreed that one of them will have to flag down a passing car. It is also agreed that it would reflect badly on the IEC if the well-known face of Dikgang Moseneke were to be seen hitching from a broken-down Uno on the side of the highway.

Louise Oliver, feisty and up-front by nature, gets out and starts thumbing the afternoon traffic. The cars pass, as does the time. Anxious and desperate, Moseneke leans over and helpfully advises, 'I think you need to do better than that.' She looks at him, at the passing cars, back at the deputy commissioner and then, with a suggestive flick of her hair, she lifts her tight skirt and tucks it in at her waist. Moseneke sits back with a smile as she faces the traffic and again sticks out her thumb. The first car to approach her screeches to a halt not ten meters from the Uno. Oliver glances at Moseneke and they both laugh.

Louise Oliver approaches the car and tells the driver she would like her friend to come along too. Peeved at being deprived of her solitary company, the driver nonetheless agrees, and Moseneke climbs into the back while Oliver chats to their rescuer in front. Moseneke, petrified of being recognised and hidden behind sunglasses, sinks low on the back seat and does not say a word. He makes his appointment with the American ambassador with minutes to spare.

CHAPTER SIX

A large meeting of the AWB is held at Trim Park in Ventersdorp. The first part of the meeting is open to the public and the media and starts with a speech by the AWB chaplain general, the Reverend Manie Maritz. The crowd take off their hats and focus on Maritz, who talks about the hand of God that led them to this country and gave them this country, this country that they must now fight for.

His voice rings out over the crowd. 'The first thing we must remember is that we are white people, but the most important thing for all, is that we believe in God who helped us out of Blood River. I say that I am a descendant, I am a white man, I am a descendant and I am proud to be a white man. I have nothing against the black man, but he is not my neighbour, he is not a member of my Volk, and that is why I say to my people that we should take up each other's hands and the hands of those who must fight with us.

'You and I will answer to God and we must answer to the question, What did you do to the property I gave you? What did you do with this country that I entrusted to you? Did you cultivate it? Did you create a legacy out of it for your descendants? We must tell God today that we will fight for what is ours.'

There is a long pause. Then: 'I want to say to you today that the revolution is at hand. Let us begin it.'

The Leader steps up. To thunderous applause, Eugène Terre'-Blanche tells the crowd 'the war is very close'. Again, he misquotes Chairman Mao Zedong and refers to '… negotiating across the barrel of a gun'. But the Leader doesn't have to worry, the crowd gets his drift.

His fighting talk continues. 'We are threatened and people are fighting against us, the powers of hell are fighting against us. We must remember that our Christian Creator would never expect anything from us which we cannot manage. He would never expect us to become a Jody Scheckter all of a sudden and become the world's best driving champion … We must sound the trumpet of the Volk and announce that we are here today. We must say the country is good, let's take it. We will look like locusts in comparison to our enemies because they are giants, but this view is not entirely of application, because the group which is threatening us is not a group of giants, and we are not like locusts.'

His eccentric rhetoric rages on, the great red flags with their ominous stylised swastikas flutter and droop. The Leader returns to his locust analogy. 'That is why I say, by means of our experience and our intellectual abilities and our spirit and the Spirit of God which runs through your veins, you can never see yourself as a locust. We are the giants then, we are the white giants.'

He tells the rally that in a month's time the flags will fly above their fatherland.

'We have seen that there are thousands of Permanent Defence [Force] members who support us. There are two hundred and fifty thousand commando and civil members of which a hundred and eighty thousand at least are right-wingers. The South African Police of which eighty per cent are right-wingers and if you add on the hundred and eighty thousand defence-force commando members and the sixty-five thousand AWB members, then we are more than prepared … Next month this time, we will become part of a new state and those three sixes will hover above our fatherland in the air … We want our own piece of land in which we can protect our men, women and children.'

He concludes his address: 'I promise you that when we have won the war, Mandela will ask us for land and then we will decide whether or not we could do away with a centimetre or two.'

The Leader looks at the crowd before him in expectation, head thrown back, his thick silver beard and blue eyes catching the light. He is not disappointed. A spontaneous roar bursts from the assembled men, seemingly lifting the array of AWB flags and banners which straighten and flick in the light wind. The men on horseback struggle to control their horses. It is a great spectacle.

The meeting is also addressed by some of the fighting generals. General Dirk Ackerman tells his men that 'there is no more time for talking, it's time for war.'

It is Saturday, 2 April 1994.

That Saturday we celebrate Simon's birthday, which is actually two days later. Caroline organises a magnificent cake and invites family, friends and his class at the Bluebird Nursery School to our home. The party starts at three in the afternoon and I get home just in time. I have made myself a promise not to miss the children's birthdays. When I arrive home, I almost rethink my vow. There is total chaos, with about thirty five-year-olds running riot.

A sizeable pile of presents is growing in the sitting room. I admire Simon's restraint as he thanks each guest for his or her gift, avoiding the undoubtedly strong impulse to rip off the paper. Instead, he calmly adds to the growing pile. As he does so, he whispers something to each of his guests. I have no doubt it is something along the lines of 'Go mad, tear the place down, destroy and maim!' I say this because the behaviour of each child changes instantly. As if possessed, they start shouting, tearing off their shirts and shoes and generally falling about in their haste to get to the jumping castle. Bedlam is the order of the day in this giant plastic mansion. For those on the floor of the castle, it is game over, as the other kids make sure that they never rise, endlessly struggling to their haunches only to be pitched back onto their faces. A bit like life, I think, as I watch in dawning terror, imagining picking up pieces of children after the party and putting them in a wheelbarrow to be re-assembled for each parent who has come to collect his or her beloved child.

Simon, big for his age and with curly blonde hair, stands close to the castle, surveying the carnage with a look that is close to pride. Then he throws himself headlong into the pile of struggling bodies. The shouts and screams shatter the sedate peace of the suburb.

I mention apprehensively to one of the other parents that it

164

looks a bit wild. 'This is tame,' she scoffs. 'They get worse as they grow older.' I shudder, remembering my mother's dictum that, with children, the first forty years are the worst.

The second part of the meeting at Trim Park is closed. The AWB crowd disperses into groups so that the commanders and generals can give briefings, check planning and confirm if their men have the necessary equipment for the insurrection being planned.

Fighting general Chris van den Heever, the commander of AWB special forces, meets with his men. Van den Heever is also a high-ranking officer in the South African Defence Force and, because of this, had earlier been tasked with obtaining medical equipment and armoured cars, known as Ratels, from the nearby military base in Zeerust. He assures his men that he has been successful and that they will receive the necessary support on the day the war starts. He believes that at least forty thousand men from the defence force will cross to their side. Further, they will bring their arms and armoured vehicles with them.

Each group is told to make their own personal preparations for the war. They must speak to their families and ensure that their wives and children are ready to leave with them for the Volkstaat. This comes as no surprise, as there has already been much talk of the sacrifice that will be needed from the men and their families. Those in employment must tender their resignations in the next few days. They will be given jobs in the Volkstaat, as policemen, traffic officers, guards and municipal officials. In their own country they will be looked after – decent work and good pay and dignity, as befits their status as Boere, the chosen people.

Van den Heever addresses officers under a tree at Trim Park. He instructs them that on Friday, 15 April 1994, they must move their people to the Western Transvaal. They must leave their houses and come with their caravans. They must bring power generators. He tells the assembled commanders that they must carry out 'affirmative shopping. In other words, you must go and buy but not pay, because they cannot claim it back from you and, as you move through and, for example, if you do not have enough money for petrol and you encounter problems while taking this petrol, you must just shoot your way through or out of the situation ...'

There will be seven assembly points in the Western Transvaal, with more than four hundred families gathering. It is said that in the run-up to the elections there will be complete chaos. In the tumult, they will create their own revolution.

The need to bring Inkatha into the election drives the major parties, the ANC and the National Party, represented by Cyril Ramaphosa and Roelf Meyer respectively, to seek compromises. Although the final deadline for the registration of parties has long passed, they make another attempt to persuade Inkatha to participate in the election. An election without Inkatha spells trouble in Natal and KwaZulu.

On Friday, 8 April 1994, Nelson Mandela, FW de Klerk and their chief negotiators meet at Skukuza in the Kruger National Park with Chief Buthelezi and King Goodwill Zwelithini.

To allay the Zulu king's fear of what might happen to him after the KwaZulu administration ceases to exist, Mandela proposes a dispensation that will establish the king as the constitutional monarch of KwaZulu and Natal. He will open sessions of the assembly, have his royal police force and receive a handsome 'allowance'. The king and Chief Buthelezi listen intently to Mandela and then request an opportunity to caucus.

An hour and a half passes, not a good sign.

When the group reconvenes, Mandela's offer is rejected. Chief Buthelezi stipulates that there can be no delinking the king from the requirements of Inkatha. Both Mandela and De Klerk prevail on the two men but to no avail. An accommodation cannot be reached.

Mandela and De Klerk decide to go ahead without Inkatha. The imperative now is to make KwaZulu and Natal as safe as possible.

If that involves taking on Inkatha and their supporters, so be it. In this battle it is now a matter of strength and cunning. The London *Sunday Times*, reporting on the failure at Skukuza, states: 'South Africa prepared for civil war yesterday.'

A state of emergency is declared in Natal and defence-force troops are mobilised. They are deployed at strategic installations, national key points and close to the major transport arteries throughout the province. A large section of the police task force is moved to Durban, and Natal Command fills with troops. The objective is to secure the province in case of attacks from Inkatha.

At the same time, intelligence reports point to an intensification in training activity at secret Inkatha camps. In the Mlaba training camp in the dense bush of northern Zululand, intelligence sources estimate the number of recruits to be about five thousand men. The province gears for war.

It is Tuesday, 9 April 1994. Eight employees of Natal Pamphlet Distributors hired by the IEC to distribute pamphlets explaining voting procedures are killed in Ndwedwe, north of Durban. They are taken to a gorge where the eight are shot and hacked to death by Inkatha supporters. Three escape. Five men are detained and charged, including the local chief.

Two weeks before the election, there is an AWB meeting at Fyndoringtjies Culture Festival Resort, a nature reserve outside Ventersdorp. It is a closed meeting of the Leader and his fighting generals. It is attended by the Kiewiet Roodt, Cruywagen, Japie Oelofse, Dirk Ackerman, the brother of the Leader, Andries Terre'Blanche, and Nico Prinsloo.

Each of the generals is allocated a region in the Volkstaat that they will command. They are ordered to bring members of their local commando to their Volkstaat area in the Western Transvaal on call-up day.

The boundaries of the Volkstaat are not specifically defined but bear a direct correlation to the areas where the right wing has been given the freedom of the town. Broadly, this region stretches in a strip from Rustenburg in the north-west to Hoopstad in the south-east. In between the towns that will fall into the Volkstaat – Klerksdorp, Schweizer-Reneke, Koster and Ventersdorp – lies the disjointed bits of land that comprises Bophuthatswana.

The discussion at the meeting centres on the need to destabilise the elections and at the same time create a psychosis of fear and panic in the country. Then people will not vote, rendering the election meaningless. In the ensuing chaos, black people will rise up and attack whites and the institutions of power. The right wing will take advantage of the anarchy and quickly establish its Volkstaat. Given their extensive military preparations and the anticipated sympathy of the defence force and police, defending this territory should not be a problem. Nevertheless, it is acknowledged that this war of liberation will not be easy. But they have God on their side. They will overcome and achieve their destiny.

The generals decide to mount a bombing campaign which will be directed exclusively at soft targets. General Dirk Ackerman gives General Nico Prinsloo the instruction to identify men from AWB special forces to construct a car bomb. This bomb must dwarf all other bombs that have been exploded in the country. It must be so big and its destructive power so great that when it detonates it will be heard in Cape Town.

The target of the car bomb is downtown Johannesburg. The precise location is left to the discretion of Prinsloo, but taxi ranks and restaurants are mentioned. The instruction is clear. The targets must be soft. The timing of the bomb, says Ackerman, is important. It must be just before the elections. The instruction is that people must die in the bomb blast, as many as possible. The Sunday before the week of the election is designated as the time. The objective is havoc.

Prinsloo has the perfect person in mind for the job. A man who is a member not only of the special forces of the AWB but also, apparently, a member of special forces in the defence force. He is one of the best-trained men in the whole of the AWB, with extensive combat experience gained in the Namibian war.

Clifton Barnard is an anomaly in the AWB. Instead of the typical short-back-and-sides haircut, he wears his hair long. He also prefers civilian clothing to uniforms and insignia. He is known as a specialist. As a result of his extensive experience and the sense of menace that he exudes, Clifton Barnard is highly respected. The fact that he is a close confidant of the Leader adds to his already considerable reputation. Prinsloo personally briefs Barnard and tells him to choose his men carefully for the mission. He is told that the attacks must be aimed at black people.

I continue to consult regularly with Dong Nguyen, Reg Austen and Michael Maley, the UN's electoral experts. Some of their stories, although hard to believe, ring a bell about the way we are doing things, particularly, when it comes to the levels of mistrust that exist in a first-time election between former enemies.

During one of our discussions relating to the secrecy of the vote, Maley recounts that such was the paranoia that existed in the first Cambodian election in May 1993 that it was rumoured that the pencils used by voters contained tiny transmitters that would tell the political parties which way the person had voted. Another rumour had it that satellites would monitor how an individual voted. There was even a story that the angel in the symbol of the Cambodian People's Party had supernatural powers and could see which way people voted. 'This got worse when the opposition party said that the angel was in fact a prostitute. Violence was threatened.'

'The fallen, the fallen,' mutters Austen.

I laugh. 'Well, we may not be quite in that league but the paranoia is also fairly bad here. Norman du Plessis told me that after they had sent the voting booths to the provinces and regions, one of the commissioners insisted that each booth should have a canopy.

When asked why, the commissioner replied that secret cameras could be installed in the roof of the voting station to record the voter's choice. The administration division was instructed to recall the voting booths, all twenty-six thousand, and fit them with canopies.'

'You are not being serious, Peter,' says Maley. 'I mean, I was just making a joke about Cambodia, but we never acted on rumours like that.'

'Michael,' I reply, 'in this country, we take everything seriously. Twenty-six thousand voting compartments came back to Johannesburg and each was fitted with a quaint little canopy. Sweet, really.'

Everyone laughs. Except that it is not so funny. It is one of the reasons I feel sorry for election administration.

The list of voting stations that was meant to have been published forty-five days before the election was given a new deadline of thirty days. That deadline has come and gone. The election is just less than ten days away and there is still not a complete list of stations. The knock-on effect for deployment of staff and provision of voting materials has now reached critical levels.

Since Bophuthatswana came under the administration of the transitional executive committee in mid-March, the crisis surrounding the siting of voting stations has deepened. This has then been compounded by the situation in the Transkei and Ciskei. Originally, just short of a thousand stations were listed for these regions. Now, based on the remoteness of some communities, an extra thousand voting stations has been agreed on. This brings the Eastern Cape total to two thousand six hundred and twelve. The impact of these late additions is problematic, as they are provisioned from the supplies already allocated to the densely populated urban areas. The administration division hopes that, despite the diversion of electoral materials to Transkei and rural Eastern Cape, there will still be enough in the volatile dormitory townships of New Brighton and KwaZekele outside Port Elizabeth and Mdantsane outside East London. I have visions of absentee-ism among polling officials in the urban areas rising like a rocket after this decision. Many of those areas have been the core of ANC support for generations and I would not want to be the one to tell voters that there are no ballot papers left.

There is also the problem of staffing. Many of the remote rural areas have few local residents educationally equipped to run the polling stations. Many of these stations have to be staffed by electoral officers from the larger towns, who have to be 'para-chuted' into the distant stations. This comes with attendant is-sues: finding accommodation and supplying communications. The outsiders are viewed by the locals with suspicion. They are not to be trusted.

The security of the voting stations has also become a major matter. The ideal is that no voting station should be used 'without reasonable certainty that the available peacekeeping agencies can ensure the safety of voters and the integrity of the voting mater-ials'. While the IEC had liaised with the police in early January around safety at voting stations, the late compilation of their exact locations meant that real and effective communication had only happened in early April.

Soweto, which houses the largest concentration of voters in the country, has two hundred and fifty stations. The SAP has checked the stations and confirmed that they can only properly secure about seventy. Finally, on Tuesday, 19 April 1994, one week before the election, agreement is reached with the SAP to reduce the number to a hundred and thirty-seven. Someone had come up with the clever idea of two-stream voting stations. This effectively almost halved their number.

In KwaZulu, the noose is tightening around the sinewy throat of Inkatha. The state of emergency in KwaZulu and Natal and the deployment of troops effectively limit any military activities that may have been intended. Of course, the seizure of large quantities of weapons from Inkatha's main training camp at Mlaba in northern KwaZulu, as well as the discovery and seizure of arms caches at other locations, further weakens the organisation's ability to indulge in the all-out conflict with which it has so frequently threatened in the past.

It has also become clear to the Inkatha leadership that they are backed against a wall. The election is an inevitability. Still Chief Buthelezi vacillates: to participate or to sit stubbornly aside? Finally, he requests international mediation between his party and the National Party and ANC. A formidable team of mediators is quickly put together: Lord Carrington from the United Kingdom, the man who had brokered the Lancaster House Agreement that ended the Zimbabwean war and resulted in its first democratic election there, and Henry Kissinger.

Helter-skelter, the Carrington/Kissinger team arrive in Johannesburg before there is even agreement on the agenda for the mediation. Discussions begin and Chief Buthelezi insists that the election be postponed. If Inkatha are to join, they want time to campaign. Both Cyril Ramaphosa and Roelf Meyer flatly refuse. This is not even a subject of discussion. As Ramaphosa puts it, the country will 'blow up' if the date is changed. The chief digs in and the process is stillborn. The disappointed mediators leave the country, and still there is no solution in sight.

It is Thursday, 14 April 1994.

With the election ten days away, Chief Buthelezi is advised by a friend from Kenya, Professor Washington Okumu, who is coincidentally in the country, that he has no choice but to fight the election. If he stays out, KwaZulu will be incorporated into South Africa, as will all of the other homelands, and he will lose his power. Far better to advance the Inkatha cause from within the KwaZulu and Natal legislature that will be constituted after the election from the parties. If Inkatha does well in the region, it could even be in the majority. Reluctantly, Chief Buthelezi capitulates at a meeting with Okumu, Mandela and De Klerk in Pretoria on Tuesday, 19 April 1994. Inkatha will contest the national and provincial elections in seven days' time.

On Wednesday, 20 April 1994, the final list of voting stations is published.

The implications of the late entry of Inkatha for the IEC and the planning of the election are enormous. I feel a little divorced from reality when I consider the challenges facing the monitoring division. But I know these pale into insignificance compared with what the administration division has to accomplish.

I phone Bheki Sibiya in Durban to get his assessment. He says much depends on whether the army, police and KwaZulu civil service will cooperate. He says he will work closely with the head of the administration division for KwaZulu and Natal, Thabane Jali, and offer him whatever assistance he needs. I hang up. I have a bad feeling about this, and I am an optimist!

The question of how to accommodate Inkatha on the ballots, which have all been printed and are sitting safely in warehouses scattered across the country, is a major problem. As luck would have it, there is a small space at the bottom of the ballot paper. It's the bottom margin, really, but it will allow a strip that is almost the same size as the other parties to be stuck on.

In these matters, size and prominence are important. Each party has to be afforded the same space. Favourite places on the ballot are the top and the bottom. De Klerk, in a gesture of magnanimity, agrees to surrender the National Party's place at the bottom of the ballot so that an Inkatha sticker can be affixed beneath it. His cabinet are vehemently opposed to this, but he overrules them. In an attempt to alert its supporters, the National Party instructs them to 'stem tweede van onder vir die kaalkopwonder'. (Vote second from under for the bald-headed wonder.)

Inkatha stickers bearing the party name, logo and the face of Chief Buthelezi have to be printed and stuck to each and every ballot paper by hand, all eighty million of them.

It is quickly estimated that the IEC will need to site, establish and equip five hundred and forty-nine additional voting stations to cover KwaZulu. Staff will need to be found and trained to run those extra voting stations. A further consequence of the Inkatha inclusion is that the workload at each of the existing ten thousand voting stations throughout the country will increase and each station will have to be supplemented by an extra two people. In total, thirty-five thousand people have to be recruited, trained and paid.

These new voting stations also need booths, ink, pencils, etc., etc. An immense task.

To make this legally possible, a special session of parliament passes the requisite legislation providing for a late registration. The last political party of size and influence has entered the election.

Abraham Christoffel Fourie attended the AWB meeting at Trim Park, Ventersdorp, both as a participant and as one of a phalanx of bodyguards for the Leader. He also attended the meeting under the tree addressed by Brigadier van den Heever and his Ystergarde commander, Brigadier Leon van der Merwe.

A few days later Fourie is told to report with his men and their families to Ventersdorp. He resigns from his job after fourteen years' service, sells the bulk of his things, and does as he has been ordered.

The men under his command gather at his house with their families, their possessions and their caravans. They are tense but excited. They head in convoy for Ventersdorp and Trim Park, where a number of others are waiting. There they are told that the AWB is moving on to a war footing.

It is Tuesday, 19 April 1994.

Abie Fourie was born in Ladysmith in Natal into a conservative family. His father was a devout follower of Dr Hendrik Verwoerd, one of the principal architects of apartheid, and he made sure that his children were raised accordingly.

Unable to continue his secondary education, Fourie left school at the age of fifteen to work on the railways in Durban. In 1967 he spent nine months undergoing his obligatory national training in the army. He enjoyed his time in uniform, and volunteered for further service over the next twelve years. He served frequently on the border and spent time in Angola fighting Swapo and the Angolan army. Despite his commitment, insubordination during a political argument resulted in his being discharged from the army.

Fourie continued working on the railways for fourteen years before moving in 1980 to Johannesburg, where he was employed at the Barlow Rand Group as a mechanic, although he had no qualification. His attempts to pass the necessary exams failed.

Politically, Fourie found a home in the AWB in 1977. He had first joined the National Party and then the far-right Herstigte Nasionale Party, but found they lacked a militant approach. The AWB, he felt, was the true mouthpiece of the Boer. Fourie even obtained a special Boere Identity Book from the AWB that confirmed him as a Boer. He was told that this document would give him residency of the Volkstaat that would be formed after the war.

The issue of the Boere ID book first arose at a meeting of the Wenkommando when the well-known Afrikaans television actor Schalk Jacobs suggested it was necessary for all Boere to have their own special Boere ID. Overawed by Jacobs's fame and personality, the idea was taken up and an ID book was soon on offer from Jacobs for a fee. He was aided in this enterprise by a woman called Elma Potgieter.

The ID book was headed 'Boerevolk' on the first page, which also contained the key principles of the Boerevolk and a statement of intent: 'The holder of this document declares that I align myself with the freedom struggle of the Boerevolk and that I will fight this struggle on the basis of the following principles' – which were then detailed. To Fourie, the words were moving and inspiring. The second page of the document set out the basic beliefs of the

Boerevolk, including their anthem, attitude to land and the form of government proposed by the Boerevolk. The last paragraph stated, 'I have read the above in applying for this document. I understand it and will commit myself to the struggle of the Boerevolk.'

The third page contained two identity numbers: the holder's South African citizenship number and the Boerevolk number. The book was printed by Potgieter Printers.

Fourie was so proud of the ID book that he used it as proof of identity when asked by his insurance company to sign some papers. When they didn't accept the book's validity, Fourie took it, along with his marriage certificate and his driver's licence, to a police station for certification by a Commissioner of Oaths. The local constable obliged, and Fourie felt that his new Boere ID was now legitimate.

Fourie's experience in the defence force and on the border is put to good use by the AWB. He becomes a weapons instructor and self-defence trainer. Over a period of ten years he graduates through the ranks and becomes a chief commandant in the Wenkommando. However, he feels that the new influx of recruits lacks the resolve of those required to fight for their Volkstaat. He refers to them as braaivleis fighters. To show his disdain for what the Wenkommando has become, he applies to become a member of the Ystergarde. Once he has passed the training course, he is chosen as one of the Leader's bodyguards. By early 1994, Fourie is the commander of the Vaal Triangle, a substantial area of the Transvaal. He lives with his family on a smallholding at De Deur near Meyerton.

He is ready for the call to arms.

Tension increases dramatically in KwaZulu and Natal with Inkatha's electioneering. The night before a major ANC rally, armed Inkatha supporters take occupation of the venue – a stadium. Police are instructed to clear the stadium but refuse on the grounds that it is too dangerous. In the ensuing battle too many men will die. The

ANC know that if they send in armed MK soldiers it will provoke a real war. This is probably what Inkatha wants.

The ANC lodge a complaint and take Inkatha to the electoral court. Inkatha are fined. But this does nothing to ease a brittle situation.

The monitoring division requests that the internal stability division, formerly known as the riot unit, occupy stadiums the night before a major rally. This solves the problem.

Johannes Coenraad Smit, a major in the Ystergarde, also receives his call-up on Tuesday, 19 April. He is fully prepared for the order, as are his men. Smit is a dedicated right-winger and has risen quickly through the ranks of the AWB since joining in mid-1991. His belief is that 'the only way to have one nation is to rid the nation of hybrids'. Smit and his men have brought their entire families with them for the 'new beginning'. He joins Abie Fourie's group.

On Wednesday, 20 April 1994 we conduct an election dry run. Ideally, we wanted to hold it a week earlier, but there have been too many unforeseen circumstances.

The dry run is a testing of all our operational systems, a mock election, really. Thousands of monitors have been dispatched to their work sites at polling stations and are due to report for duty as they would on election day. This will test our transport system, telecommunications, issuing of equipment, and functioning of the thirty-two operations centres as well as our information technology systems.

I have been at the office since five o'clock this morning. The bulk of the work is being supervised by Phiroshaw Camay and Eddie Hendrickx aka Eddie the Belgian. Hendrickx is conducting the simulation with passion. In Brussels, he says, they would do a dry run before any major event in the city. It was a routine part of their training. For us it is far from routine. We have one shot at it and then three days to fix our problems before the main act begins on Tuesday.

I am sitting in the ops centre when Judge Kriegler and some of the commissioners arrive to check how things are progressing. Fortunately no crisis hits us while they are there and they leave nodding their approval. In truth, the entire day is like that. The systems work. We have some minor problems with jammed faxes and phones that don't work, which Willem Ellis takes personally. I try to mollify him but he is a perfectionist and promises that it will be sorted out by Sunday night. The only other hitch involves two car crashes in separate incidents. Thankfully, no one is hurt and the damage is not extensive.

With few exceptions, the monitors do their job and file their reports in the format provided. We gather in the early evening and have a few drinks, which Solveigh Piper and Vanessa Henry have organised. It is probably the last chance that we will have to relax before the final countdown to the election. We toast the dry run's success and congratulate everyone on their hard work. Some of the commissioners join us; the atmosphere is almost festive. I glance at Eddie the Belgian and raise my glass saying, 'So, Eddie, we are looking good then.'

'It is just a *dry* run, Peter,' he replies. 'Just a dry run.'

awb Lieutenant Etienne le Roux, under the command of Kommandant Abie Fourie, is told to report to Trim Park, Ventersdorp. When he gets there he is instructed to set up camp on the nearby farm of Clifton Barnard.

Le Roux grew up in a very conservative household. The son of a civil servant, he was conscripted into the army in 1972, an experience which convinced him that 'anything' must be done to halt the forces of darkness in the form of the anc and, even worse, the South African Communist Party.

Le Roux joins the awb in 1988. It confirms to him that the Boers are God's chosen people and the organisation's military camps convince him that these people mean business.

It is on one of these training camps in December 1993 in Clocolan in the Orange Free State that he meets Piet Koekemoer, a blaster from the mines. Both men are subsequently admitted into the ranks of the elite Ystergarde.

In early 1994, he attends secret meetings organised by the Leader and his fighting generals. Le Roux supports the pervading sentiments that the proposed election will hand over power to the ANC. The Boer heritage will be lost. At one of these meetings his group is shown a document which lists those right-wingers to be killed by the government's security forces in an attempt to neutralise the right wing. The document is compelling. Le Roux is shocked that the security forces would do this but is told that this is the threat facing them as a Volk, and their only alternative is war, a war on their terms. The belief is that if the right wing can create enough chaos in the country and instigate a black–white conflict, then, in the ensuing carnage, they will establish their own state. In the war to come, black people are to be the targets. Blacks, particularly MK, will retaliate and a fire will sweep across the land, out of which the Volkstaat will be born, rising from the ashes white and Christian, principled and pure. This vision resonates with Le Roux.

He is pleased to hear that in the new Volkstaat those who fight in the coming revolution will be given jobs, status and authority. He hopes to become a policeman. He is told the call-up will come in April.

The call-up comes from Johan Vlok, who is in the same order group as Le Roux. Le Roux closes down his business, and with his wife and children, moves to the rendezvous.

He is not alone as the men and families of the AWB commence their exodus to the Western Transvaal, the area of the new Volkstaat. They gather at many locations (among them a holiday resort at Koster near Klerksdorp), but mainly on farms, including the farm of Manie Maritz, the chaplain general of the AWB.

On the afternoon of Friday, 22 April 1994, a convoy of trucks and trailers, caravans and cars wends its way over dirt tracks to Clifton

Barnard's farm. Because of a lack of toilet and washing facilities, the women and children are soon moved to a farm with better facilities at Ottosdal, belonging to Jan de Wet. The men are ordered to a game farm in the Magaliesburg that belongs to Brigadier Leon van der Merwe. From here the Ystergarde will launch hit-and-run attacks on selected targets across the Witwatersrand.

The farm is a hive of activity and quickly assumes the appearance of a military base. Guards are posted at key entry points. Strict instructions are given that no one is to leave the camp without permission.

In the late afternoon General Nico Prinsloo gathers the men. He tells them there is no 'turning back'. He reminds them of the oath they took on joining the AWB: 'If I walk ahead, follow me, if I turn around, shoot me. So help me God.' No one is to leave the camp without permission.

Prinsloo instructs that communication lines are critical and must be established as a matter of urgency. The network is based on a relay system that will stretch across the entire Western Transvaal. The command centre at the game farm will send messages to Ottosdal, from where they will be dispatched to Schweizer-Reneke, relayed on to Hoopstad and then to Brandvlei. The radio channel to be utilised is Bravo 25. However, radio personnel battle to establish their communications network. It is grudgingly accepted that the system has a serious malfunction. This is a major blow. To keep the channels open, Prinsloo will drive on a regular basis to headquarters in Ventersdorp to get instructions from the Leader.

The gathering at the game farm is replicated at many venues throughout the Western Transvaal. At the holiday resort at Koster, about a thousand right-wingers have assembled.

The following day, Saturday, 23 April 1994, a number of the AWB fighting generals arrive at the game farm. Clifton Barnard is among them. He recruits Le Roux and Piet Koekemoer and a man called

Koper Myburgh for a special operation. They transfer explosives and a number of homemade pipe bombs from a Volkswagen Golf to the boot of Le Roux's car. Barnard instructs Le Roux to drive to a farm called Koesterfontein some fifteen kilometres away. The farm belongs to Myburgh's father.

At the farm they stack the material on shelves in a workshop. Barnard tells the men that they are to make the bomb that starts the revolution, a car bomb so massive that it will rock the city of Johannesburg and plunge the nation into panic. 'It is the beginning of the terror.' He adds, 'People must be killed in these explosions in order to demonstrate the seriousness and to convey the message … The more people you kill, the greater the message is …'

In Ulundi on this Saturday three ANC canvassers are killed by unknown gunmen while handing out election leaflets to a crowd. They are part of a group accompanied by IEC monitors. Eventually Chief Buthelezi is prevailed upon by Nelson Mandela to intervene and restore order. Only when Buthelezi arrives is the crowd persuaded to disperse. The election group leave Ulundi in police armoured vehicles.

It is the intention of the AWB special forces to steal a number of vehicles to use as the 'casings' for car bombs. To this end, volunteers are drilled in the hall on the game farm on how to hijack vehicles. The instruction is by Jannie Kruger, a lieutenant in the Ystergarde. Commandant Johan 'Duppie' du Plessis also joins in the car-theft classes to point out the areas in Krugersdorp where vehicles can easily be stolen.

The hijacking tuition includes a simulated exercise. Four chairs are placed in a square, two by two, to represent the sitting occupants of a car. The methodology is not too complex. Under the watchful eye of their instructor, the two in the back are told to jump out of the car. One heads for the driver of the car to be commandeered while the other keeps his gun on the passenger or passengers. The driver and passengers are then roughly evicted by the pair, who leap into the vehicle and speed off. They are instructed to shoot if necessary. This is serious. The driver in the AWB bakkie is to follow the stolen car in case it encounters problems.

Unfortunately, the vehicle-theft campaign founders on the Saturday afternoon when the two bakkies break down on the way to their destinations and have to be towed back to the game farm. However, a Mr Breytenbach donates his old Audi to Clifton Barnard, telling him to 'do with it what you want'.

At Koesterfontein, under the direction of Piet Koekemoer, the men construct the car bomb. The problem of the inner housing of the bomb is solved by using an old iron lawn roller that they find lying near the workshop. With a blow torch, Koekemoer cuts open the roller and bends the 'cap' upwards. He places one hundred kilograms of Anfax explosives and diesel into the iron cylinder, mixing them slowly. Thereafter Koekemoer places twenty sticks of Watergel plastic explosives in the centre of the cylinder. A fuse is then inserted and the cap bent back to seal the roller. The men gingerly carry this tube of explosives to Mr Breytenbach's blue-grey Audi, remove the spare tyre, and place the tube in its well.

More explosives – Anfax and diesel – are packed around the roller. Gradually the boot fills with explosives under Koekemoer's direction. Pieces of iron and explosives are packed close to the car's petrol tank. Finally, fuses are inserted in the explosive around the roller, bound together and led to the front of the car through the back seats. The fuse will take about six minutes to burn.

The intention is to light the fuses from the front, get out and leave fast in the backup vehicle. The Audi is a gigantic bomb.

To maximise the blast, the men require a corner in Johannesburg with few open spaces, and lots of people, black people. The splintering debris and flying shards of glass from the shattered windows will wreak a havoc of their own. The men discussing the target refer to the Church Street bomb detonated by the ANC in May 1983 outside the South African Air Force headquarters in Pretoria. This bomb should make that one look like a firecracker. This bomb will signal the start of the Third Boer War of Liberation, and the people will rise up.

It is agreed that they will drive into Johannesburg the following morning and search for the right spot. Tired, the men unfold their sleeping bags, and prepare for sleep. It is late on Saturday night, 23 April 1994.

CHAPTER SEVEN

The AWB men rise early the next morning. They breakfast and drive off in two cars. Etienne le Roux is in the lead car. He has radio communication with the car carrying the bomb to alert them should he encounter any police presence or roadblocks. Koper Myburgh and Clifton Barnard drive the Audi car bomb. Koekemoer stays behind at the farm. He intends making some pipe bombs while they are gone.

Le Roux knows Johannesburg; he's the only one among them who does. The precise location has yet to be determined.

The car-bomb convoy heads for Krugersdorp, through that town and out on to Ontdekkers Road, left past the Rand Afrikaans University and the South African Broadcasting Corporation, over the Braamfontein hill and down into the city. Le Roux turns into Bree Street.

The street is flanked by high residential buildings and buzzing with shoppers and hawkers, a blaze of colour as the shops display their wares on the pavement. Residents cluster on the balconies of their apartments, leaning over, sharing the morning's news and the day's prospects. It is a perfect autumn day in Johannesburg.

Le Roux finds the right parking spot for the Audi and indicates to Barnard and Myburgh, but they ignore him, motioning him on. He drives a little further and points to another vacant parking space. The Audi slowly turns into a parking spot in front of the Monte Carlo Hotel, a busy establishment with a vigorous clientele who rent the rooms on an hourly basis.

Le Roux drives on and stops around the corner.

Myburgh and Barnard leave the Audi and walk quickly away. Two black street children hurry after the men and tell them, 'Mr, that car that you have parked there, it's burning.' One of the men stops, looks at them, and casually answers, 'It's not burning, there's

184

a bomb inside.' He disappears around the corner, leaving the street kids staring at the smoke coming from the car.

It is ten to ten on Sunday morning, 24 April 1994.

Le Roux is joined by Barnard and Myburgh and they drive off. The bomb that is smoking in the car parked on the corner of Bree and Von Wielligh streets in downtown Johannesburg is huge. It is well over a hundred kilograms worth of bomb.

I am at home this Sunday morning, having decided that I will go into the IEC only at ten. I regard this as a day off, spending precious time with Caroline and the children. The next week is going to be frantic as we hurtle into the voting and counting days. I savour this time at home, reading the newspapers and playing with the children.

Shortly after ten I get a phone call from the operations centre: a bomb has just exploded in Johannesburg. It is carnage, bodies and bits of bodies everywhere.

'You better get into the ops centre now,' says the nervous voice.

On my way into town, I listen to Radio 702. They have interrupted normal broadcasting to report on the bomb. Their reporter is on the scene describing the devastation.

At the IEC headquarters there is an urgent meeting of the commission to discuss the bomb and the tense security situation in the country. It is agreed that meetings will take place at the highest level with the police and also the defence force. Extra security is also requested and deployed around the IEC building.

The bomb that explodes in Bree Street at ten minutes to ten that morning is so powerful that the blast blows some bodies ten storeys high.

Mrs Seako, a shop owner whose shop is close to the blast, is urgently called at home by the white prostitutes who work near her business. They have an informal agreement to keep an eye on her premises. Mrs Seako rushes to the area and sees that a nearby shop belonging to her friend Freda is destroyed. She enters to find her friend dead. Her own shop is completely destroyed, too. Inside is the dead body of Yaliswa Rita Seako, a relative. Out on the debris-strewn street she finds her cousin Thokozile Fani, dead. Fani was on her way to attend a service at the Methodist Church a few blocks off.

Mrs Seako stumbles on two small street children, both horribly injured but still alive. They tell her about the man who left the smoking car and what they said to him.

Mrs Sifiso Freda Ngwenya leaves home early on the Sunday morning. She works in a shop on the corner of Bree and King George streets. She is in Bree Street when the bomb explodes. She regains consciousness in hospital with severe injuries, her jaw virtually blown off, and her leg fractured and torn by shrapnel.

Susan Ann Keane is a committed South African who welcomes the coming election. She is at the beginning of her career, having completed a bachelor of social science degree, a higher diploma in third-world development and planning, and a master's degree in town planning. Keane is known among her peers as a deeply caring person who has made a valuable contribution to the fight against apartheid. She is in her car driving past the smoking car when it explodes, killing her.

Mr Khumalo parks his car in Bree Street, then walks towards Morkels furniture store. He notices a car coming towards him, an Audi, smoking. The car parks in front of the Monte Carlo Hotel. Khumalo continues on to Morkels. Two minutes later the Audi explodes. He is severely injured, suffering serious wounds to his head, legs and feet. His uninsured car is completely destroyed.

Two policemen stationed in Bree Street for a march that is scheduled to take place later that day are also injured as they emerge from a shop.

Mrs Gumbi, a teacher at the Roman Catholic School of Saint Teresa's in Rosebank, has a flat at thirty-five Maxwell Hall, a residential building in Bree Street. She is in the bathroom when the car bomb explodes close to her apartment, which faces the street. She is temporarily blinded, the clothes torn from her body by the blast, her body lacerated by glass splinters. She is rescued by her son Umfundo, who is also severely injured. He wraps a towel around his blinded and bleeding mother and, together, they stumble into the street. He faces a scene of disaster.

The bombers drive back to Koesterfontein and take a shower in the main house of the farm.

They then report the mission's success to General Nico Prinsloo at the game farm.

The three bombers know that the Bree Street bomb is the signal to right-wing forces for the war of liberation to begin. Le Roux wants to ask Prinsloo if the Leader has yet claimed responsibility, but feels it would be presumptuous.

At the IEC we go about our duties with deliberate intent, focusing on what we have to do, avoiding discussion of the bomb that exploded a few blocks away. It is a trauma that we all think about, but do not speak of. We cannot afford to be distracted, there is still too much to be done.

A meeting has been called in the monitoring division – yet another, to identify areas of potential breakdown on election day. We also receive a report from our troubleshooting team that has spent the past week in the Umtata office. We've been having staffing problems there. David Storey, the team's leader, urges that unless someone with the requisite skills is found to manage the ops centre, our function could be jeopardised in the region.

We go through a feet-shuffling exercise. This is a job for which few will volunteer. Suddenly Colonel Jules Koninckx, the policeman from Belgium, sticks up his hand. 'I'll go.' There is silence. Storey says, 'Jules, do you know where Umtata is?'

'No,' replies Jules. 'But how bad can it be?'

More silence.

'Well that settles it then, thanks very much, Jules,' I say quickly.

'We owe you one.' To which there is a sudden chorus: 'Absolutely, Jules, and good luck.'

The reports from the rest of the country are encouraging. In the Northern Transvaal, Riel Pienaar, based in Pietersburg, has performed outstandingly. He is responsible for a large and difficult region that also has right-wing problems, yet we hardly ever hear from him. His reports come in dead on time and whenever I speak to him he is positive and nothing is a problem. Attie van der Merwe from the Eastern Transvaal is a similar performer. Both of them have been shipped out to take up their positions for the duration of the election and are permanently based there, away from their families. And they are not the only ones.

Our big worry, though, is KwaZulu and Natal. Not that the Eastern Cape and Transkei don't keep us awake at night as well.

Kgomotso Moroka, who heads up the complaints and investigations department, confirms that they have received over two thousand complaints. Thus far the vast majority have been resolved through mediation. As we get closer to the election, the complaints have dropped off.

That is the thing with this election, I realise: there are fairly normal complaints that can be resolved through mediation, and then there are the lunatics setting off bombs in the middle of the city. There is no middle ground. It is either complaints about election posters or gigantic bombs.

A knock disturbs my reverie. Vanessa Henry comes in.

'I have been watching you,' she says, 'and I think you are going to need this over the next week.' She hands me a large square box on which is written in bold black letters 'Election Survival Kit'.

'Thank you, Vanessa, that's very kind of you,' I say, opening the box. Neatly packed inside are a few thick bars of chocolate, a bottle of whisky, caffeine pills, an inflatable airline neck cushion, and painkillers. I burst out laughing, asking if there is any particular order in which they should be taken.

On the game farm a closed planning-meeting in a small hall is attended by Johannes Smit, Clifton Barnard, General Nico Prinsloo, Brigadier Leon van der Merwe, Abie Fourie, Jan de Wet and Duppie du Plessis. The commanders confirm that the success of the Bree Street bomb will be built on by a widespread bombing campaign, with the objective of killing as many people and causing as much damage as possible. Again, it is stressed that congested black areas will be the target.

There is also discussion about building a massive bomb in a trailer that can be towed to the next target. Pipe bomb missions will also be dispatched. These missions will consist of three-man units.

Planning for the trailer bomb runs into difficulties because they do not have a trailer. The problem is solved by Clifton Barnard, who suggests that they use the Leader's trailer. This suggestion is greeted with silence as they imagine the wrath of the Leader when he finds out his Karet trailer has been blown up by his own men. Prinsloo recommends that they tell the oubaas his trailer is to be used for operational purposes. As it turns out, the Leader is furious when he learns that he is about to be a trailer poorer.

At Koesterfontein, Piet Koekemoer begins building another bomb. He takes a full, nineteen-kilogram gas bottle, binds a fuse around it and places it in the middle of the trailer. He is being helped by Etienne le Roux and Johan 'Vlokkie' Vlok. Following the same methodology as for the car bomb, the men help him pack forty sticks of Watergel plastic explosives and a mixture of Anfax and diesel around the gas bottle. They then place pieces of metal that will serve as shrapnel in the trailer, packing it as tightly as possible.

While they're about this job, Koper Myburgh arrives to pick up the pipe bombs and transport them to the game farm.

That night the men at the game farm watch the eight o'clock news on television. The Bree Street bomb is given much coverage, with video footage of the bodies of the dead and the carnage. The men are cheerful, some even make jokes. With such a bold start to the war, they cannot be stopped. The newsreader says that this bomb blast is a major blow to the election process.

After the news, there is a meeting of General Prinsloo, Brigadier Leon van der Merwe, Koper Myburgh, Duppie du Plessis, Abie Fourie and Johan Smit about the use of pipe bombs in the surrounding towns. The commanders agree that the missions must leave early the following morning, Monday, 25 April 1994.

It is agreed that volunteers will conduct these missions. At a general meeting, the men are briefed by Myburgh on the pipe bombs: explosives, nuts and bolts have been packed into these pipes, which are of varying lengths. One end of the bomb is welded closed, from the other tapers a fuse. He tells them how to ignite the fuse and that it will burn for about three minutes. Missions will be conducted in Randfontein, Carletonville, Krugersdorp and Pretoria. There is no shortage of volunteers.

Abie Fourie's brother, Gert, is part of the group designated to bomb Pretoria along with Peet Steyn and Jaco Nel. The four pipe-bomb groups are told to choose targets where they will cause maximum damage to people and buildings.

On the game farm and at the other assembly points of the AWB in the Western Transvaal, the men believe that the Leader will soon claim responsibility for the bombings and trigger the revolution. They believe he has a reason for keeping quiet and that there is surely a higher plan that he cannot share with them at this point. But there is growing concern that the forty thousand men from the defence force have yet to defect.

In the IEC operations centre it is reported that nine people have been killed and ninety-two injured in the Joburg bomb blast. Sitting at the desk next to me is a young girl, who starts sobbing. She looks barely eighteen. She is a volunteer and has been with us for about two weeks. Eddie Hendrickx looks at her and unsmilingly motions with his head towards the door. She gets up and leaves the centre. I see his point – this place has to keep calm – but I feel sympathy for the youngster. This is the start.

Back in the ops centre downstairs, I ask Hendrickx if he and Jules Koninckx ever completed their emergency evacuation plan for all the Belgian nationals in the country. He looks at me and smiles. I don't press it.

We fear what is to come.

At midnight, forty-eight hours before the start of the election, all campaigning by political parties stops according to a stipulation in the Electoral Act. It is a time of waiting.

CHAPTER EIGHT

It is Sunday, 24 April 1994.

David Storey accompanies Jules Koninckx and the small team that will run the ops centre in Umtata to the Transkei. They leave in a Barlow Rand plane very early in the morning. The plan is that Storey will help them settle in and fly back in the early evening.

They arrive in Umtata to find chaos, with soldiers roaming the streets and no semblance of any functioning administration. Koninckx is unfazed by the mayhem and spends the day introducing himself to staff and fine-tuning systems in the ops centre.

Briefings are held and the regional heads of departments plan the days ahead. There is much tension as everyone knows that the state of infrastructure in the vast Transkei is poor and that ensuring proper logistics for the election will be a massive challenge.

We start the election week by doing a final check of our systems. In the monitoring division things are a lot calmer than on the streets, where there is palpable excitement, tension and fear.

Some whites fear that there will be pandemonium after the election and that the place will disintegrate into violence and anarchy. Shoppers, both black and white, with trolley-loads of canned goods and other essentials, tell reporters that they are worried foodstuffs will no longer be available after the election.

An IEC monitor shows me a list of supplies that people in a suburb on the West Rand are being advised to stockpile. I gaze at the list in fascination: Epsom salts, margarine, seven packets of soap powder, shampoo, Sanpic, nylon thread, fishing line, tweezers, Jeyes fluid, biltong, and vegetable seed.

'Well, at least these people are going to be clean and sanitised after the election – that's a good start for the country,' I say, noting the emphasis on items relating to hygiene.

'Ja,' says the monitor, a young black student from the Rand

Afrikaans University, laughing. 'These guys think we are going back to the dark ages where we are going to have to hunt and fish for our food.'

The general mood varies. Some say it will be fine. Others worry about an uncertain future for the 'new South Africa', as some have taken to calling it.

Among black people there is an air of intense anticipation, an almost unbearable excitement. What's certain is that everyone is thinking, eating and sleeping this election. It is pumping in our blood.

And, of course, a lot of important people have come to town; this is not an event to be missed. Former presidents, foreign ministers, heads of political parties, diplomats, movie stars, well-known personalities famous for being famous, heroic activists and general hangers-on have all swarmed to this light like moths.

The foyer of the Carlton Hotel resembles a saloon from Johannesburg's gold-rush days. The hotel is *the* place to stay and be seen. The cognoscenti arrive for meetings, hold meetings, wait for meetings, swap tables to attend new meetings, drink coffee, slurp tea, often iced. The hotel's flagship restaurant, The Three Ships, is constantly full, booked weeks in advance.

Over breakfast, lunch and dinner, the heads of international observer missions and political analysts discuss the coming days. Who will be in the new cabinet? Who will be the minister of finance? Who will be what? Each one has an impeccable source close to, if not in, the inner circle.

And why shouldn't they share in this glorious moment? This is, after all, an extraordinary event that will commence tomorrow with a special voting day for the elderly, the infirm and those in hospital. It is the freeing of a nation from bondage, the last country in Africa to be released from its own form of colonialism. What a thing to celebrate!

At Koesterfontein Etienne le Roux, Clifton Barnard and Piet Koekemoer start the morning by working on the trailer bomb.

Koekemoer realises that the fuse will not be as easy as it was on the Bree Street bomb. He improvises and leads a wire from the trailer into the car. He calls it a 'crisis detonator'. Le Roux removes the chassis plate number from the trailer but, inexplicably, leaves on the number plates.

Barnard states that if they run into a roadblock, the bomb must be detonated. However, the men in the car towing the trailer are concerned that they might be killed or injured should they have to blow up the trailer bomb. Koekemoer reassures them that once they have sent the charge down the wire, they will have time to run away. The men are doubtful, but no one wants to take this further with the forceful Clifton Barnard, who might question their commitment to the revolution.

Etienne le Roux in the lead car will determine the precise target, preferably a black taxi rank. Germiston is the target town. Jan de Wet, whose Toyota is pulling the trailer, must follow. Vlokkie Vlok is to travel with De Wet. The men in the cars can communicate with each other via radios stolen from the defence force.

Vlok will detonate the bomb. He is an employee of the AWB, having joined the organisation as a member when he was seventeen years old. He worked at AWB headquarters before being trained as a bodyguard for the Leader. With the rank of captain in the Ystergarde, he has been responsible for organising guards at the Leader's house and at head office. His AWB salary of five hundred rand a month he regards as a godsend and he blames affirmative action for his inability to find a job elsewhere.

Vlok is instructed by Koekemoer on how to detonate the bomb. There are two fuse wires leading from the trailer. He is to wind each wire around the terminals of a car battery. After a short while the bomb will explode.

Before they leave, the men shovel soil into the trailer to compact the bomb. The trailer is hooked up to Jan de Wet's car and the detonator wire from the trailer fed through to the car. Before they drive off, the men pile loose bits of metal into the trailer.

Piet Koekemoer stays behind, watching as the two-car convoy leaves the farm in the crisp early-morning light. Dew sparkles on the ground and glints silver on the spider webs that mesh the khaki veld.

Le Roux, in the lead car, is accompanied by Duppie du Plessis. He will be driving the next bomb so this is his training run. Le Roux drives slowly to Germiston and the targeted taxi rank. On this busy Monday morning the place is crowded with people queuing for taxis. It is eight o'clock. In the traffic congestion the two AWB cars become separated and the radios fail to work. Panic stricken, Le Roux and Du Plessis decide to leave the area.

In the car towing the trailer bomb, Vlok sees a parking spot and De Wet stops the car. It is a tight situation in the dense traffic and they will be unable to make a quick getaway. So De Wet drives further on, in search of another parking space. He finds one and stops adjacent to it. They unhook the trailer and push it into the parking space. Vlok ignites the bomb and they drive off.

Mavis Phungula, a resident of nearby Katlehong, works at the Fair and Quick Bulk Supermarket in Odendaal Street, Germiston. She is seven months pregnant and although uncomfortable is still able to work. At about quarter to nine in the morning, she sees a car stop near a parking space in front of the supermarket. Two white men leave a trailer in the vacant space.

Mavis Phungula wonders if the men aren't salesmen and the trailer full of products. She carries on with her work but she feels uneasy, so she returns to the trailer and inspects it again. The two men have gone. She hears a knocking noise coming from the trailer, and, scared, heads back into the shop. There is a massive explosion and Mavis Phungula feels 'the whole earth opening up'. She is lacerated by glass shards, her eardrum bursts, and she blacks out. When she regains consciousness there are bodies on the floor of the supermarket, which is awash with blood and body parts.

Paul Ontong is nineteen years old and works in a shop opposite the supermarket. He is fifteen metres away from the blast and is killed instantly.

De Wet and Vlok are two blocks away, stationary, waiting for the red light to change when the bomb explodes. They report the success of their mission to AWB headquarters at eleven o'clock.

The report of the Germiston bomb blast is received in the ops centre with appalled silence. There are ten dead and at least forty injured, some of them very seriously. It is just the start, as news of attacks on polling stations, of bombs, and threats of bombs comes in. During the day, six polling stations are completely destroyed, while a number of others are damaged. Further reports of sabotage of voting equipment and isolated violence in election areas are also received. Each one is logged and dispatched to the relevant police headquarters for action. With each incident the stress in the country mounts. The violence appears to be escalating into an onslaught.

Nonetheless, we go about our work, painstakingly making sure that everything is in place for the next day. Members of the armed forces and police who will be on duty on election day, Wednesday, 27 April, also vote tomorrow. So do prisoners.

This is an election from which no one is to be excluded, a provision which applies to South Africans living abroad. Voting will take place at most South African embassies around the world and also at select venues in certain cities. In New York, temporary structures have been erected on the lawn in front on the United Nations. In Tel Aviv, it is the show grounds. In Australia, twenty-two polling stations have been set up; there are twenty-five in the United States.

We are reassured by the administration division that they are ready. A quarter of a million IEC employees, ninety-three thousand policemen and sixty-seven companies of soldiers are in place to make sure that events at the more than ten thousand voting stations proceed according to plan.

The IEC communications office has put out an advertisement which boldly reads: 'You're ready. We're ready. Let's do it.'

The pipe-bomb squad dispatched to Krugersdorp, consisting of Pieter Hanekom, Philip van Voller and Pieter Duvenhage, are unsuccessful in their mission; their bombs don't explode. The unit commander, Hanekom, returns to the game farm late on Monday night complaining bitterly about defective materials.

The Randfontein squad consists of Johannes Andries Venter, Cruywagen and Clint Ellish. They leave a pipe bomb in a public toilet next to a black taxi rank. The bomb injures six people.

The team sent to Carletonville throw their pipe bomb at a black taxi rank in Westonaria. The bomb kills James Ncube, Alfred Dayele, Peter Mogoshe, Phillip Plaatjies and Alex Maziba. Many others are severely injured.

The Pretoria pipe-bomb squad of three is led by Captain Jaco Nel, with Lieutenant Petrus 'Peet' Steyn and Lieutenant Gert Fourie.

Fourie, who attaches much significance to sharing a birthday with the legendary Boer leader and president of the Zuid-Afrikaansche Republiek, Paul Kruger, sees himself as a man of destiny. At the age of seventeen he was conscripted into the army and told that it was his duty to fight the ANC–SACP alliance as they wanted to make the country ungovernable and, ultimately, take it over and cause violence towards its citizens. On leaving the army, he joined the right-wing Herstigte Nasionale Party in 1976, but it was only when he joined the AWB that he realised he had found a political home.

Fourie became fanatical about the establishment of a Volkstaat. To this end, he was prepared to make many sacrifices. After the meeting at Trim Park in Ventersdorp in February, he emptied his house and, with the little money that he had, bought a caravan. Fourie meticulously prepared the vehicle for the trek north. His three sons were taken out of school. He also gave up his job as a barman, working his last shift the night before he took his family north.

Fourie had come off a four-hour shift of guard duty when he was ordered to join Nel and Steyn on the bombing mission.

They decide to target a black taxi-rank, but there is a heavy police presence. Instead, at Nel's suggestion, they visit two women at an apartment in Sunnyside who are preparing to leave the city for a holiday resort near Hartebeespoort Dam, where AWB people are gathering. The women say that they are worried about staying in Pretoria as they fear attacks after the election.

After a cup of coffee, the men arrange fake number plates for the car, buy Steyn a pair of shoes, and shop for food. They then return to the flat the women have vacated and wait for nightfall.

Once it is dark they drive through Pretoria, searching for a target. It is not easy. There is still an exceptional police presence on the streets, particularly in the areas where there are large groupings of black people. The men are tense, aware that one wrong move will get them arrested.

They decide to bomb a café on the corner of Bloed Street and Seventh Street. The café is crowded and there's a queue of people buying food. Black people. Nel orders Steyn to bomb the café. Steyn lights the fuse, walks to the door of the café and throws the bomb inside. He rushes back to the car and they drive off.

Nel, at the wheel, is shaking, having a type of breakdown, unable to drive properly. At one point he turns the wrong way into a one-way street. Nel decides to head for the holiday resort at Hartebeespoort Dam to calm down. They find the women they'd met earlier in the day, and the women then depart with Nel while Steyn and Fourie cluster round the fire with some women and children. They are joined there by two blind men who lost their sight in an explosion during the war in Rhodesia. One of the men brings out his guitar and sings sad songs of another time, of loss. At two in the morning Nel returns, looking more relaxed. It is time they returned to the game farm, he says.

Joyce Baloyi, Samuel Masamola and an unidentified man die in the explosion at Sannie's Café. Twenty-nine people are injured.

It's early evening in Umtata. David Storey meets the Barlow Rand pilots in the foyer of the Holiday Inn and they discuss their route to the airport. Their conversation is interrupted by shouting in the streets outside the hotel. The incident is calmed down but it delays their departure and by the time they get to the airport it is dark.

The place is almost completely deserted and the runway lights are not working. The chief pilot shrugs; they will simply have to take off in the dark.

Storey, an uneasy flier at the best of times, splutters, 'But you won't be able to see the runway.'

'We've got no choice,' replies the pilot. 'We can't leave the plane here overnight.'

The three men climb into the plane and taxi to the end of the runway. The pilot turns the aircraft, looks at his co-pilot and his passenger, then heads the plane into the rushing darkness. They take off without incident.

Inexplicably to the seventy men at the game farm, the Leader does not claim the AWB's responsibility for the bomb blasts. His silence bewilders the men, and some question the delay. After all, the bombs are meant to signal the start of the war.

This unease is replicated on other farms where the AWB forces have gathered. These men have left their jobs, as have their wives. They have sold their homes, taken their children out of school and moved to the Volkstaat with all their remaining possessions.

But the Leader remains mute.

When the Pretoria squad fail to return, Kommandant Abie Fourie fears they have been caught. Everyone is on edge. After discussions with the other commanders, a decision is taken to move the entire detachment early the next morning to the Waterval Shooting Range near Rustenburg.

At three in the morning the three men return to the game farm.

I sleep for about three hours that night, fitful stuff, not the real thing.

CHAPTER NINE

It is Tuesday, 26 April 1994.

For Dikgang Moseneke the day begins very early. He has only had a few hours' sleep and he is exhausted. His first phone call is from Chief Buthelezi.

'Advocate, my brother,' says the chief, who always addresses Moseneke formally. 'I have trusted you throughout this whole process and our relationship is a close one. You assured me that Inkatha would always be treated fairly and that the IEC would run a free and fair election.'

'Yes, Nkosi,' says Moseneke, dread curdling in the pit of his stomach.

'I am thinking of withdrawing,' says the chief.

Moseneke is silent, then scrapes out: 'What is the problem, Nkosi?'

Chief Buthelezi replies, 'I have just seen the thin sticker that has been made for Inkatha which will be stuck to the bottom of the ballot paper, and my head looks like a little tokoloshe, all squashed up. How will people vote for me if I look like a tokoloshe? I am thinking of withdrawing.'

Moseneke examines the ballot paper closely. Unsure as to whether the chief is serious or joking, he has to admit that the chief's head is a little scrunched up. Also, the sticker strip isn't as broad as those of the other political parties on the ballot.

'Nkosi,' he says, 'I think your head just looks that way because the sticker is very narrow and that gives it the effect that you talk of. But I also think that it is just this batch of stickers. We will see if we can fix it in the other batches by printing a broader strip which will give your head more space.'

The conversation continues for a while until the chief, feeling placated, puts the phone down.

Moseneke's day has begun.

I am up at four and at the office thirty minutes later. The operations centre is gearing up for the big day. While we are apprehensive, the number of special voters is small compared to the number that will vote on the Wednesday and Thursday, but that is no reason to be anything other than anxious. Especially regarding the prisoners.

There has been much discussion among the commissioners about whether prisoners should be allowed to vote. Some argue that they have forfeited the right to be involved in their society. But what about trial-awaiting prisoners? Should they vote? And if we let them vote, would the sentenced convicts cause trouble?

Popcru, the union for prison warders and police, states that there will be trouble if prisoners are not accorded the right to vote. The Popcru leader, a man with the wonderful name of Goldenmiles Bhudu, is adamant that prisoners should vote.

I know Bhudu, as my law firm once acted for Popcru and, of course, for the man himself. He is a flamboyant individual. When campaigning, he has the habit of stripping off his shirt to reveal a perfectly muscled torso, wrapping himself in thick gleaming chains and then locking the chains with police handcuffs to an iron bar or railing outside the court at which his protest is directed. Bhudu is a familiar presence in front of the Supreme Court. On occasions, he has been arrested and bundled, clanking and shouting, into the back of a police car and it is the job of someone in the firm to ensure his release. He is a charming man whom one cannot fail to like, chains and all. His cautionary has to be taken seriously. In an election already racked with bombs and violence, you do not want the prisons to erupt in riots and flames. Consequently, all prisoners have the vote.

The men on the game farm leave early on the morning of Tuesday, 26 April 1994 for the Waterval Shooting Range near Rustenburg. Although the Pretoria bombers have returned, the order to strike camp has not been rescinded.

Jan de Wet is told by General Prinsloo to drive separately from the main AWB convoy. The make and colour of his car has been identified on radio news bulletins as the Germiston car bomb vehicle. It is the subject of a massive search by police and security forces.

De Wet is the first to arrive at the Waterval shooting range, joined shortly by a large contingent of AWB men from Natal, under the command of Miles Sharp. General Prinsloo orders De Wet to remove the tow bar from his car. At least that is one less identification detail. De Wet reluctantly obeys.

The convoy from the game farm arrives but the morale of the men is low, even gloomy. The commanders struggle to organise the men, most of whom mill around. More groups arrive, adding to the confusion. There are also distressing signs of dissent. They are questioning their commanders. When will the defence force join them? Have they defected in their tens of thousands as had been foretold? Where are the armoured cars? Why has the Leader not proclaimed the start of the war so that the Volk can rise up?

From reports on the radio, most of the men are aware that the bombing campaign has started, but it is not enough. They don't get the sense that the war is happening or that enough is being done to prosecute it. They feel isolated and at a loss stuck out on this shooting range in the bush, sleeping rough with few facilities.

Their spirits rise with the arrival of the Wenkommando bearing chops, wors and steak. The men prepare the fires and soon the meat is sizzling, small plumes of blue-grey smoke rising into the leaden sky, a closed canopy above them.

The fighting generals realise that the troops need more information. They brief a few men with the precise details of some of the bomb blasts and tell them to pass it on. The men, buoyed by the braai and the bombs, regain their sense of purpose.

The ops centre is functioning smoothly. Phones ring, reports are typed. The large maps on the wall locating the voting and counting stations remain free of the red pins that would indicate incidents or systems failures.

The television in the ops centre shows pictures of mobile IEC polling teams at a white old-age home. That it is inhabited by white people is not surprising, as the Nationalist government has invested little in homes for black people per se, never mind homes for aged black people. The picture shows a black polling team assisting a row of pensioners. Some of the pensioners look a little bemused, staring at their black nurses and then at the polling officials enquiringly as they make their mark. It is almost as if they are asking for help in voting. Others, more sprightly, are deliberate in their actions.

An old man, shrunken but still dapper, has taken the opportunity to wear his medals, presumably from the Second World War, on a dark grey suit. As he emerges from the voting booth, he is asked for a comment. He turns to the cameras and says, 'I never thought that I would live to see this …' He pauses to collect his thoughts. I hope he won't make a racist or silly comment that will spoil the moment. I hope he will not say something unbecoming of a man who fought fascism. He wipes his mouth with a white handkerchief and continues '… and I am grateful that God kept me alive to be here to witness it. It should never have taken so long.' Tears well in my eyes. I look around the room self-consciously and see the same reaction in many of the staff.

The reports from the prisons let us know that all is calm. Prisoners are subdued, almost respectful, as they make their mark. The usual noise and clamour of shouting inmates and warders, crashing doors and yells is absent. I think to myself that if I were a prisoner, I would also be pensive, particularly today.

Radio and television broadcasts report on the nation's sick and elderly, painstakingly taking their time to vote. In the hospitals, patients shuffle in their pyjamas and sagging gowns to the voting facilities. At the massive Baragwanath Hospital in Soweto we see footage of patients waiting in queues, patients being ushered by assistants, black and white, into the booths to vote. When some emerge they are sobbing and the camera pans to the polling officials and hospital staff, and they too are crying, not openly, but silently, wiping away their tears as if they are an unwelcome distraction from their important task. There is emotion everywhere. Each scene is flooded with it.

We watch old ladies in bed being helped as they vote for the first time in their lives, weeping. And looking at the pictures, I want them to get well and get out of those places, so clinical and cold. Now is the time to get better and enjoy what they have never had before, to walk in the street freely. To feel the sun.

It is still early in the day but it is encouraging that there are few reports from monitors or the press of any voting problems. The systems seem to be working. There is a sense of optimism in the ops centre and in the building. With each passing hour, the tension eases. People sit back at their desks and take note of the accounts coming in.

At midday we hold a final planning meeting for tomorrow, the first day of general voting. The mood around the table is upbeat. Too confident. I don't like it.

'I do not want to be the one to dampen the mood,' I say, 'but today is the easy one. Firstly, the number of voters is miniscule compared to tomorrow and, more importantly, the administration division knows exactly how many voters there are in those prisons, hospitals and old-age homes, so they knew how many ballots were required and how much equipment. No polling station that opens tomorrow will have that type of information.'

Heads nod round the table, the mood lowered.

Idiot, I think to myself, perhaps I shouldn't have done that. But then again, we have to be realistic and prepared for the worst.

'It doesn't really matter, Peter,' says Phiroshaw Camay. 'At this stage we have done all that can be done. The country is excited, optimistic, even if they are fearful. People are not sleeping, everyone is waiting for tomorrow. Tomorrow is when it all happens.'

I reply, 'I am glad to hear that others are not sleeping, but we all know what this country is like. The mood can turn in a second.'

Everyone agrees. We know it to be true.

By mid-morning the good cheer in the ops centre is much diminished as monitors report 'significant systems failures in a number of voting stations'. I go cold as I hear the words.

Come late afternoon, the maps on the wall have developed measles. I am feeling pretty sick myself as the implications of the problems sink in. The issues are myriad. Voting stations opening late, some by many hours. Lack of voting material, allegations of irregularities and incredibly slow voting processes. To make matters worse, huge numbers of ordinary voters pitch up to vote, unaware that this day is only for special votes. After queuing for hours, they are turned away, angry and disappointed.

The political contenders are also not slow to complain about shortages of electoral materials in certain places. It worries me that some polling officials don't think they have sufficient ballots for the next day. Their requests for more are being refused.

I meet with Piet Coleyn and offer him help in addressing any blockages. I voice my concern about lack of materials.

'If you want, Piet, I can send monitors in cars to voting stations to meet with some of the heads of the polling stations, and if they need backup supplies of voting materials, like ballots, ink, ultraviolet machines, we can deliver those from the regional depots.'

Coleyn is incredibly calm. 'Peter, we do have a few problems, par for the course. I have spoken to my regional polling officers and there is no reason to panic,' he says.

'Look, Piet,' I reply, 'I know you have done this before many times but this is different. We have between five and ten per cent of voting stations reporting serious problems. They can't function, and these are only the special votes. What will happen tomorrow when the whole country pitches up to vote? Can you handle that? And how can we help?'

He looks at me in a measured way. 'There will be problems tomorrow but we can handle them,' he says firmly.

'But how are your reserves, Piet?' I mean the reserves of voting materials, ballots, ink, ultraviolet lights, the extra materials that were ordered and deliberately set aside for contingencies.

'Peter, there are no reserves. They were used for the one thousand six hundred extra voting stations in the Transkei and the additional five hundred and fifty in KwaZulu. There is precious little for emergencies,' he says. A door slams shut in my head. Darkness.

The conversation is over. I look in his eyes and I see a tired man living with the knowledge that he is going to jump off a cliff, and if he doesn't, he will be pushed.

'Piet, call me if you think we can help. I mean it,' I say.

He nods.

The final report for the day shows breakdowns at ten per cent of voting stations. I discuss this with Judge Kriegler. He is exhausted and appears resigned. Our course is set.

I return to the ops room and tell everyone to get a good night's sleep. From now on, it is likely to be a rare commodity. We are due to start at four the next morning.

At the Waterval shooting range, Clifton Barnard tells Piet Koekemoer that another device is required: this one is destined for Jan Smuts International Airport. The instruction emanated from a meeting of a number of the fighting generals at the game farm on the evening of Sunday, 24 April 1994. Their decision: to create an international incident by bombing the primary gateway to the country on election day, 27 April 1994.

Piet Koekemoer applies himself. An old-model, dilapidated Peugeot is to be the bomb. Etienne le Roux examines the car and discovers that the coil is overheating. He replaces it with the coil from his own vehicle. One of the tyres is also slowly deflating. He has the puncture repaired in Swartruggens.

In the late afternoon some of the men at Waterval request

permission to visit their wives at De Wet's farm. Their restlessness has returned; they are missing their wives. Etienne le Roux is opposed to the idea, concerned that it might compromise their position. However, Brigadier van den Heever consents. Relieved, the men pile into a number of cars and head for De Wet's farm and the women encamped there.

On the evening of Tuesday, 26 April 1994, the Leader meets his fighting generals at AWB headquarters to receive their situation reports. The picture is a discouraging one: some senior commanders have disappeared or deserted. Morale is low. The heady days of early April have gone. Weighing heavily on them is the failure of the men in the defence force to defect with their weapons and equipment. Worse, the police have betrayed them, infiltrated their ranks and have arrested some members.

In the face of such adversity, the Leader and his fighting generals conclude that the war should be cancelled and that all attacks should cease. Certainly, with the prospect of arrest imminent, now is not the time to claim responsibility for anything. The order is given that the AWB battalions must scatter, hide on the farms, find refuge wherever they can.

The order to revoke the revolution and cease hostilities is meant to be relayed to all AWB detachments. But they forget to rescind the order to bomb Jan Smuts International Airport.

At midnight on Tuesday, 26 April 1994, in cities around the country, the old South African flag is lowered for the last time and the flag of the new South Africa, brilliantly coloured, is raised. It is an event of great significance, the passing of an era from a time of exclusivity to one of inclusivity and sharing. Actually, the ceremonies around the country are not that well attended. They seem a mere formality. I don't bother to attend one or even watch it on television. Our real future starts in the morning, or is meant to.

CHAPTER TEN

It is Wednesday, 27 April 1994.

I am in my office as I watch the sun slowly rise, the first rays lighting up the mine dump which has the Top Star Drive-In on it. As the sun climbs, the dump loses its golden gloss, turning a grubby brown. Despite the comfort of my office, I feel cold deep inside. On the spur of the moment, I head down to the street to get the sun on my face.

I light a cigarette and stand, head tilted to the nascent sun, feeling the pure warmth relax me, seeping in.

I think back to my interview for this job three months ago and the reservations I'd had about whether it could be achieved. Today is the test. I feel privileged that I was involved in an endeavour to free a nation. I will probably never again play a role in something as important as this election.

The over fifteen thousand trained and accredited monitors of my division have long been dispatched, mostly to the polling stations. The telecommunications system linking them to regional, provincial and the national ops centre is immense. I hope that the problems we encountered in the dry run have been sorted out.

Many of the commissioners are already in the provinces to which they have been allocated. Gay McDougal is accompanying Nelson Mandela when he casts his vote. For her, this is the realisation of a dream. As an African American at the forefront of the international anti-apartheid movement, she had thought this moment would never come.

The monitors radio in reports of people who've been gathering since four-thirty at voting stations. Long snaking queues wrap themselves around and around the polling stations. It is a perfect day, already warm when the stations open at seven o'clock.

In the sprawling, undulating Soweto, some voting stations

have close to ten thousand people lining up to vote. The voices of the monitors at Orlando and Jabulani are tense and nervous as they radio in their reports of voting stations far from ready to open at the appointed time. They worry about the reaction of the thousands of voters who have been there for hours. I share their concern, given my experience, mostly negative, with the psychology of crowds.

But this is different. The queues assume their own hierarchy, with the elderly and infirm being pushed to the front, followed by women with babies. Residents emerge from neighbouring houses carrying chairs, which they offer to those in the queues. Political party marshals, mostly ANC, although not wearing their party colours, walk slowly up and down the queues reassuring everyone that they'll get to vote. Repeatedly, monitors are asked to describe the mood of the crowds so that we can get a sense of the potential for violence. From Thokoza to Soweto, they reply that the people are calm, patient. The atmosphere is almost one of devotion.

In some white areas, the queues are shorter. Elsewhere they stretch over a few kilometres. These queues are a mixture of black and white, the wealthy and the destitute, domestic workers and their employers, construction staff and their bosses. These queues all reflect the same characteristics: patience and respect.

In the ops centre we are drinking coffee. A clerk, a student volunteer from Wits university, carries around a tray of sandwiches for those who have not had time to breakfast. I look at the big clock on the wall. Five to seven. The time has come; this event, which must not fail.

And then the bomb threats come in. Dozens of them.

In the early hours Etienne le Roux is awoken by Clifton Barnard. Le Roux is to drive the lead car, a borrowed blue Toyota. Commandant Duppie du Plessis and Jannie Kruger, the hijacking instructor, are in the battered Peugeot, the bomb car. Le Roux explains to

Du Plessis that at Jan Smuts airport he will take the road to the arrival and departure terminals while they park the Peugeot in the airport parking garage.

Everything goes according to plan. There are no police road blocks. At the airport Du Plessis parks the Peugeot on the top level of the underground parking arcade. Somehow, as they make their way to the terminal buildings where Le Roux is waiting for them, Du Plessis and Kruger separate. When Du Plessis meets with Le Roux, Kruger is still missing.

The men are close to panic. In the parking lot close to them a bomb is about to explode. They decide to give Kruger two minutes. Their wait is interrupted by a massive boom as the bomb detonates. The ground shudders. Kruger is abandoned as Le Roux and Du Plessis drive away at speed.

I am in my office having a cup of coffee, discussing the planning for the day with Thele Moema from the information and verification department. It is difficult to know how seriously we should take the bomb threats. Clearly they are a tactic to disrupt the election process at a number of voting stations. In truth, they are achieving their desired effect, as the bomb squad runs ragged from station to station.

We discuss how the recent bombs had exploded without warning. There had been no advance threat. We agree that the right-wing strategy has worked to some extent. Now the bombs do not have to be made and placed: an anonymous phone call will do the job and achieve the objective – fear and panic. I put it bluntly to Moema: 'The issue is, Thele, how brave is this electorate? As a people, how much more can they take?'

Moema, as is the wont of those in the intelligence game, is more philosophical about the bomb threats and disruptions. 'Peter, as a nation, we can take anything. History has shown us what we can bear, and it is endless. This is no longer about risk, not for black people or white people. We have gone beyond risk or jeopardy.'

I agree with him. When you are in the abyss, there are no lengths to which you will not go. There are few shadows.

Even so, Moema agrees that we have to take the threats seriously. 'They will delay the elections in certain parts, but it is only a delay. People will come to vote, bombs and all, the election will go on.'

He tells me that they have made a breakthrough on the right-wing front and that the police expect to make a series of arrests. 'By the end of the day we will have wrapped them up. We will have put a stop to this thing. It is over for these guys. They may still conduct sporadic attacks but we will have taken away their ability to wage war.'

Spoken like a spook, I think as I sip my coffee.

We're disturbed by Phiroshaw Camay rushing into my office. 'A huge bomb has just gone off at Jan Smuts. The damage is very serious and there are many injured,' he says in a quiet, emotionless voice.

'Jesus, how many dead?' I ask in shock. I am thinking, Not again, not every day – this is the third day in a row and that only in Johannesburg.

'We don't know how many dead. They have stopped all flights coming into the airport while they check for more bombs. The airport has been cordoned off. I'll keep you updated,' he says, heading back to the ops centre.

'Under control, Thele?' I say, looking at him.

'They are arresting them now as we speak,' he says.

'Well they missed these ones and blowing up the country's premier international airport is quite something to let slip through their fingers.'

'I know, I don't know how they got through,' he says, shaking his head.

Jan de Wet meets with a number of husbands and wives on his farm. The women are unhappy with their lot. There have been disagreements and squabbles. They have now instructed their men to tell De Wet that 'they have had enough and that they want to go home'. De Wet drives the despondent spouses into Ventersdorp to AWB headquarters.

He walks into the Leader's office to find him ashen-faced. Eugène Terre'Blanche has just learnt that General Nico Prinsloo and Brigadier Leon van der Merwe and the Pretoria bombers have been arrested by the police.

The Leader instructs De Wet to rush back to the Waterval Shooting Range and tell the men that if they are arrested, they must keep quiet and use their right to silence. De Wet leaves at speed. On his approach to the shooting range he is flagged down by an AWB member who warns him that the police are arresting people at the range. De Wet heads for his farm to pick up a few belongings before he goes on the run.

At fifteen minutes past five in the morning, the South African Police swoop on the Waterval shooting range. They arrest the entire AWB contingent, including Leon van den Heever, the organisation's kommandant-generaal. General Nico Prinsloo is taken to the Protea Police Station in Soweto. The police seize explosives, sixteen machine guns, over thirty thousand rounds of ammunition, detonators, hand grenades and fire arms.

At the same time, the AWB men in the Koster assembly area are arrested and detained. Major Smit, who is visiting his parents in Pretoria, is arrested by a special police task-force at their home. The squad of right-wingers dispatched to the Eastern Cape to conduct a prolonged bombing campaign in the province are also arrested. The airport bomb in which eighteen people are injured goes unclaimed.

Phiroshaw Camay knocks on my door to tell me that the police have just disarmed a large bomb at the main voting station in Potchefstroom. 'Listen, Phiroshaw,' I exclaim in irritation, 'I am getting scared to answer my door. Each time there is a knock, it's you telling me stories about bombs all over the place. Bring me some good news, man!'

'Hey, Pete,' he says, ignoring my mild humour, 'do you want the news or don't you?'

'Yes,' I say, tired now, and the day has hardly started. 'Bring it whenever you get it.'

The bomb scares continue. Not one or two but hundreds, and each time, the voting station or building has to be evacuated so that the bomb squad can do their sweep. Some places have multiple bomb scares. But we have to play it safe.

At other voting stations shots are fired. Voters drop to the ground, refusing to lose their place in the queue. Once the shooting has stopped, they stand and dust themselves off.

Meanwhile our ops centre receives excited reports of other right-wingers being on the march with guns, threatening to shoot anyone in their path. At Viljoenskroon they have barricaded crucial access points to the town. At Bothaville, we hear, they intend setting up a machine-gun post to control access to the area. Rosil Jager, an IEC commissioner, persuades them to abandon their plans.

Bomb threats are not the only challenge the election faces. Throughout the morning we are inundated with other messages: The queues are too long. We need more ballots. The ultraviolet lights are not working. The polling officers have not arrived. The crowd has been waiting so long and the voting station has not yet opened; they are getting angry. We are trying to calm the people but they are threatening to burn the building – get security here fast.

On my fourth cup of coffee, I see the red points on the maps multiplying. It is the beginning of a pandemic.

I phone Ebby Mohamed in the Western Cape. He is calm and cheerful but also reports systems failures where voting stations opened late or there are shortages of voting materials.

Charles Nupen phones in from Durban. 'Look, it's happening. It's just happening very slowly,' he says wryly.

Etienne le Roux and Commandant Duppie du Plessis switch on their car radio to hear that they are the subject of a massive manhunt by the police. The news bulletin has details of the early-morning police raid on the Waterval Shooting Range.

Le Roux is at a loss. He cannot understand why the Leader or the fighting generals haven't claimed responsibility for the bomb blasts. He'd been expecting it after the first Bree Street blast but there was nothing. Now, after the third bomb and the pipe bombs, he can't understand why the Leader doesn't signal the start of the revolution.

Le Roux and Du Plessis realise they are now fugitives. They too go on the run. Le Roux plans to move from farm to farm at night to avoid arrest.

Gert Fourie, the Pretoria bomber, on his way back from seeing the women at De Wet's farm, stops at AWB headquarters to catch up on news of the war. He finds the Leader flustered and emotional. Eugène Terre'Blanche's voice lacks the iron that has always impressed Fourie. 'Men, you must flee and you must keep on running,' he tells them.

Gert Fourie does just that.

A few hours later Kommandant Abie Fourie and his men stop at AWB headquarters. They had spent the previous night with their wives at De Wet's farm and are now returning to Waterval Shooting Range.

Fourie finds the Leader alone in his office, head in his hands, shoulders slumped. In a hoarse voice he tells Fourie of the arrests.

Ponderously, Terre'Blanche walks with Fourie to address the men waiting listlessly outside. He informs them of the arrests, and then, in a rising fury, laments that 'these generals of mine ate dirt, they dropped us, they left us in the lurch ...' His chest heaves. 'Bliksems,' he shouts with the passion of a man whose dream has died.

He stares at his men. 'Here is money. Buy some petrol and do not let them catch you, even if you have to shoot your way clear.' Before they depart Terre'Blanche tells them that if they get caught, they have the right to keep silent because Section 29 of the Internal Security Act has been changed in their favour. He praises them as heroes of the Volk, the true freedom fighters.

The men return his gaze blankly, scarcely believing his words. The war is over. So quickly? Fourie looks at the father figure of the Leader and feels abandoned, as if he has become an orphan.

The men depart. Fourie ends up on a friend's farm. She tells them of the arrests. Fourie stays there one night, then, like his brother, goes on the run. His war is over.

There are serious problems being reported from all over the country. By midday, a number of voting stations have still not opened, while others have already run out of supplies and closed, much to the anger of voters, many of whom started queueing before sunrise.

In the administration division's office I talk to Yunus Mahomed. He has dark rings under his eyes and has clearly had little sleep. Along with Piet Coleyn and Norman du Plessis, he is in crisis-control mode as their staff field continuous calls for extra supplies as well as the urgent dispatch of polling officials to voting stations. I tell Mahomed that we have people who can ferry supplies on an emergency basis.

'Thanks, Pete,' he says, 'we will call on you but at the moment we are just trying to get a sense of the extent of the problems. The need is less on getting supplies to voting stations. The real issue is that stocks of election materials are running out. The problem is that the managers in charge of the regional warehouses have given certain voting stations more than they should have in terms of ballots and ultraviolet lights.'

'But didn't they issue according to your instructions for each voting station?' I ask.

'Yes,' he replies, 'but after the problems that we had with special voting, many heads of voting stations simply demanded that they be given extra ballots as reserves. They didn't want to have angry voters. Some of them even threatened the depot managers, who just gave them extra. Some voting stations have too many ballots and others not enough. It's a nightmare.'

There is desperation in his voice as he grapples with the disaster.

'At the moment, we are trying to determine exactly how much stock we have and where it is. The other problem is that we cannot make contact with some of the regional warehouses. They are simply not answering their phones. So even determining what we have is difficult.'

Back in my office, I call Imraan Haffagee, the head of specialist monitoring, and tell him to get his monitors to the regional and district warehouses countrywide to find out what is going on. If we can get that information to the administration division it may help them with their planning. If the warehouses are empty, we are in deep trouble.

Haffagee tells me that speculation is already rife that the election has been sabotaged. People are openly speaking of a conspiracy around the voting materials, that the warehouse managers have destroyed ballots and deliberately given out wrong amounts to polling-station officers.

'The rumours are not only out there,' he says, 'they are in the IEC. Everyone suspects sabotage.'

He is right; rumours abound.

'Let's get the facts, Imraan. Find out where the supplies are, if they exist,' I say, deliberately swallowing the last three words.

My concern is that while the people in the queues are patient at the moment, the longer they spend in the hot sun in lines that move very slowly, the less tolerant they will become.

At the moment, though, the mood is buoyant and respectful. We hear stories of black people leaving the voting stations with tears streaming down their faces. Of a white couple, in tears, saying to a cameraman, 'Finally, we are able to feel proud of our country.'

Caroline phones to tell me of the footage the ITN crews are getting. Of seasoned anchormen from the biggest news channels in the world clearly emotional as they record and describe the historic day.

An elderly black man tells the interviewer from ABC News in America, 'Now I can die. I have voted in my country.'

White residents in a suburb close to a voting station in which the queues are mainly black put out tables on which they provide glasses of water and sandwiches. People close to voting stations open their homes for people in the queues to use the toilet. A car arrives at a voting station on the West Rand and a man climbs out, saying that he owns a shop, and then distributes dozens of umbrellas as protection from the burning sun. ANC marshals dispense the umbrellas to those most in need, the elderly and women. The queue breaks into applause as the man drives off.

The queue at the Bryanston Laerskool in Johannesburg is two kilometres long and it, too, is quiet and patient as gardeners line up with their suburban employers, teachers and school cleaners. Hawkers, wares still in hand after voting, wander through the parked cars in the school grounds trying to make a sale, but in a solemn kind of way, almost deferring to history.

Nobel Peace Prize laureate, Archbishop Desmond Tutu, votes in the ghetto township of Gugulethu. He emerges from the voting station and with great emotion tells the international press that he 'felt two inches taller … We are the rainbow people. We want the whole world to know that we have done it.' Animated with excitement, he says that he couldn't sleep last night and started making his preparations for the day at two o'clock in the morning. 'The day I had been waiting for had finally arrived … I could have touched the sky with my happiness.'

Nelson Mandela votes at Ohlanga High School in Inanda, north of Durban. In the voice that has become instantly recognisable, he says, 'We are starting a new era of hope, reconciliation and nation-building.'

PW Botha, the former hard-line prime minister, who missed his opportunity to 'cross the Rubicon' and embrace change in the mid-eighties, thereby subjecting his country to many more years of racial oppression and violence, votes near his home at the Wilderness near George. He jumps the queue and, lips pursed, refuses to speak to reporters before stomping back home, a bitter and lonely man.

President FW de Klerk, hailed as a visionary, is the last president to represent the National Party that has ruled the country since 1948. He votes at the Arcadia Primary School in Pretoria and talks of the 'golden era' that lies ahead for all South Africans.

In Dawn Park near the home of the murdered Chris Hani, the queue stretches for more than six kilometres. At places it is eight abreast. There is no violence or anger. Some in the queue chatter excitedly, others are quiet as they privately reflect on the events that have brought them to this point. It is a day that belongs to everyone.

I think of Chris Hani, a remarkable man who could've played a great role in the new country. He should be there, in that queue.

I think of my colleague and friend, Bheki Mlangeni, killed by a security-police parcel-bomb. He, too, should be there, voting in Jabulani with his wife Seipati.

I get a phone call from a client of mine, Jabu Masina, one of four MK fighters I had represented in a major treason trial at Delmas. They had been part of an ANC assassination squad reporting directly to Chris Hani. After a dramatic trial, three of the four had been sentenced to death. We had successfully appealed against the death sentence and they had later been released. During the course of their imprisonment and trial, strong bonds of friendship and camaraderie had developed between us. Masina tells me, 'Today is the greatest day of my life, my dream has come true and I am so happy.' I ask him where he is and if he is celebrating. He replies that he is on duty guarding the home of Walter Sisulu in Orlando West, Soweto. He is calling from the house phone. The celebrating will come later. We talk and make an arrangement to get together. After the call, I shake my head, thinking that it is

218

a miracle that the four men are still alive, never mind voting in their first election.

Police report that there are virtually no incidents of crime. 'Even the criminals have taken the day off to vote,' quips one of the supervisors in the ops centre.

And the people move in their millions to the voting stations: the sick pushed in wheelbarrows, the elderly in steel shopping trolleys pushed by children. Donkey carts stand in the queue, with voters sitting up against the sides. In the Orange Free State some farm workers come to vote on their horses. Taxi drivers, often irascible and bandit-like in their behaviour, fill their taxis with voters and do not charge as they deliver them to the polls. They make repeated trips. No one wants to miss this time, this day of redemption.

In the ops centre, matters are less sanguine. At many voting stations, supplies of ballots are running very low and they will soon have to close. At midday, John Kleine, Phiroshaw Camay and Eddie Hendrickx enter my office as I am eating a toasted bacon-and-egg sandwich, breakfast.

'I don't think that this is sustainable, Pete,' says Hendrickx in his direct manner. The bacon turns to dust in my mouth. I know what he is saying but I have to hear it, like a death sentence.

'What do you mean?'

'He means that there are too many breakdowns at the polling stations,' says John Kleine, who is now running the ops centre. 'The failure rate of stations is now sitting at close to twenty per cent and climbing. In the PWV [Pretoria-Witwatersrand-Vereeniging] area, the place with the highest potential for violence, there is a twenty-five per cent systems failure. What is worse is that a number of the voting stations that are operating, particularly on the East Rand, will soon have to close as they are running out of ballots. It is a nightmare out there.'

It's a bloody nightmare in here as well, I almost shout in desperation. 'Voting is meant to close at seven tonight, and even though there is still tomorrow, we have a situation where huge chunks of the electorate will not be able to vote because of the shortages of materials. What is the administration division saying about this?'

'They are working flat out to address it, but it is too late and, frankly, they have underestimated this whole thing,' says Camay.

'What is Imraan Haffagee coming up with on the ballots? Is he finding them in the warehouses?' I ask.

'He says that the warehouses that they have got to are largely empty.'

I light another cigarette, taking the smoke deep into my lungs, as if it were the last cigarette of a condemned man. Which it just might be with things going the way they are.

'The ballots cannot be found,' I say out loud, pointlessly, and with a small degree of dementia, bitterly realising that what has been keeping me awake for the past three months has come to pass.

'Well, some have been found,' says Hendrickx, straight-faced. 'We received a report in the ops centre that a Cape Town businessman had reported a large quantity of IEC boxes left at his storeroom near Cape Town Airport on Monday night by two well-known transport companies. The drivers of the trucks asked the businessman to store the materials. The man, knowing nothing about storing anything for the IEC, later opened the boxes and found that they were filled with ballot papers. He phoned the police, who came and collected the materials.'

'How many ballots were there?' I ask.

'Nine hundred thousand,' says Camay.

'Jesus, that's a lot. So what is the explanation?'

'It appears that the drivers of the trucks were given the wrong address,' says Hendrickx.

'Very funny, Eddie, you are kidding me, right?' I say smiling. At a time like this, a joke is useful.

'Peter, I am not a joker,' he says in his thick Belgian accent. 'This story is true.'

I mouth a silent profanity as I throw my half-eaten toasted egg-and-bacon sandwich into the bin like a missile.

A short meeting with Judge Kriegler. He says he has been getting reports of systems failures. He wants to know how bad it is.

'It is a serious problem, Judge,' I say. 'The breakdowns are such that a lot of people will not be able to vote. Even if the administration division is able to reduce the amount of non-functional voting stations in the next few hours, it will be too late. It cannot be done in the time available.'

He looks at me intently, lost in thought, and then says that he needs to hold a meeting of the commissioners. I promise to keep him updated about things in the field.

By two o'clock, things in the field are not good. In fact, some would say they are stuffed. At twenty-two per cent of voting stations countrywide there are 'significant deficiencies', while in the cities and townships around Johannesburg, the failure rate is thirty per cent. In some provinces, voting proceeds more or less smoothly. Zac Yacoob, the commissioner allocated to the Northern Transvaal, reports that the province is functioning reasonably well. They are shuffling ballots and materials between the voting stations according to turnout. Proactive and getting good information from the voting stations, Yacoob, based in the operations centre, assists where he can. He makes it clear, though, that their ink will run out soon and that they need a lot more urgently.

The Western Cape is operating at ninety per cent efficiency. The Orange Free State is at eight-seven per cent, the Northern Cape under the leadership of Steve Kahanovitz is at a hundred per cent and the North West at ninety-five per cent. The problems lie in the Eastern Cape, operating at eighty per cent, and the Eastern Transvaal, also at eighty per cent.

But, if this is bad, then the headache problems are the region around Johannesburg, the industrial heartland of the country, and KwaZulu and Natal. They stand at seventy per cent and seventy-five per cent respectively. Both those areas have the potential to explode and burn. Easily.

It is clear that there are still too many people to vote. Millions of them. There will not be enough time even if the polling stations close at midnight. Telling people who have been queuing since four in the morning that they cannot cast their ballot and must come back the following day – which is an ordinary working day – is not worth contemplating. I am glad that I'm not in Judge Kriegler's shoes, although my own footwear is starting to feel distinctly uncomfortable.

In the afternoon the commissioners take the brave but necessary decision that the following day should, like today, be declared a public holiday. They realise that a decision of this nature will need the support of the private sector. Calls are made to the heads of the big corporations and the unions, who agree to support the IEC decision.

As does the Transitional Executive Council, which urgently requests State President FW de Klerk to declare the Thursday a public holiday. The public announcement made on all radio and television stations has a major effect. It takes the heat out of the situation and lowers the political temperature.

Kriegler holds a press conference and is roundly criticised for the administrative mess and systems failures. The press, having borne the brunt of Kriegler's biting judicial sarcasm in many earlier press conferences, take their revenge, taunting the judge with his boast of 'we are ready, let's do it'. His response is honest. His exhaustion clearly apparent, he admits the failures but also emphasises the steps that the commission has taken to address the issues.

In addition, the commission gives instructions that voting stations do not have to close at exactly seven that night. They are requested to stay open until everyone who is inside the station's inner perimeter has voted. Effectively, this means that stations will stay open until most of the people in the queue have voted.

The commission also takes the extraordinary step of agreeing that additional ballots, ink and ultraviolet lights should be ordered as a matter of urgency from local suppliers. Gone are the strictures of security.

Despite this, I still worry that they are too late and that we will not be able to get the supplies in time. My thinking is interrupted by a message that I'm wanted at an emergency meeting in the commissioners' boardroom. Gathered there are Yunus Mahomed and Piet Coleyn from the administration division as well as a number of commissioners. The meeting is chaired by the judge, who is in a very bad mood. Who wouldn't be, in his position? In fact, his bad mood cheers me up a little, if not for long.

He says to me, 'Peter, we want you to convene an emergency task team and ensure that every single voting station, particularly in the Witwatersrand, gets election materials.'

I look at my watch, wishing that the hands would move magically in the opposite direction. It is already late afternoon.

'Use whatever means you need to get the supplies and also to get them to the voting stations. This includes the South African army and air force. The administration division will assist where they can, but they are so stretched that this operation must be run by the monitoring division.'

I nod, mainly because I'm speechless.

'Another thing,' says Kriegler. 'We want your monitors at voting stations to place themselves at the disposal of the polling officers and help out where they can.'

'We have no problem in doing that, Judge, but you realise that this will blur the distinction between monitors and the administration division that the Act prescribes.'

He looks at me in a measured way. 'We understand that, but this is necessary to pull off this election. Those polling officials need assistance and the monitors are well trained and know the voting procedures. They are the only people who can assist in this situation. We will use National Peace Accord people to fulfil the role of the monitors.'

We leave the boardroom in silence.

In the mid-afternoon, the estimate is that we need to print at least nine million more ballot papers. To do this, we have no choice but to approach the Government Printer in Pretoria. Earlier rejected by the commission on the basis of their perceived lack of independence and capacity, they quickly open their premises that night, after a phone call from Norman du Plessis, and get their presses rolling. Other local printers, earlier scorned by the IEC for their lack of expertise and capacity, have been asked to print millions of additional ballots. The printers respond magnificently. Without a murmur, managers and workers open their factories, prepare their printing plates and get their presses rolling.

The problem of insufficient ballots had first arisen in Natal and KwaZulu in the late morning. Charles Nupen, realising that the province was running short of ballots, had phoned IEC headquarters in Johannesburg and requested that the air force urgently fly down extra supplies of ballots and ink.

He is told, 'There are no ballots left.'

'My God, you must be joking,' he responds. 'Most of this province has yet to vote and there is nothing left! Inkatha will think this is done on purpose to take away their vote and they will go crazy. Are you sure?'

The man, with the voice of an undertaker confirms that, yes, he is sure.

'What about the other provinces, don't they have surplus?' Nupen asks desperately.

'No, this is a crisis,' answers the man.

Nupen, exhausted and on edge, shouts into the phone, 'This is not a crisis, it is a national disaster', and slams down the handpiece.

In mid-afternoon Nupen is told that he can ask local printers to print extra ballots down there. He hands the task to his trouble-shooter, businessman Terry Rosenberg, a volunteer.

Rosenberg tracks down his contacts on the beach. Still wearing slip-slops and baggies, they open their printshops and get to work.

One of the companies, Fishwicks, uses the slogan, 'Print beyond limits.'

'We are going to put their slogan to the test,' says Nupen.

Extra ink is requested from the Police Forensic Laboratories headed by General Lothar Neethling. Norman du Plessis remembers that the police laboratories had manufactured the ink for the Namibian election in 1990. I mention to Eddie Hendrickx that in the 1980s the Police Forensic Laboratories made lethal poisons which were used to kill anti-apartheid activists. We know a number of people who were murdered by their poisons. This is a strange situation. We are now relying on them to manufacture ink that will help save the election that will usher in a new government. 'I hope they don't get their formulas confused,' I say. As it happens, they are able to supply only a limited amount and they soon run out of the key ingredients.

Du Plessis phones the chemistry department of the University of Pretoria, who immediately open up their labs. Lecturers and a number of post-graduate students commence manufacturing the ink. By three o'clock in the morning the university lab has made enough ink to supply the entire country. They are simply amazing.

Ink ran out in the late afternoon in Sekhukhuneland in the north. They filled the ink bottles and stamp pads with water and told the voters that their ultraviolet lights were not working. They then marked the thumbs of each voter with water, telling them that it was invisible ink. The electoral officers reported that it 'worked like a charm'.

In Durban Charles Nupen remembers that the ultraviolet lights had also been used in Lesotho. He phones the authorities in that country and borrows lights. A military plane flies into Maseru to pick them up.

The group around the small conference table in my office is a grim one. The mood has also been affected by news from the ops centre that on the East Rand, the most volatile and violent area in the country, many voting stations have run out of materials and closed early. Tens of thousands of angry people have gone home without voting. They make it very clear before they leave that they will return the next day, and if they cannot vote, they will burn down the voting station ... with the officials inside. Understandably, this has affected the morale of the voting staff, who do not want to go to work tomorrow morning.

Eddie Hendrickx does not blink as I relay the request from the commission. In fact, he shows absolutely no emotion whatsoever when I tell him that I want him to head up the emergency task team to source and distribute election supplies. I tell him that Phiroshaw Camay must be on the team with a few others, including Vuyo Ntshona, the head of monitoring for the Witwatersrand area.

Thele Moema and Dries Putter, both of whom are present, are to get us information on the hotspots, the places where security needs to be deployed to safeguard the IEC stations and officials through the night. Dries Putter is also requested to contact his sources in the military. He phones General Gert Opperman, the officer coordinating all military support for the election. General Opperman assures him of the support of the military and that they will lay on whatever transport is necessary to get the supplies out. This includes troops to protect the ballots.

We agree to work in shifts. As far as supplies are concerned, we are mostly talking about ballots, ink and ultraviolet lights. In some areas pens, pencils, paper and paperclips are also needed.

We have teams sourcing these items and the manufacture of extra supplies. We have a team focused on planning and distribution. This team also lines up people, cars, armoured vehicles, delivery companies, couriers and fixed-wing planes and helicopters.

The teams are told to liaise with the administration division to ensure that there is no duplication. We set up our emergency office on the floor that houses the telecommunications department. They provide us with a bank of phones within a few hours.

We agree to hold progress meetings every two hours throughout the night. I am on standby to unlock blockages and to phone the right people to get supplies. I look at Eddie Hendrickx, thinking that this man from Brussels actually looks like he's enjoying himself.

While rushing between offices, I come across a tall, gaunt young man with a wild look in his eye and a very pale face. He is sitting at a desk. 'Are you okay?' I ask, worried that he may have had a traumatic experience and need help. He introduces himself as Antony Altbeker and says, 'Yes, I am fine. It has just been the most unbelievable day.'

'I know,' I respond, 'a great day for the country but we still have a lot of problems.'

Before I can stop him, he blurts out, 'My day started yesterday with special voting.' I can see that he wants to talk, so I stand and listen.

'I was assigned by my supervisor Selma Browde to an old-age home in Germiston by the name of "Our Parents' Home". All white, a different world that moved in slow motion; it was like going back in time, I tell you. Surreal. One old lady said she wanted to vote for Jan Smuts's party and which one was it. I think I told her it was the ANC.'

He smiles. 'No, just joking. I told her that there were different parties now and that his party was long gone. Anyway, I came back here yesterday afternoon and told Selma that I didn't volunteer to work in old-age homes, I wanted to be where I could make a real contribution. She looked at me in a funny way for a while

and then said, "Oh, so you want to be in the thick of it. Fine, report for duty at four o'clock tomorrow morning and you will be
driven to a polling station in the middle of Alex." I said, 'That's
fine, I will be there."'

By now a group of people have gathered around us.

Altbeker continues, 'So, I meet the rest of my team here at
four, damn cold, and we are driven to this polling station in Alex.
By seven in the morning, there are five thousand people in the
queue and there are no ballots at the voting station. We start to
crap ourselves. By nine, the numbers have grown even more and,
hell, I know that we are in deep shit so I ask the ANC head marshal
if I can borrow his car and go to IEC headquarters to get ballots.
The ANC guy stares at me as if I am mad, and then he looks at the
long lines of voters waiting in the morning sun and he says he
will lend me his car for ten rand. I thank him, give him ten bucks
and drive here like hell.

'I go to Selma and tell her that I need ballots urgently otherwise
there will be violence at that polling station. Selma looks at me.
Her face is white and she is in a terrible state. She tells me that the
election has been sabotaged on a massive scale and that war has
broken out on the East Rand. I start to cry in despair and terror.
I shit myself, thinking, This is it, the apocalypse, our nightmare.
But after a while I gather myself and I still think that I must try
and find ballots. So I go to the administration division floor and
start checking in the rooms. A lot of them are empty but in one
corner room I see a large box and when I open it there are ballots
inside. I steal the box of ballots.'

'You did what?' I ask in horror. 'You stole ballots? Shit, are you
mad?'

'Yup, I knew that war had broken out on the East Rand and I
thought that if I could get ballots to Alex, we could stop the war
there.'

I shake my head.

'So, I steal the box and in one of the other rooms I find two rolls of Inkatha stickers. I steal those too, and I wrap the lot in my coat and smuggle it down to the ANC guy's car and drive to Alex. As I am driving, I am thinking, We are now a country at war with itself. I am completely petrified and I swear to myself that if, when I get close to Alex, I see smoke rising, I will just get out of the car and run all the way into Johannesburg. Crying from fear, I think that I am going to die.

'Well, there isn't smoke coming from Alex so I carry on. I get back to the voting station to find that all of the supplies have arrived except for the Inkatha stickers, which means that voting still cannot take place. Truly, I tell you, I am treated like a hero when I produce the two rolls of Inkatha stickers. I get told to take one roll to the voting station down the road and as I walk past the long queues at the other voting station, the voters see the Inkatha roll in my hand and they start clapping and cheering me. I don't think I ever felt so good in my life.

'Back at my own voting station, I phone my folks to warn them that war has broken out and that they must take shelter where they can because it is going to be very dangerous. My dad tells me that he is watching CNN and that it all looks pretty calm to him – he can't see any war. I tell the other staff at the voting station about war breaking out and they all laugh at me. I laugh with them because I feel so relieved.

'At five in the afternoon Helen Suzman arrives at our station to see how things are going. She asks me if we have enough supplies of voting materials and I tell her we have tons of the stuff and will sell it to the highest bidder. Phew, she crapped on me from a dizzy height and told me to grow up and not be ridiculous. I apologised a lot to her.

'I stayed there until everyone had voted and then reported back to Selma at IEC headquarters, who seemed to have forgotten that she had told me that war had broken out on the East Rand. Again, she gave me a funny look and then sent me out to the East Rand with Rehad Desai to deliver supplies to a voting station there. My

God, what a drive. On the way there I was so hyped with adrenaline that we had two crashes, both times into police vehicles. The second one I was going too fast and we crashed headlong into a parked police caravan filled with cops. Fuck, they were woes, really angry, they came out crouching like you see in the movies with their guns drawn, all in action mode. They thought they were being attacked and when they saw it was only me and Rehad, a Jewish boy and an Indian, they got even more furious and threatened to shoot us. Hands above my head, I told them that I was only twenty-four years old and was working for the IEC. They let us go and, unbelievably, our car still worked, so we delivered the supplies and came back here. And now I am finished. I mean, what kind of day is that?' He holds up his hands in supplication.

The meeting of the task team at seven is quick and clinical. Representatives of the defence force and police are also present. We now have much more information and so are able to make informed decisions. It is clear that the sections have put their two hours to good use.

In a stroke of genius, the task team, assisted by the men and women from Telkom, realise that the one organisation which can get to most voting stations very quickly is Telkom. It has an extensive network of technicians with their own transport in every town and they are in telephone communication with their head office. It is agreed that these Telkom technicians assisted by Post Office delivery vans will be the primary distributors of the materials. We just have to procure the materials and get them to the technicians.

On the security front, we agree that in certain areas we can no longer rely on civilian managers for the protection and issuing of materials. They are too prone to persuasion and intimidation. We will bring in the military. Highly trained men with semi-automatic combat rifles will be less amenable to undue pressure.

Buoyed by the meeting and with twelve hours to get materials to the voting stations, I return to my office to find my door open. This is unusual as it is normally locked when I am absent. Ireen Avidan standing outside, her face white, says, 'I am not sure you should go in there.' I go in nonetheless.

A small group of concerned-looking men and women in IEC bibs stand near the window. At the conference table are seated another four men. The men at the table appear angry and very impatient. David Storey is also in the room, tight-lipped and staring at me.

'Yes, gentlemen, and how may I help you?' I ask in a serious voice, thinking I don't know how these guys got past security, but this is a huge breach.

'We are polling officials from voting stations in Katlehong and these are a committee of voters from the area who have brought us here,' says one of the men in an IEC bib.

'I know Katlehong well, but what are you doing here?' I say. One of the men at the table, a stocky, well-built man in a yellow T-shirt says in a clipped voice. 'These IEC people are our hostages. The officials at one of the voting stations have also been taken hostage. The voting stations in Katlehong have run out of ballots and ink and the ultraviolet lights do not work. We hold the IEC responsible – they are sabotaging our election. We have come here in taxis using our own money to tell you that if we do not return to the voting stations in a few hours with ballots and other supplies, our comrades will kill the officials that we have hostage there.'

I look at the IEC officials. 'It is true,' they say in unison. I need this now like a hole in the head. Here I am involved in a critical exercise that will hopefully pull us back from the brink and suddenly I'm being invaded by a self-defence unit from Katlehong plus their hostages, who want to camp out in my office. I mean, can this thing get any worse? My question is soon answered.

'No,' shouts the stocky guy loudly, 'it is not just them who are hostages. It is also the two of you,' he says, pointing aggressively at Storey and me.

The last person to vote at the city hall in Durban on that Wednesday night is Dikgang Moseneke. He arrives in the early evening from a trip with Gay McDougal by helicopter up the coast to Ulundi, the former capital of KwaZulu. Along the way, they stop at various polling stations, checking on how voting is proceeding. For Moseneke, it is an emotional and humbling experience. He moves from station to station along the beautiful jagged coastline, the pristine beaches and lush green hills lining an interior that history had soaked in blood. The roar of the beating rotors cocoons him. He retreats into a detached, thoughtful silence. From the air he can see the long queues like pieces of string leading to the polling stations.

His pensive mood is broken when they land at a remote voting station in KwaZulu. As they alight from the chopper, they are surrounded by a throng of young women and men wearing traditional garments. Each has a string of beads slung diagonally across his or her chest. Gay McDougal, flustered by the nudity of the young women, tells Moseneke to close his eyes. It is not proper to look at the breasts of the women. Moseneke refuses, pointing out that she is eyeing the muscled torsos of the young men.

The city hall is almost empty when Moseneke finally casts his vote. In the silence of the great chamber, this man who was sent as a prisoner to Robben Island for ten years at the age of fifteen makes his two crosses deliberately, slowly folding the two ballot papers into small squares. The moment is not as emotional as he had imagined. He feels a great calm as he walks from the hall.

From my Peace Accord days I know that Katlehong is one of the most dangerous places in the country, with Kumalo Street, the road that runs through it, a virtual channel of fire. In the media it has been described as 'the drag of death'. It is a place where life is cheap and violent death a frequent reality. Which is why I'm a little nervous about this delegation.

'Guys, I appreciate your problem and I can try and help you

but you are in the wrong place. You report to the administration division and they are the people who must help you. Let me get someone to guide you down there,' I say helpfully.

The stocky man looks at me and rattles off in Zulu, a language I don't speak. One of the IEC officials, Phindile Nzimande, translates: 'He is saying, "If you want the cart to move faster, you must hit the strongest oxen."' In other circumstances it would be a flattering gesture. What it does is conjure up another African proverb: 'You don't shout at the crocodile when you are still in the river.' We are in deep water here. This has to be dealt with sensitively, without police or army. The self-defence units in Katlehong are strong, well armed and not afraid to fight. Security intervention will only inflame a situation that is already smouldering. It could start a small war.

The key imperative is that these people need to vote the next morning and they need election materials in order to do so.

It suddenly strikes me that half an hour earlier Imraan Haffagee had reported that a warehouse situated in the Dunnottar Military Base near KwaThema on the Nigel–Springs Road had voting materials. His report lying on my desk gives a contact name, Scholtenmeyer, and a telephone number. I reassure the kidnappers that I am not phoning for assistance, and get hold of Scholtenmeyer. It is not an easy conversation. Initially, he doesn't know if he has the materials. Then he admits he might have some 'stuff'. He slurs his words. It occurs to me that Scholtenmeyer is drunk.

'Mr Scholtenmeyer,' I say, 'let us understand each other. I have people being held hostage here because of a shortage of electoral supplies. At the voting stations, IEC officials will be harmed or killed if we do not get supplies there tonight, and you are being obstructive. I am sending these men with a police escort down there and you will open up your warehouse and hand out any supplies in it. If you don't, I will have you arrested tonight for attempting to sabotage the electoral process. Is that clear?'

'Yes, sir,' he says loudly, 'extremely clear.'

233

I notice that the slurring is gone. 'They will be there in forty-five minutes and I expect you to be waiting outside your warehouse with the keys ready to open it.'

Putting down the phone, I say, 'Right guys, we will give you directions to the warehouse and organise for police to escort you there.'

I want to get the police on to this so that if things turn nasty, they will be on hand to protect the IEC polling officials. The escort will not only safeguard the officials but also the ballot papers, should they find any in the warehouse.

'This is progress,' says the stocky guy. 'We need to get to the warehouse fast.'

'I agree, but first wait for your police escort. I can't just let you go and pick up ballot papers.'

I call through to Captain Rossouw in the ops centre and request the escort. She tells me that it will have to be traffic police as the police are already stretched to the limit.

'No problem,' I say.

The stocky guy says, 'Not so fast, this could just be a trick to get rid of us.'

Irritated, I respond, 'Listen, you have heard me and I have done my best to help you. Now you must let us run this election. We are dealing with crises all over the country.'

'That is your problem,' he says. 'One of you will come with us as our hostage until we have delivered the supplies to the voting stations in Katlehong.'

My eyes meet with David Storey's. I know I have to make a choice here. Fortunately for a decisive man like me it is not too difficult. Hesitating for all of two seconds, I say, 'This man will go with you,' pointing at Storey, who does a double take and then nods with resignation.

I justify my choice on the basis that I have to run this entire division and distribution of ballots through the night and I cannot be stuck in Katlehong for the next five hours.

While the kidnapper delegation waits, I tell Captain Rossouw that the traffic policemen's real duty is to protect the IEC officials and David Storey.

She says that she will notify the reaction unit in Thokoza. I also arrange for a group of IEC monitors to meet the cavalcade at the entrance to the military base.

Thirty minutes later, I phone Storey on his mobile phone. 'How is the hostage?' I ask with a smug laugh. Despite the gravity of the situation, it has a light side, a light if hysterical side. It is not often that you get a chance to offer up your good friend as a hostage.

'Very funny,' he says. 'You should know that on the way down from your office, we ran into Vuyo Ntshona in the lift.' Ntshona is the head of monitoring in that region. 'For good measure, they took him hostage as well.'

I ask if everyone is alright.

Oh yes, says Storey, they are travelling in a cavalcade of minibus taxis with traffic police in cars and on bikes in front and behind. The traffic cops ensure right of way through the intersections, and the cavalcade sails through at speed, sirens blaring. I can hear the sirens as he speaks.

'Good, it is not so bad then?'

'I could get used to this,' he says. I can imagine the smile on his face.

An hour later David Storey phones. He has confronted Scholten-meyer, a stocky man with a red face and a brandy-blue nose. Scholtenmeyer is drunk and refusing to open the warehouse. While we're talking, the warehouse keeper disappears. I give the order to break in.

Inside the warehouse are racks of shelving and stacked neatly on them containers filled with indelible ink, hundreds upon hundreds of them. There are also a large number of ultraviolet lights. The IEC officials feel they have uncovered a treasure trove.

They break open a second warehouse to find piles of ballots – not huge amounts, but sufficient to supply a number of voting stations.

Certainly, there are now enough supplies to ensure the release of the hostages and to provision the East Rand voting stations. The election in the area will continue.

It has to be said that IEC officials have got used to being on the receiving end of public anger. Most incidents, as did this one, end well. Some don't. In Soweto, an IEC driver ferrying monitors and supplies is stopped outside his house by criminals who demand his car keys. He refuses. He tells them the car is being used in the election. When he again refuses to give them the keys they shoot him and flee. Unfortunately the IEC official dies from his wounds some hours later.

At IEC headquarters, the task team is working flat out. Voting stations with surplus ballots and other materials have been identified, and these items are being brought to us. Voting stations that have run out of ballot boxes are being supplied with canvas postal bags instead – some seven thousand.

As the Telkom technicians around the country have become our main distributors, it is up to the Telkom staff on the task team to get their cooperation. They huddle in a corner with Telkom staff directories containing names, addresses and phone numbers. I hear them speaking in Afrikaans as they wake people up at midnight. 'I am sorry to disturb you but we need your help. It is a national emergency. We need you to be available for the next twenty-four hours to deliver electoral supplies.' Often there is a silence and then I hear our operator saying, 'Baie dankie, oom, ons waardeer dit baie.'

Eddie Hendrickx conducts the midnight meeting of the task team. I like his meetings; they are short and sharp, rarely taking more than thirty minutes. He listens to reports, gives instructions and the meeting is over. He spends his time moving constantly among the task-team members, speaking quietly to the heads of the sections, listening, commenting.

On the hour, every hour, food and coffee are brought through by monitors who have been called in from the field. Vanessa Henry walks from section to section, asking the task team if there is anything they need, dishing out her never-diminishing hoard of sweets to those in need of a boost. She is cheerful, as if she is at a garden party.

Vuyo Ntshona, released after the hostage drama, returns to headquarters and immediately gets involved with the task team. He, too, is showing signs of extreme fatigue. In addition to his work with the task team, he is also coping with reports from the ops centre regarding areas of actual or potential violence. He'd hoped that his teams could rest from nine o'clock in preparation for the next day, but mostly this is not possible.

It is now after midnight and monitors are still being sent to flash points. Through it all, Ntshona is calm and professional.

He and I know that this additional work will stretch everyone to their limit. Will they hold up? Once the voting stops, the counting starts. We have days and nights of arduous work ahead of us.

In the run-up to the election, we had worried about the army and air force. There were concerns that they might sabotage the day by not delivering supplies of material and people where they were needed. With a few isolated exceptions, they are, in fact, magnificent, and rise to the occasion.

Earlier in the evening, Allan Repshold, the IEC official liaising with the air force, had secured air transports that would operate throughout the night and next day. The chief of the South African Air Force, Lieutenant General James Kriel, had sanctioned the deployment of as many aircraft as were needed.

With the air transport laid on and waiting, all that remains is for the supplies to be delivered to the handover points. Most of the air traffic is destined for the Eastern Cape and Kwazulu and Natal.

I am impressed by the SAAF's commitment to making this work. They are treating this like a military rescue operation, not an event that will result in their losing power and handing the country over to the very people they have been fighting for decades.

At the Dunnottar Military Base, David Storey needs to get the voting equipment from the warehouses to the voting stations in Katlehong. The traffic police refuse to help him, saying that it is too dangerous. They depart, leaving the IEC officials in the hands of their kidnappers at the military base.

In desperation, Storey phones a colonel he knows from his days in the Peace Accord and requests a military escort into Katlehong. An hour later a truck arrives with about fifteen soldiers. The convoy of IEC cars follows the truck to the Katlehong police station.

It is close to midnight when the convoy reaches the police station. The majority of the supplies are placed in a secure storeroom. The rest are to be delivered to the voting station where the hostages are being held.

But now the escorting troops refuse to venture any further into Katlehong. It is too dangerous. There is nothing for it but for the weary IEC monitors to deliver the equipment themselves. They watch in disappointment and disgust as the troops clamber into their truck and leave.

A short while later, the small convoy of IEC cars also leaves the police station and winds its way through the dark streets of the township. Here and there, they see men with guns moving between the houses, their faces covered with scarves.

It has been agreed that once they have completed their delivery, they will return to the police station. They need to make other drop-offs at the remaining voting stations in the area. Phindile Nzimande stays behind at the Katlehong police station to divide and supervise the delivery of ballots. She works through the night. The ballots and equipment are delivered to the voting stations and the hostages are released.

The staff at the polling stations in Katlehong get no sleep as they receive the ballots, ink and lights, and prepare the voting station for the next day's voting. There is no point in going home. The voting station has to be ready for voting at seven o'clock, just five hours away.

Exhausted, David Storey drives to the Natalspruit Hospital in Thokoza. He stops in the hospital's grounds and sleeps for an hour in his car before driving back to IEC headquarters. He joins Eddie Hendrickx's task team sourcing and distributing election materials.

Khosi Ndlovu, the head of the monitoring division's transport department, liaises with the task team, calmly issuing orders for cars and drivers to handle the emergency distribution of supplies. The monitors, summoned through the ops centre, arrive in their cars. They have been up since four the previous morning.

I phone Jay Naidoo and tell him that we need drivers and cars. He contacts the unions to help us. Our calls for help are answered by many. Students, pensioners, trade unionists, church people, friends of IEC officials, parents, sundry motley individuals, hundreds of them, arrive in their personal cars at the side entrance of 41 Kruis Street to pick up and deliver supplies. They have been told to be there at four o'clock in the morning, but many get there earlier, patiently waiting in the dead of night. A long queue forms. The supplies are piled into the cars. Each is accompanied by an official from the administration division or a monitor to safeguard the material and ensure it arrives at the right place. Many volunteers make more than one trip.

It is a monumental effort. No arguments, just raw dedication. It is the IEC's Dunkirk.

In Pretoria exhausted managers at the Government Printer and their staff work through the night to print the ballots. A grim commitment informs their labour each focused intently on his or her task, knowing the urgency, and the consequences of failure.

The professor supervising the manufacture of ink at the Pretoria University chemistry lab phones to tell us that they do not have sufficient containers. Solveigh Piper contacts André Lamprecht of Barlow Rand, who contacts a senior manager at Nampak, the Barlow Rand subsidiary that makes containers. He meets a dead end. Nampak produces only branded containers. He phones Pete Surgey of Plascon and asks if their subsidiary Polycell can help out. Yes, they can. They have unmarked containers, but can the manager be reached? Can the factory be up and running in the next two hours?

More calls are made and within an hour the managers from Polycell and technical staff are preparing the lines for operation. The police collect the large vats of ink from the chemistry laboratories at Pretoria University and deliver them to the Polycell factory.

The first supplies of ink bottles are received at IEC headquarters at three o'clock. Other larger batches are dispatched to the air-force planes at Waterkloof air base outside Pretoria. At four in the morning, the final bottle comes off the filling line at Polycell and the line is switched off. It is done. The men look at one another in exhaustion, and in triumph. The last air-force plane carrying the ink to the provinces lifts off at seven o'clock on the morning of Thursday, 28 April 1994.

The printer in downtown Johannesburg that is printing ballots phones just after midnight to say that he has completed his batch. Imraan Haffegee and a team of specialist monitors are sent under police escort to collect the ballots. They return at two o'clock.

Soon afterwards, the ballots start to arrive from the Government Printer. They are delivered to a large area that the task team has cleared in the underground parking. The entire area is secured by the army. Ten heavily armed soldiers guard the entrance.

The incoming materials are received and logged. In an adjacent area, supply orders relayed from the task team upstairs are checked and fulfilled. Once a batch is complete, it is moved to the entrance of the parking area where its contents are again checked against the order. The batch is then loaded into a volunteer's car, signed off and dispatched. It is a clearing and forwarding operation of great scale.

Eddie Hendrickx and Phiroshaw Camay move like generals

among the teams, giving instructions as they check that no mistakes are made.

The IEC officials who deliver the materials to the air force are instructed to travel with the supplies until they are handed over at their destinations. The feedback to the task team is that air-force personnel are extremely cooperative at the bases. They have been briefed to expect the IEC and have men on hand to assist with loading.

While all of this is going on, I talk frequently to Charles Nupen down in Durban, who, along with Dikgang Moseneke and Gay McDougal, is also dealing with a desperate situation. There is some relief in sight. Early on Thursday morning, Nupen tells me with pride that by two o'clock that morning, the two Durban printers he had dragged off the beach had printed three million ballots, enough to supply the entire province.

At daybreak I am in the dispatch area in the parking basement below. I see a line of cars snaking away down the street for many blocks and Eddie Hendrickx, sharp and alert as ever, his shirt still neat, calmly directing the situation. Given the urgency and tight time scale of the operation, the attention to detail is extraordinary.

The drivers have acknowledgement-of-receipt forms and phone numbers if they get lost. There are people upstairs on phones whose sole job it is to give directions to lost drivers. I chat to Hendrickx, who tells me that the dispatch operation has been under way since four o'clock.

'Look over there,' he says pointing to a corner. I see Judge Kriegler, the sleeves of his white shirt rolled up, helping to load the boxes of materials as they arrive. There is a faint smile on Hendrickx's face as, turning to me, he says, 'You know, Peter, I think this is the most inspiring thing that I have ever done in my life. Yesterday, I was in the lift coming up to our floor and there was an elderly black lady in the lift. Apparently, she works on one of the floors for the IEC. I don't know what her job is. We started talking and she looked at me with tears in her eyes and said, "I am so happy today. This is the first time in my life that I have voted and it may be the last time, but I am just so happy." She looked at me, holding my arm tightly, and she thanked me for coming here to help organise the election. And I felt so proud, I tell you.'

'Well, Eddie, she was right. We do have to thank you for coming here and helping in the way you have. How are we doing?'

'According to our estimates, we will have delivered ballots to the majority of the voting stations in this region by seven this morning and all by nine o'clock. They will not have full supplies to last them all day as there is simply not enough to go around. Each station will get enough to see them through to about midday. We will be resupplying during the course of the morning and the afternoon.'

I shake my head in wonder. The man is a miracle worker.

CHAPTER ELEVEN

It is Thursday, 28 April 1994. I am in my office as the sun creeps softly through the city. This is it, I say to myself. We have to finish it today and then, once the count is over, I will sleep for a month. For the moment, I just need to get through the day. Strong coffee and a toasted egg-and-bacon sandwich will assist that process.

I phone Caroline to see how she is. She tells me that she has just arrived at the ITN offices in Melville and is making preparations for the day. She is focused on her work and even a little cheerful now that the end is in sight. ITN film crews have inundated her with requests for interviews with senior politicians. They're getting irritated when their wishes are not granted. The truth is that most serious radio and TV stations around the world have sent their top people here and they all want that critical interview with people like Mandela, De Klerk, Roelf Meyer and Cyril Ramaphosa.

Over the last three months, I have hardly seen Caroline and the children. I promise myself that when this is over, that will change. If these days will only pass. If we can just get through it.

By nine o'clock, reports coming through the ops centre confirm that most voting stations in the Johannesburg region are operating, although there are still some isolated problems. Thankfully, the dreaded East Rand is quiet, with few incidents reported.

In spite of now having ballots, KwaZulu and Natal remain in a state of crisis, particularly in the north where the Empangeni region still indicates a thirty-one per cent failure rate.

It also seems the hostage contagion is spreading. A group of disgruntled volunteers registered to observe and report on the election have taken hostage Bheki Sibiya, who is the head of monitoring in KwaZulu and Natal. They are angling for payment. Fearing for the safety of his colleague, the deputy director of monitoring, Steve Collins, phones Colonel Vernon Hunter of the police reaction unit. They both have Motorola 'bricks'.

A short while later Colonel Hunter and his heavily armed men arrive. They storm into the church and head for the altar where Sibiya is being held. His kidnappers quickly disappear, and Sibiya is rescued.

The situation deteriorates further in KwaZulu and Natal when IEC officials working at the main polling station in Durban demand extra money. If they are not paid urgently, they will not allow the voting to take place. Dikgang Moseneke is appalled by the lack of patriotism being shown by these young men and women. He feels they are literally holding the nation to ransom. He berates them for their lack of commitment, cajoling them. 'Okay,' he says, 'if that's what you want. Don't work, we will stop the election in this province, and you will be the people that did it. It is on your heads. Now what are your names?' There is a stunned silence from the youngsters, who say that they need a moment to caucus outside. They return to tell him they will go back to work.

I laugh out loud when Charles Nupen tells me this story, imagining Moseneke, regal and dignified, tearing into the youngsters. Nupen is fulsome in his praise. 'Pete, Dikgang was simply amazing. He stood there and faced them down, a large crowd, very hostile. There was this huge standoff and then they blinked. Shit, it was close.'

Radio reports tell of an incident, confirmed by the ops centre, of a white man opening fire on people in the queue outside the voting station at Taung in the Western Transvaal. Braving the shots, voters stormed the car and set it alight with petrol. The man was badly burnt and would have died had the police not rescued him. The man was arrested and placed under police guard in Rustenburg hospital.

Later in the day, fifteen magisterial districts in the Western Transvaal, the region that was intended as the Volkstaat, are declared 'unrest areas'. This declaration gives the security forces extraordinary powers of arrest, search and seizure.

While I have always opposed emergency provisions such as these, I welcome this one, particularly after Thele Moema and Dries Putter give us a detailed briefing on the insurrection planned to take place in the Western Transvaal. Unfortunately, right-wingers are still clustered on a number of farms. Security forces are taking no chances with these men. Moema tells me that identified farms will be systematically swept and searched until the area is 'clean'.

By midday, eighty-five per cent of counting stations are functioning properly, with the main problem spots being in remote rural areas where it is difficult to fly in additional supplies. Air-force choppers deliver to drop-off points, but the issue is getting the materials to the voting stations. In areas where there are few roads, this takes time. With the rest of the country looking good, all efforts are directed at Venda, Lebowa, Gazankulu, the Ciskei and the Transkei, all former homeland areas where the infrastructure is, at best, poor.

In the cities, by mid-afternoon, the printing presses slow and come to a halt. The job is done. The local printers have printed an additional nine million three hundred thousand ballot papers, an extraordinary achievement.

The challenge is now to get the ballots to the former homelands. By three o'clock, sixty-five per cent of stations in these areas are still having problems. To compound matters, there is often no electricity, which makes voting after dark impossible. After consultation with the political parties – a five-hour meeting during which they complain bitterly about the problems and irregularities – the commission decides to extend voting for another day in the areas of the Ciskei, Gazankulu, Lebowa, KwaZulu, Transkei and Venda.

State President FW de Klerk makes the official announcement of this extra voting day. The parties are at one another's throats. The ANC accuses Inkatha of setting up pirate voting stations which they control and run to the exclusion of other parties. Inkatha accuses the ANC of the same crime in the Eastern Cape. The smaller parties complain about intimidation, no-go areas, vote rigging, and 'stuffing' ballot boxes. The National Party is vociferous in its criticism of the ANC, again focusing mainly on the Eastern Cape.

In the early evening, my personal spectre, the East Rand, rises to rattle its bones. It had been agreed that the hostel dwellers in Katlehong, Thokoza and Vosloorus areas would vote in their hostels. The reason being that the hostels were Inkatha. Having these people vote in the townships would be a recipe for war. It is now dark and one of the hostels hasn't voted due to the late delivery of materials. The hostel has no electricity. No lights. The situation is deteriorating, with the hostel dwellers threatening to vote at a polling station in the middle of Katlehong. They are dressing and arming themselves as if for war.

It is imperative that lights be delivered to the hostel fast, before the impi moves out. As word spreads of the hostile hostel dwellers, nearby residents flee their homes. The local ANC self-defence units prepare to defend the area.

There is a standoff at the Thokoza police station. The police refuse to take the trailer containing the lights into the hostel. It is too dangerous, they claim. An army colonel arrives and berates the police brigadier for neglecting his duty. Their slanging match ends when the colonel arranges for Wits Command to send a platoon. An hour later, the troops arrive, hook up the trailer and take it into the hostel. They set up the lights and voting commences. Just before midnight, the army and polling officials leave the hostel. Voting is complete.

Late in the evening, the ops centre confirms that with the exception of a few voting stations, the elections in the Eastern Transvaal, the Northern Cape, the Orange Free State, the PWV and the Western Cape have been successfully completed.

To make this happen, the South African Air Force carried out sixty-six flights, including the transport of forty-six tons of ballot papers and equipment. In addition, aircraft offered free of charge to the commission by well-known businessman Johan Rupert of the Rembrandt Group flew one hundred and thirty-three hours during the election, of which sixty-eight hours were in emergency response to direct requests from the national and provincial operations centres.

Despite the remarkable work of the IEC task team in issuing temporary voting cards, hundreds of thousands of voters turned up with either invalid or no identification. This had been anticipated. Stations capable of processing temporary cards had been established close to the major voting stations where problems were envisaged. From 25 to 29 April, the issuing stations handled almost one and a half million temporary voting cards.

Late that night, a couple of us gather in my office, dog-tired but elated. Zac Yacoob has just flown in from Pietersburg. He tells us of his experience in the Northern Transvaal over the two days, the drama, the elation, the patience and dignity of the voters as they waited to cast their votes. He tells of the air-force planes bringing in ballots and ink. He is particularly complimentary of the role played by the defence force as he recounts a conversation he had with one of the regional commanders in the area. 'Our role is not to make political decisions,' the man had told him. 'Our job is to make political decisions work, and that is what we will do in this election.'

'They were damned impressive, the way they came to the party,' says Yacoob emphatically.

'The majority of the country has voted,' I say, raising my glass of whisky. We drink to this.

CHAPTER TWELVE

Friday, 29 April 1994 is a slow day as we wait for the voting to finish. It has been decided by the commission that the counting should not commence until all voting has finished. In our view, this is not a bad thing as it gives the administration division time to fine-tune their preparations for the count.

In the monitoring division, the lull lets us gain some sleep and also check our deployment of monitors assigned to the count.

In late February, we had realised that after a number of days of voting our monitors would be exhausted. This led to supplementary monitors from an NGO – the Independent Mediation Service of South Africa – being trained to assist our staff. The election department of the service is run by Dren Nupen, a determined and skilled elections expert.

At one of its first meetings the commission had decided that the counting would not take place at the voting stations. Rather, ballot boxes would be taken by polling officials in the company of monitors and observers to the six hundred and seventy counting stations around the country.

For practical and security reasons the counts in the major cities are to be conducted at a single venue. Each of these metropolitan counting stations will have multiple counting streams. Thirty-seven counting streams are planned at Nasrec in Johannesburg, thirty at the Pretoria show grounds and twenty-eight at the Durban Exhibition Centre.

The procedure provided is for votes to be counted in batches of three thousand. Once the batch tally forms are completed and signed they will be transmitted to the results-control centre at IEC headquarters in Johannesburg. On completion of the counting process at the counting station, a final tally form reflecting all the votes counted at the particular counting station will be filled in, and sent to the results control centre. The control centre will reconcile these results to the final tally form and then input the information into a top-secret program that will add the tallies to the counted votes already received for each party.

Once the results contained on the batch forms have been in-putted and checked in the control centre, the information will be relayed by direct Telkom link to the IEC communications and press centre at Gallagher Estate in Midrand. Gallagher's, as it is known, is a giant and very swish conference centre. The main hall and adjoining meeting rooms have been taken over by the IEC. Desks, computers and banks of phones have been set up for the local and international press. Another area has been set aside for refreshments.

On one wall is a massive display screen on which the names of the political parties are listed in the order in which they appear on the ballot form. As the results are received from the control centre, they are displayed. It is a showcase of technology and so-phistication, an illustration of the abundant resources of the IEC, and hence the country. Showing off a bit, actually.

In Johannesburg, thirty right-wingers are brought to court and charged with nineteen counts of murder and close to two hundred charges of attempted murder. The charges relate to the AWB bomb-ing campaigns over the past few weeks and, specifically, the election week. The press describes a few of the men as 'defiant' and full of bravado. The majority are described as 'scared looking'.

At midday, Judge Kriegler gives a press conference. He calls the three days of voting an outstanding success. Admitting that the IEC's administration had major problems, the judge is frank in his appraisal and also spends time thanking the police and defence force for their assistance in a time of crisis.

Nelson Mandela, interviewed on SABC television, says he is confident that the election will be declared free and fair.

There is much speculation in the media about the results, particularly whether the ANC will get a two-thirds majority. This will enable them to change the interim constitution, should they feel inclined. Despite repeated assurances from the ANC that they will not change the constitution, the tension in the country is palpable as the fears, particularly of whites, feed on rumour and gossip. The country is wound up ahead of the counting process.

In the late afternoon, Imraan Haffagee presents his report on the supply and distribution of voting materials and equipment to the voting stations.

The severe shortage of ballot papers in certain areas had led to rumours of sabotage. In short, the hoarding and stealing of ballot papers, lights and ink were part of a plot to derail the election.

As the two worst-hit areas are the volatile East Rand and KwaZulu and Natal, the conspiracy theory being touted in the media comes down to a grand right-wing plot to convulse the country in war.

Against this background, we asked Haffagee to investigate.

His report is comprehensive and clear. The administration division's plan was to arrange for the distribution of materials from central storage sites to the provincial and sub-provincial storage sites. From these sites they were to be sent to the voting stations.

The plan, Haffagee finds, worked well in many parts of the country, but in others its implementation was poor. In fact, the plan was only disseminated after 16 April. Even then it failed to be passed on to key officials. Simply put, the administration-division people in the provinces needed more warning and knowledge of the plan.

The late notification of the most important link in the electoral chain, the supply and distribution of supplies to voting stations, was compounded, according to Haffagee, by 'a lack of appreciation of the size and difficulty of the task'. This resulted in certain of the more populous areas not being allocated sufficient ballots and other materials. Also, the late appointment of key administration division staff at provincial and sub-provincial levels and a lack of team work in the national office mitigated against the efficient running of the division.

The report finds that 'sufficient quantities of materials were, on the whole, procured by the administration division. Shortages of most items could be attributed to poor distribution rather than insufficient stocks.' The shortage of uv lights was attributed to the late entry of Inkatha into the election, necessitating a large increase in the number of voting stations.

Shortages of ink were attributed to both distribution difficulties and actual shortages. In addition, the ink appeared to have been mishandled.

'But, my God, Imraan,' I burst out, 'this is just such basic stuff. Are you telling me that these are the reasons for the mess?'

He clears his throat in that quiet polite way of his and continues, 'Actually, these are the high-level reasons. It gets worse,' he says, avoiding my eyes. He tells me there were also communication problems between national and provincial administration division offices; convoys were delayed because secure storage sites weren't located in time; and convoys arrived at a number of storage sites to find no administration division staff of appropriate seniority to meet them. In some cases officials were not aware that materials were due to arrive.

Haffagee's report makes recommendations for the next elections.

'To hell with the next election, Imraan,' I say irritably. I am so tired that it is hard to think of the future. 'Who gives a shit about the next election? That is years away and we will all probably be dead by then. I am interested in what went wrong here and who was responsible. What about the East Rand? What happened there?'

He refers me to page seven of his report, which points out that there is an ongoing investigation into the culpability of various individuals. 'Hah,' I say derisively, 'I want that Scholtenmeyer's head. He was in charge of a packed warehouse and he sat there getting pissed.'

'That is one of the cases we are looking into,' says Haffagee, 'but there are more general problems that affected the entire area.' I grunt and read on.

'Administration division officials at provincial and sub-provincial levels with responsibility for procurement, storage and distribution of electoral materials were not sufficiently briefed on their responsibilities. They did not have enough forewarning of the matters dealt with in the [national office plans]. Nor did said plans provide sufficient detailed instruction. This led to some deputy provincial electoral officers and those in the districts failing to fully grasp what was required of them in the distribution chain.'

I fume. 'I would like to fully grasp them around the bloody neck.'

Finally, the report notes 'insufficient experienced warehouse staff to run the ten main warehouses situated within the Witwatersrand'.

'Oh my goodness, what a mess,' I say. 'Why didn't we pick all this up before? Why didn't we see it?'

'There is a simple reason,' says Haffagee, 'and that is that the plans were so secret. The administration division was petrified that if the location of the storage places were known by too many people too far in advance, people would get to those places and destroy the materials.'

'Please, Imraan,' I sigh, 'don't give me that. This thing started with the late siting of voting stations and now it continues with the provisioning.'

'Peter,' he says, 'I am not arguing with you; in fact, I agree.'

'I'm sorry,' I say. I don't want to fight with the messenger. I don't want to fight with anyone, actually.

The next morning I am feeling much better, rested after a good night's sleep. I cuddle up next to Simon, holding him tightly then tickling gently, embracing his wriggling warmth as we giggle. I repeat this with Isabella, then we both pile into Simon's bed. I pretend to be a monster, grabbing at them as they try to escape from the bed. They shriek with laughter and joy at the game, desperate to escape the growling, snuffling, tickling monster that their father has become. They run yelling from the room only to return and throw themselves on the bed, willing captives in a game that I know must end soon. I sneak a glance at my watch. There is just time for a quick breakfast and then a fast drive to be at the IEC before seven, when the counting begins.

In the next room, Luke and Dominic are making a hell of a racket in their cots, writhing to an inaudible beat, disco slugs, as they lie on their backs, outstretched arms frantically clawing the air, heads moving constantly as if on springs. They're using their newly discovered strength and movement.

Caroline sits them up and they grip the wooden bars of their cots, shaking them like furious prisoners. Except, they are wide eyed and smiling, almost conscious of the havoc they are about to create as they warm up for the day. I give them a big kiss, soaking up that soft, fresh baby smell.

In the kitchen, I quickly make eggs and bacon, toast and coffee, a Saturday ritual. Except today there is no time to relax with Caroline and discuss our leisure options. Today is different. It is the count.

I meet with Dong Nguyen, Reg Austen and Michael Maley of the UN for coffee in my office at ten o'clock. We talk about the mountains of ballot boxes, thousands upon thousands of them, at the major counting centres in the cities. They have been 'dumped' there in recent days by polling officers gaga with fatigue. Many of them have not even been signed in. Our monitors for the count, who have been at the counting centres for the last few days, report long queues of polling officials wanting to hand over their ballot boxes as quickly as possible. They also report that the receiving officials have been unable to control the exhausted and often ill-tempered polling officers. To make matters worse, where the number of voters had far outnumbered the number of ballot boxes, officials had made use of a variety of random containers, most of which had no seals.

We had raised our concerns with the administration division about this, as had a number of the commissioners. We had been told that they were instituting emergency measures to sort out the jumble of boxes so that they could be counted in their allocated streams. We also know that counting officers have been working nonstop to sift through the boxes so that when counting began at seven this morning, they were in some kind of order. But it was an impossible task, for the simple reason that the necessary documentation does not exist, and it cannot be created post facto.

Maley, Austen and Nguyen are quick to tell me that the failure to properly receive and document the ballot boxes at the counting centre means that there can be no reconciliation with the batches of votes checked against the originating voting station. Maley is appalled that no reconciliation will be possible.

'Jesus, Peter,' he says, 'this means that there can be no checking where those ballots came from. They could come from anywhere.' His Australian twang lifts at the end of each sentence.

Austen, fresh out of Cambodia, is more cavalier in his approach. 'The real issue, Peter, is whether there is hard evidence of the fraudulent "manufacture" of ballots and the "stuffing" of boxes. If there is evidence of this on a grand scale then you have a problem with no reconciliation taking place. If not ...' he shrugs his shoulders. 'As long as the amount of votes generally reflects the will of the people ... This is not a perfect election, there have been problems. Of course recons are preferable, but they cannot stop this electoral process from coming to a result.'

Nguyen chips in. 'I agree with Reg. This is not an election where the result is going to hang on a few or even a few hundred thousand votes. As long as the votes are counted properly and efficiently tallied and added, the result will be a fair one. And that is all that counts.'

I think, This is where the will of the people bit comes in handy.

Phiroshaw Camay joins us from the ops centre, saying that counting has been delayed at a number of stations because of staff problems.

'Staff problems.' I frown. 'What kind of staff problems, and where?'

'Well, they are not really IEC staff,' he says hesitantly, 'but they want to be. That is the problem.'

Exasperated, I say, 'Please explain'.

'Well, a group of people down in Durban have prevented the count from starting because they want to be employed as counting officials and be paid for it.'

'This is completely ridiculous. They are not trained and cannot now be employed. Call in the police and have them arrested and removed. Shit, every Tom, Dick and Harry wants to stop this election because of money. It's insane. This is not Christmas. It's our first democratic election.'

Durban is not the only place where the count is delayed. At Mount Frere in the Transkei, the political parties are deadlocked about the location, staffing and organisation of the counting station. In Lebowa, the local community objects to the composition of the counting officials, saying that they are biased. Generally, however, the count proceeds and the results flow into the results-counting centre. At first a trickle, then a deluge. We are worried that the top-secret results-control centre will struggle. All okay, Piet Coleyn reports at midday. 'The system is coping.'

Sitting in my office on Saturday, 30 April 1994, I have to give the administration division due credit: the system seems to be working and the feed of results to the supersonic media centre at Gallagher Estate is steady and consistent. The media, hyped by some of the voting problems, calms down. The ANC takes an early lead, with the smaller parties not doing too badly, because many of the early results come from the urban areas where they have reasonable support.

In the late afternoon, I hear reports that the results-control centre is struggling to cope with the traffic volume. Piet Coleyn, his skin almost grey, puffs on one of his interminable cigarettes. 'You okay, Piet?' I ask.

'No,' he says, 'we have problems in the centre, the systems are not coping.'

'But, Piet, five hours ago, things were working. What has happened?

'It is simple, Peter. A lot of the smaller counting stations have now finished and they are sending in their results. There are just too many and we do not have enough facilities to receive them. I don't know how long we can keep going.'

'Keep going, Piet?' I have to control my voice. 'Keep going before what?'

'Before everything crashes,' he replies dully.

'You must be joking,' I say weakly, struggling for breath.

He merely shakes his head slowly from side to side with the look of a man who has come to the end of his tether.

'Look, Piet, I know you don't like help and you are the election expert, not me, but we have people in the monitoring division who have run a lot of elections. People from the UN and the European Union. They know what they're doing. Just let them come in and assess how your systems are working. Who knows, they may be able to suggest something. Perhaps fix it. You can't lose anything, Piet.'

I suggest Fred Hayward from the UN puts together a small team that can report to both of us.

Coleyn agrees.

In the early evening, the commission issues the wise and practical instruction to all counting stations that 'where reconciliation would inordinately delay the commencement of the count, counting officers were to note all objections and deficiencies, but proceed with the counting process …'

The reason this is both wise and practical is that if the law were strictly observed, the count would not be able to take place at certain of the major counting centres in the big cities. This would result in hundreds of thousands, if not millions, of voters being disenfranchised through no fault of their own. Such an eventuality would be both unwelcome and unfair, not to put too fine a point on it.

It is about eight o'clock at night when we call Fred Hayward to a meeting in the monitoring division's boardroom. Hayward is one of those electoral experts who lives and breathes elections. Clean cut and clear eyed, he is a man who takes his craft seriously.

'Look, Fred, there have been some developments with the count,' I say. Silence as those around the table look at me cynically. 'Developments' is probably not the way they would have put it.

'Piet Coleyn recognises that they have real problems in the results-control centre and that they are battling to cope with the volumes. He has authorised a small team headed by you to go in and conduct an assessment. Fred, this review must examine the functioning of the centre from a risk perspective and make recommendations on how it can be improved. We have to prevent a systems breakdown. If they are in trouble, we must help as much as we can. I will speak to the judge and get clearance for this before we go in.'

'Finally, they are letting someone see their super-secure system. Isn't it a little late with the election on its knees?' says a head of department sarcastically.

'It's never too late,' I respond sharply.

Hayward says, 'When do you need the report?'

Tomorrow morning six o'clock, I tell him.

He nods, almost eagerly. I like that, a man who looks forward to working through the night.

The phone call from Fred Hayward comes in the early hours of the morning. I am so tired that the luminous hands of the clock next to my bed are a blur and I can't see the time. I am nervous. I desperately want to know what he has found, but I do not want him to give me the details over the telephone. I tell him I have a meeting with Zac Yacoob and Ben van der Ross at seven. We can discuss his report then. In a calm voice, almost flat, he says, 'I think you should postpone the meeting, you need to hear this first. We have a real problem.'

CHAPTER THIRTEEN

I am in my office sipping bitter coffee and watching the sun rise, once again, as I wait for Fred Hayward and his team to arrive. My cigarette tastes sweet and good with the strong coffee, as a Camel Plain should at this time of the morning.

It is Sunday, 1 May 1994.

I'm beginning to hate watching the sunrise. I have seen too many in the last few months and I don't mind if I never see another one.

Hayward is a taciturn fellow – this must be serious if he thought it necessary to phone me in the early hours of the morning. I wonder how many more crises the IEC can take. How many more the country can take.

Hayward tells it quickly. I prefer it that way. In his typically methodical way, he has spent the night identifying not only the problems, but also the solutions. I focus on the problems as I listen.

The officials running the record-control centre admitted that the centre 'was not fully prepared to receive and enter results from all the counting stations. No record of confirmations (of results) was being kept on the computers.'

The confirmation record identified which voting stations and counting centres had sent through their results. Without it, we had a final tally of results but would not know which counting centres had sent in their results.

Hayward found that there was no mechanism for differentiating batch totals (sub-totals) from the final tally. Also, some counting streams had been given identical numbers; consequently, distinguishing one total from another was difficult or impossible. To make matters worse, counting-station results were disappearing in the control centre and between the counting stations and IEC headquarters.

He also discovered that the results-control centre did not have enough fax machines and computers for capturing, verifying, and tallying election results.

'Surely that is enough, Fred. Hell, man,' I protest at this litany.

He continues in a torrent. 'I have also found that there is an inability to easily add counting streams set up late in the process, confusion of spoilt ballots with total number of people voting and failure to provide an easy mechanism for determining missing data [i.e. counting stations which have not reported].'

He reckons that the administration division has not anticipated the volume of results. Although the monitoring division has mentioned the problem to the results-control-centre planners and offered additional overflow fax capacity, our offers were turned down. Hayward concludes, 'Many of these problems would have been discovered if a dry run had been undertaken.'

'Nice,' I say. 'Thanks for being so diplomatic. Why don't you just say that we can't be in more shit than we currently are?'

'I thought I would leave you to tell the commission that,' says Hayward.

The meeting with the available commissioners and the judge is short. They accept the findings in the report and instruct the monitoring division to implement the recommendations and solutions set out in Hayward's report.

I leave the meeting in need of more coffee and a Camel.

Yet another task team is pulled together at short notice. We appoint Phiroshaw Camay to run it with the close assistance of Fred Hayward and others. If we have any more task teams, I think, we will need a task team to appoint a task team. The odd thing is that the task teams, as in most organisations in a state of crisis, all seem to consist of the same people. But that's task teams.

The results-control-centre task team immediately focuses on some of the activities which will bring quick relief. Extra staff are shifted into the control centre and additional material resources, like faxes, are immediately bought and connected. While part of the team addresses the material issues, others address the processes that are contributing to the breakdowns.

By midday, a 'revised plan for counting' as well as a priority list for the revised count is implemented. This instructs all counting stations to stop counting batch totals and focus only on final tallies.

Hayward's report recommends that the best way to sort out the confirmed versus unconfirmed results is to set up an alternative computing system which will record confirmed reports. It will also provide printed updates of unconfirmed and confirmed results. We set this up in a separate confirmation centre. Here the confirmed reports from counting officers and counting stations will be received. The centre will also confirm results by a variety of mechanisms, including radios and telephones.

In spite of all the new measures, we still fear further breakdowns. A backup is needed: a system to verify that the numbers that the results-control centre inputs into their computer program are checked and confirmed in terms of their totals. This will ensure that the results on the tally sheets are correctly allocated to the political parties. And, importantly, that they are correctly added up.

If this is done and the counts of the results-control centre and the monitoring verification centre match, we will be sure that there has been no interference or manipulation of the count. Establishing a manual verification process to run behind the electronic count becomes the responsibility of Fred Hayward, Eddie Hendrickx and Phiroshaw Camay.

In essence, we will receive the tally sheets that have been faxed in to the results-control centre and we will manually record and input them into a stand-alone set of computers. We want to check the results-control centre's results and ensure their integrity. It is there to keep them honest, just in case.

Results flow in throughout Sunday and Monday. The instruction to the counting centres to only send through final tallies has removed much of the confusion and made the job of the counting officers simpler. The additional fax machines have unblocked the logjam and a team moves regularly along the long row of clicking machines uplifting results, noting them and delivering them to the technicians responsible for entering the data on the banks of computers in the results-control centre.

The confirmation centre is slowly piecing together the jigsaw of confirmed results and, where confirmation has not been received, they use alternative checking methods.

Things appear to be going smoothly. There is a steady stream of results from the counting stations. The situation in the counting stations is approaching a state of order. The senior people in the administration division are looking more cheerful. Norman du Plessis is now playing a key role in the running of the administration division. He's a stocky, jovial man, with a cigarette permanently between his lips. A hundred-a-day man. In my view, he is one of the few excellent electoral technicians in that division. If there had been more Normans we would probably have avoided many of the catastrophes. Then again, organising an election in three months was a bridge too far from the start.

At the main counting centre in Durban, a major row between the ANC and Inkatha has developed. Counting stops. The dispute is sparked by the arrival of dozens of ballot boxes, all of which contain neatly piled stacks of votes. They are all folded in exactly the same manner. In electoral terms, this is called 'stacking'.

These boxes come from areas that are Inkatha dominated and controlled. The ANC objected. These votes are clearly fraudulent. Consequently, the boxes have been set aside in a large pile in one corner of the counting centre. Inkatha has taken great exception, and the counting has stalled. The stakes are not small. There are many votes at risk and neither of the parties will budge. Inkatha threatens to pull out of the election if the votes are excluded.

By the time Charles Nupen arrives to mediate, the parties are not speaking to one another. Nupen gets them talking, but there is no resolution. The mediation is interrupted by the arrival of Pravin

Gordhan, a senior leader of the ANC in the province and nationally. Gordhan, a highly respected political activist and leader, was also one of the convenors of the multi-party negotiating forum.

Gordhan consults alone with the ANC representatives. Fifteen minutes later, he instructs that the disputed boxes can be included. 'Let them in,' he says. 'They can be counted.'

Nupen is flabbergasted, as are the counting officials. They stare at Gordhan. 'Let them in,' he says again. With that he leaves.

It is an extraordinary strategic intervention by Gordhan, which allows the count to continue in circumstances where many would have been happy to see it stall and fail, thereby discounting the election in the province.

At about midday on Monday, I hear a roar from a crowd in the street outside the IEC. They appear to be mostly young people, shouting and waving placards. These people are polling-station workers who were paid during the election days but now feel they deserve a bonus. When their initial demands at their local and regional IEC offices met with no success, they marched on IEC head office.

Renosi Mokate, the CEO of the IEC, quickly arranges a meeting of a few commissioners, who refuse to accede to the demands. Dikgang Moseneke, whose reputation in this messy area has grown considerably since his success in facing down the Durban crowd, is assigned the thankless task of conveying this information.

Suave and impeccably dressed, as ever, in a crisp, dark-blue shirt, Moseneke stands before the angry and vociferous crowd. He is accompanied by security personnel, whom he instructs to stand back a few metres. Alone, he engages with the leadership. The encounter is angry and brief as Moseneke sharply tells the polling officials that they will be paid for the work they have done, but nothing more.

'But, comrade, you are being insensitive,' he is told.

Moseneke replies that they are wasting their time. With the crowd now silent, he strides back into the IEC building. As he enters the doors, there is a roar of anger, and the crowd try to storm the building. The security detail at the front door, which includes troops, take up defensive positions. This stops the mob, which, after a while, disperses.

I return to work, as do the other viewers who have watched the incident from the safety of the upper floors.

Unfortunately, the incident is not over. An hour later Moseneke drives his sleek new black BMW out of the underground parking into a side street. He is headed for a meeting in Pretoria. About twenty disgruntled individuals are waiting for him. They empty refuse bins on his car, and attempt to shatter the windows. Moseneke puts his foot flat and speeds away, chased by a furious mob hurling bottles and cans. It is a close call and a reminder that this process can turn very ugly very quickly. And these are our own employees.

The verification centre is in a long rectangular office next to the ops centre. The tally sheets are brought up in bundles from the results-control centre below, signed for, logged and then sorted into ordered piles for entry into the closed computer system. It is methodical work. Because the manual count is progressing slowly, we commission more computers and operators. As laborious as the process is, it is vital. We need to confirm the electronic count being conducted downstairs. We're two days behind them.

The press appears to have accepted that we have got through the worst and are reporting a successful election.

I hear from a senior journalist that on late Saturday afternoon, the influential *Sunday Times* had two front pages. The one detailed all the election's failures and was extremely negative of the whole process. The other hailed the election as a triumph, a victory for democracy. Only at the last minute did the editorial committee go with the story of triumph. I am glad they did.

The results feed to Gallagher Estate is also working well. Some of the commissioners even have time to drive to the plush conference complex and pump the flesh of the media. Everyone is assured that all is well and that the count should be complete in the next day or so.

Around the country, the political focus shifts to the inauguration of the new president, scheduled for Tuesday, 10 May 1994 at the Union Buildings in Pretoria. There is no doubt anywhere in the nation that the ANC will win and that the country's new president will be Nelson Mandela. The only issue is by how much the ANC will win.

In the monitoring division, we are slowly relaxing. Incidents of violence have reduced drastically as the voting results are made public. Of course, there remains pressure to finish the count as quickly as possible. For one thing, the parties want to know how many seats they will have in parliament.

The commission has made the seat allocation the responsibility of Jorgen Elklitt from Denmark. He is one of the world's experts in this highly complex area. After the results and seats have been annou nced, parliament will be convened so that the president and other office bearers can be elected. The inauguration is, after all, only seven days away. And this is not an event that can be moved. The invitations have been sent to heads of state and other dignitaries. The time frames have no margin for error, given that we are now in the late afternoon of Monday, 2 May 1994.

It is tight. But we estimate that just on two thirds of the votes have been counted, so we should meet the deadline. All the systems are working, not necessarily free of problems or stress, but they are working. The crash in the results-control centre that we had dreaded has been avoided. Everyone has a spring in their step. This renewed energy is valuable, especially in the ops centre, which has been working twenty-four hours a day for the last seven days. Most of the personnel there have reached the point where their ten-thousand-yard stare has telescoped to a much greater distance. But they do the work.

I go home early. It is a while since I've been home before my children have gone to bed. Luke and Dominic are asleep early;

Simon and Isabella will be in bed by about seven thirty. If I hurry, I should be able to make it. I leave the team in the ops centre ticking over. They've ordered pizzas for dinner, preparing for the long night-shift ahead. We are almost there.

CHAPTER FOURTEEN

It is Tuesday, 3 May 1994.

It is a beautiful day.

I have slept well.

While I'm breakfasting with Caroline and the children, my bleeper goes.

The message reads: 'You need to get here now. We have a real problem. Michael Yard has found something.'

I no longer want my breakfast.

I leave the table with a sick feeling in my stomach. I phone the ops centre.

'What is the problem?'

'It is in the results-control centre. This cannot be discussed over the phone.'

Stillness descends on me. My blood has become ice as my heart pounds, leaving me strangely breathless.

I rush out of the house.

On the drive into town, the dread keeps me staring straight ahead, trying not to speculate. But I can't help it. Has the results-control centre crashed inexplicably? Have our worst fears come to pass?

I park in the basement and take the lift to the ground floor, and then another to the secure floor of the ops centre. Fred Hayward is waiting for me.

We enter my office, he closes the door.

'Someone has hacked into the counting program in the records-control centre,' he says. 'It has been compromised.'

'With what result?'

'The votes of three of the political parties have been multiplied.'

'My God, by how much?' I am trying to remain calm, avoiding the terrifying and unspeakable thought that if the count is compromised, there is no election. It will have to be run again.

'We don't know yet, but at least by a couple of per cent for each of the three parties. It could even be by as much as ten per cent of the national vote. We will have to run a detailed check. We are pulling everyone in.'

I let this sink in.

'Which parties have had their votes multiplied?' I already know what he's going to answer.

'The Freedom Front, the National Party and the Inkatha Freedom Party.'

I am partly right. I had thought that it might be all of the main opposition parties, any party that would reduce the votes of the ANC. The objective is clear: the changes will not stop an ANC victory but will ensure that the ANC are well below the two-thirds majority that would give them the power to change the constitution.

'Has someone told the judge?' I ask.

'Yes,' says Hayward, 'he has been told. He is upstairs in his office now.'

'One thing: can this system continue to operate or is it totally compromised?'

'You don't understand, Pete. The whole system has been hacked into. It is not just compromised. It is finished. The person who did this might do it again once it is found out that we know. The person who has done this has got in. He has the keys to the kingdom. We don't know who this person is. It could be anyone, anywhere. It could be one of the staff who originally worked on the program and installed it. It could be one of the staff who currently works on those computers every day in that secure room. It could be a senior person or a junior. It could be anyone. It could be a group. It could be someone sitting in Bangkok.'

'I should be sitting in Bangkok right now. When did the hacker go in?'

'Early this morning. We don't know the precise time yet but we think between five and six. We're working on it. Neil Cawse, an expert checking the system for fraud, ran a report which reflected a big increase in the total number of votes counted.'

We're stuffed, I think without saying it. This is the end. Things could not possibly be worse. This is enough to halt the electoral process. It is our nightmare.

I make my way with Phiroshaw Camay to Judge Kriegler's office. He is waiting for us.

Kriegler is sitting at his round table wearing a white neck-brace. He turns to me in that stiff robotic way that the brace compels. His hands shake more than normal. He uses both hands to hold his cup of coffee. His voice cracks as he speaks.

I tell him I need more time to get a full report but that the preliminary advice is that the electronic count has been irrevocably compromised. The counting has to be immediately stopped and the counting system in the results-control centre shut down.

I tell him this and he nods, fixated on his coffee, his face grey. 'Is that what you are saying? Close it down?'

'We don't think you have a choice. The system has been hacked into. There has been a fraud,' says Camay.

Kriegler stares silently at him.

'I will have to call a meeting of the full commission. This is a big decision.'

'Judge, you understand that if the results-control centre is closed down the flow of results to the country will stop. That will have massive consequences. People will think that the election has been stopped or hijacked because the ANC is winning. I must tell you that there could be very serious unrest. I mean, we have to take the country into our confidence here. How you break this to the media is critical.'

'I know,' he says. 'We will discuss that in the meeting. Will you both be there? We need to know how this can be taken forward and I want a full report on the fraud from you.'

I leave his room thinking that the election cannot be invalidated. We cannot go back.

Phiroshaw Camay and I stop in at the ops centre to talk to Eddie Hendrickx. The talk in the room stops abruptly as we walk in. There is a pathetic sadness on their faces. The same dejection that I feel but try not to show, that it may all have been for nothing. The despair seems everywhere: a disease that kills hope and crushes the spirit.

In the verification centre I tell Hendrickx that it's almost certain that the commission will close down the results-control centre and stop the electronic count.

'They don't have a choice, the system is fucked,' says Camay bluntly. I have known him for some time, through good days and bad, but mostly bad, and I have never known him to swear. Not even in the worst days of the Peace Accord and the violence on the East Rand, not with an Inkatha impi bearing down on him and bodies on the ground have I seen him panic. Some people just don't panic. I have now heard him swear for the first time. Aside from that he is composed, and I wonder if I can keep my own.

'Can the verification centre take over the count and run it on a manual basis as we have been doing?' I ask them.

'I think we can do that,' Camay says, nodding slowly, speaking in that measured way he has. 'It will be difficult, but I think we can do it. You know we are running a few days behind the electronic count so it will take us a while to catch up. This is a hell of a thing, Pete.'

'A hell of a thing,' I say. 'A hell of a thing. That someone has hacked into the national electronic count and cooked the results beyond recognition, yup, that is one hell of a fucking thing.'

Hendrickx smiles. It is a thin one.

'I think you'd better prepare your staff to take over the count.'

The meeting with Fred Hayward in my office is short. I tell him that our top internal experts and independent external experts are to conduct a forensic audit of the fraud. And it has to be done today. It cannot wait. These people must be prepared to work through the night. I need their report by eight o'clock the next day.

A few hours later the investigation team has been drawn up. It consists of six people. Two are from the IEC, with one being familiar with the administration division's IT system. The third expert from the IEC, Fiona Menzies, is an independent consultant with no previous contact with the IT system. The fourth person is Michael Yard, who has been seconded to the IEC from the International Foundation for Electoral Systems in Washington DC. The remaining members are IT experts from a government department in Pretoria, with no previous contact with the IEC.

They are instructed to maintain an event-and-action log throughout the investigation and keep all data samples with original paper records. The team is given a detailed briefing on their mandate. It is stressed that their investigation is a matter of national security and any breach of confidentiality will be prosecuted.

The investigation is scheduled to commence at 10 o'clock.

The commission meets later in the day and halts the electronic count. The results-control centre is secured and sealed. Only Hayward's investigators will have access to it. At that moment the results feed to Gallagher Estate stops, the big fancy electronic screens go blank. The commissioners know it will be two days before we can catch up.

I leave them to digest the indigestible.

They have to tell the political parties and the public. I feel sorry for the judge; this news will be difficult to divulge, and even harder to swallow, particularly in this hungry country.

Now that the verification centre is taking over the count, we need to ensure that the system is totally secure. In the words of Eddie Hendrickx, 'Once the hacker or saboteurs know that the results-control centre has been closed down and the count moved to a new centre, they will come after it. It will be the new target.'

Hayward adds, 'You must remember that whoever did this was working on the premise that this single act would stop or derail the count and the election, which is exactly what it has done. In that respect, the hacker or hackers have been successful and achieved the objective. But the one thing they did not take account of is the verification system and that it would be capable of taking over the count.'

I realise we will need twenty-four hour protection. Once the information is public, we will be a target. The new counting area is moved to a space outside my office. Arrangements are made with the army to guard all access points. We are taking no chances. The stakes are so high that I break into a sweat every time my thoughts flit in the direction of this new count also being compromised.

The move to the new area takes just over an hour. As always, IT is exceptional and by two o'clock we have a blocked-off set of computers for inputting the results. The only difference is that their numbers have doubled.

Eddie Hendrickx, Phiroshaw Camay, Fred Hayward and I meet to plan the workflow. A roster system of continuous shifts is devised that will run for the next few days until the count is complete. Additional data capturers are obtained and briefed. In essence, they are told that they are no longer conducting a check on the count, they are conducting the count. If they fail, there is no count and no election.

I see determination on the faces of the programmers as they listen to the briefing. They are a mixture of old and young, some of them student volunteers from the local universities. As I look at them, I see a microcosm of this new country that will be born if this count can be made. They are African, white, Indian and coloured. When they talk after the briefing it is in the languages of this country, African, Afrikaans and English, with all of the wonderful accents of their rich cultures. Each one of them has gone through a strict vetting process. In the verification centre they have already proven themselves trustworthy and resilient.

Even so, we are taking no chances. We get experienced external auditors to stand behind each data capturer as they input the results.

The auditors on each shift rotate to eliminate any chance of collusion. A strict no-talking rule applies, unless a mistake is noticed.

The commission decides to relay the bad news to State President FW de Klerk and Nelson Mandela. They need to be told about the fraud and what is being done to rectify the situation. After that they face the Transitional Executive Council and the key political parties. Then a press conference.

I am (thankfully) not part of the Mandela and De Klerk briefings; however, I hear later that while they were profoundly irritated, they were philosophical and mature in their response. In truth, they had no choice. Both men quickly realised that this was not about the gaining of political advantage, it was about the survival of the entire country.

Each face a major question: can they control their supporters?

The real issue is how the country and the world will react when the results to Gallagher Estate suddenly stop dead. I suspect that the first reaction will be incredulity, then anger as people leap to the conclusion that there has been a fraud, that the election has been stolen.

There is a good chance that people will react badly. A good chance of renewed violence. Having gone through the aftermath of the Chris Hani assassination, I know how easy it is for violence to spread.

Judge Kriegler's press conference is his toughest to date, which is saying something. He needs to explain the blackout, but he also can't release too much information. To reveal that there is a hacker in the system would be to cast doubts on the entire process, which could lead to panic and violence. He has a difficult line to tread.

He manages. He admits problems with the count. He says it has been 'penetrated' but leaves it at that. 'Penetrated,' I think. Well, that is one way of putting it. A journalist at the back of the hall loudly uses a different word. This lack of information creates a problem in that, as we all know, journalists do not like to be kept guessing. So, they take it out on the poor judge, again. Like a bulldog with his big white collar of a neck brace, he stands his ground, refusing to divulge anything more. They go for him. It's not pretty, but then not many dogfights are.

Outside my office, there is a low hum as the teams working on the new count get into their stride.

We have dispatched Vuyo Ntshona and Alan Brews to the big counting centre at Nasrec to help the exhausted officials, some of whom have not slept in days. They attempt to bring some kind of order to the counting. Tempers run short as frustrated party agents and observers overstep the mark by attempting to get involved in the process.

As the day draws on, the smaller and medium-sized counting stations wrap up their counting. We receive their tally sheets by fax and sometimes as wads of paper delivered under police escort.

In the provinces where the counting is virtually complete, it is clear that the voter turnout has been extraordinary. Based on the estimated electorate in each province, there was a turnout of eighty-seven per cent in the Western Cape, eighty-three per cent in the Orange Free State, the Eastern Transvaal was eighty-five per cent, the Northern Cape ninety-two per cent, Northern Transvaal eighty-four per cent. Although the results are still coming in from the Eastern Cape, it is estimated that the turnout there was more than ninety per cent. In the PWV, also still counting, the turnout was well over eighty per cent, while in Natal it was eighty per cent in a count that is ongoing.

Given the country's exceptionally low literacy and educational levels, electoral experts estimated there would be high numbers of spoilt ballots, as high as ten per cent. They believed this might even influence the results for some parties. With over two thirds of the count completed, the rate of spoilt ballots stands at less than one per cent. Personally, I'm not surprised at the low number of spoilt ballots. The ballot paper was designed to overcome such issues. In short, people didn't need to read. They just had to know what they wanted.

As nightfall approaches, the teams outside my office grind on. The data capturers are relieved every few hours, as are the auditors. We take it hour by hour, sheet by sheet. Although the piles of tally sheets appear not to have been reduced, I can see from the numbers on the screens and from reports from the auditors that with every hour, we are gaining on that fixed point where the electronic count stopped.

On the night of 3 May, I sleep in my office. Phiroshaw Camay sleeps on a small bed that he has set up in an office next to the new count-and-ops centre. In fact, we don't sleep.

CHAPTER FIFTEEN

I meet with Michael Yard of the forensic investigation team in my office at eight o'clock on Wednesday morning, 4 May 1994. He is exhausted, his eyes bloodshot and outlined by thick black lines of fatigue.

He hands me a two-page report.

'Is that it?' I ask.

'That's all you need,' he replies, an unhealthy rasp in his voice. 'I'll talk you through it.'

I pour him some coffee and we sit at the small conference table, the sounds of early traffic filtering through the sealed windows as the city splutters into life.

'The hacker went in between 05:56 and 06:41 on the morning of 3 May and made changes to the vote count of three parties. Neil Cawse picked up early that morning that there was a significant increase in the number of total votes counted nationwide [in the order of one to four million].'

I nod dully to show that I am listening, but it is an unwilling comprehension as I listen to him telling me how the electronic count has been tampered with and altered.

'Shit,' I says at one point, 'surely this couldn't have been easy to do. I mean, the administration division told us that this was an incredibly sophisticated system, foolproof, the Fort Knox of systems, completely impregnable. You can't just get into a highly protected IT network and change national election results.' There's an unnatural whine to my voice.

He goes on: 'The total votes for all parties at each counting station was also changed, but doesn't match the sum of the vote totals for individual parties after the changes to these figures were made. The new total for all parties per counting station is in between the original correct figure and the sum of the votes per party for the counting station after the changes. So the program was doctored to increase the votes of the three parties by about point thirty-three per cent.'

'So what were the changed results? Hell, I can't believe that we are in such kak.'

Deadpan, he looks at me and says, 'The changes upward are between two point five per cent and four per cent for the Freedom Front, approximately three per cent for the National Party and between four and five per cent for the Inkatha Freedom Party.'

There it is. Silence. I break it. 'You and the team are sure of the extent of these changes?'

'Oh, absolutely. These were consistent across our data sample and there are always increases to the vote count.'

It is worse than I thought.

Solveigh Piper joins us in my office. I give her the report. She shakes her head, pursing her lips. 'This is history, it is already past,' she says. 'We are fixing this. We have no choice but to go on and make it happen. We will get to an honest result.'

No one speaks for a while as we sit there. I can hear the data capturers working away.

I turn to Michael Yard. 'Can you find out who did this?'

He points me to the report. 'The NT file server on the network is capable of generating a log of who logged onto or out from the network, and the time that this happened. We checked this log and found that this information is only recorded from 18:10 on 3 May. From this we conclude that this logging process was either cleaned out as of this time, or was only turned on at that time.'

'Nice … very nice,' I say, bitterly. 'So we can't trace who did this. It is a successful "hit and run". Surely we must be able to find who did this?'

Again, Yard gestures to the report, which simply states: 'No logs or other audit trails were found that could help in isolating the cause or source of the problem.'

I need to get this report to Kriegler and the commission.

As I walk out the door, Yard says, 'You know, Peter, this hacker did quite an incredible job. I mean this is damn clever stuff. One hell of a job,' he says, the admiration in his voice unmistakeable.

'Thanks for your and your team's hard work, Michael,' I respond, 'but do me a favour, leave out the compliments for the hacker. This is not the time for professional envy.'

He smiles ruefully.

The judge doesn't take it well.

After relaying the report of the forensic investigation to Judge Kriegler, I hold a meeting with the intelligence heads. This is a time when we need the security situation to be firmly under control. There is a real concern that with every hour that the country does not receive election results, the potential for violence increases. This stress is not helped by reports from the ops centre that there have been violent incidents on the East Rand and also in KwaZulu and Natal.

Through Caroline, I hear that news crews believe the election has been sabotaged and will have to be held again. There are also rumours that the right wing, with the support of the military, has staged a coup and will soon make an announcement. Another story claims the government has stopped the election and will declare martial law. Yet another buzz has it that the IEC has messed up the count and another election will be held in eight months' time. Like the violence, the speculation mounts.

As with many rumours there is a kernel of truth to some of the stories. The problem is, we know this because we are on the inside. But the general public doesn't know what to believe. Newspapers report that after the announcement that counting had stopped, there was a rush on goods in foodstuffs in some areas. In a number of rural areas, farmers cluster in groups for security, fearing that black militias will drive them off their land. Swart gevaar stories abound. The frozen election results place the country in limbo. Fear feeds on fear and the political mercury rises.

The spooks tell us that security forces have been placed on

high alert. Moema reports increasing tension in the townships and that while leaders are appealing for calm, groups of people, mostly youths, are gathering and asking why the election has been stopped. Even though they have been given the reason, they do not believe it. The gatherings are being monitored from a distance, our police liaison tells us.

After discussion, Moema is asked to get ANC organisers to these nascent assemblies. They need to be addressed and defused before they become unmanageable. It is up to the political parties to control their supporters.

At midday, a friend calls from London to ask why the election has been stopped. Short of sleep and desperate with worry, I swear at him unreasonably. What does he mean by saying that the election has been 'stopped'?

'Well, that is the word on the block here,' he says. 'It is believed that the count has been sabotaged and that the election has been stopped and will have to be held again. Some journalists are saying privately that the IEC and the political parties are too scared to announce it because they know the place will blow.'

Feeling about to explode myself, I say, 'That is complete horseshit. There has been a problem with the count and the results are delayed. But this election is definitely not cancelled, so tell the people on the block that.'

I put down the phone and walk out to the counting team saying, 'No pressure folks, but the whole world and a lot of this country do not believe that we can complete this election. We are going to prove them wrong. How are we doing?'

Data capturers and auditors turn as one and say, 'Fine.' But they say it in that pointed way which makes me even more worried. Although the piles of final tally sheets do appear to have shrunk significantly.

I head upstairs to brief the judge and find Cyril Ramaphosa waiting outside his office. He too looks gaunt and stressed. He says the ANC has everyone in the field trying to calm the situation.

He asks when the results will flow to Gallagher Estate again. Sometime tonight, I reply, with more hope than I feel. He looks at me, shakes his head. 'I hope we can hold it.'

Later that afternoon, on another report-back to Kriegler, I find Roelf Meyer waiting outside his office. My discussion with him is similar to my earlier one with Ramaphosa.

The judge, feeling the pressure, asks me with an edge in his voice if there is anything that can be done to help speed up the count.

I tell him that we have to get this one right. Which translates as, No, we can't speed it up. 'If this count fails, Judge,' I say, 'there is no backup count. This is it.' He looks at me and nods.

Back downstairs I find security and the two armed soldiers manning the door against a small group of men. They introduce themselves as representatives of political parties. 'Which ones?' I ask. They tell me. They belong to a smattering of the smaller parties. They want to see the counting process. They do not believe it is happening.

'What, you think this whole thing is a con, a charade?' I burst out.

Yes, they respond. The entire process is being rigged and hijacked by the ANC and National Party and they are the ones giving the IEC orders.

'Gentlemen,' I say, 'I can promise you that there is a count being conducted, right outside my office, in fact. But for security reasons I cannot show it to you or any other political party. This is not a smoke-and-mirrors show. I can also assure you that the connection to Gallagher Estate will, in all likelihood, be resumed tonight, although I cannot give you an exact time. Hopefully the count will be concluded soon after that.'

There is animated discussion. I suggest that if they have any further problems they raise these with the judge. If they do, he will not be happy to know I referred them.

On television is another interminable panel of election experts giving their expert views on some specific area. Actually, I feel some sympathy for them. They are doing their job, one which has been made harder by the work of the hacker. Their schedules have gone for a burton, their analysts are repeating themselves.

Unfortunately, some of these analysts add to the mounting public hysteria. They have it on good authority that a deal is being done between the political parties on the election results. I think a deal would be a good idea. We could then stop the counting and go home to sleep. But in the real world there is no deal, not even talk of a deal. So the count goes on and the incidents of violence increase.

By late afternoon, there are marches on the various provincial IECs. Rumours abound of cars and buildings in flames. Information is relayed to the political parties, who quickly react, dispatching ANC leaders to potential flashpoints, calling meetings, addressing crowds.

Jay Naidoo uses the extensive communications machinery of Cosatu, sending shop stewards from workplaces all over the country into the hotspots to appeal for calm.

In the ops centre, we have a sense that the fabric is slowly but irrevocably tearing.

An emergency meeting of the interparty security committee is held in the early evening. Sitting there is an old adversary of many years, Adriaan Vlok. He is, as always, friendly, showing the forced affability of a man who has transgressed and is about to cede power to his former victims. 'Will the security forces be able to hold the line?' I ask him.

'Peter,' he says, 'we will do our best, you can rely on us.'

I shouldn't have asked, I think to myself.

Phiroshaw Camay never seems to take a break. Eddie the Belgian and Fred Hayward are constantly reconciling tally sheets or quietly directing the auditors.

Camay and Hayward conduct spot checks on the final tally sheets. On one occasion, scanning a recent tally sheet torn from a fax machine, Camay laughs out loud. It is from a small town in northern KwaZulu and the overwhelming majority of votes are for the IFP.

'I know this town and area,' he says. 'There is no ways that it has that number of voters. These figures are definitely padded, hugely.' He picks up the phone, dials the number on the tally sheet and asks to speak to the person in charge of the count. A woman is called to the phone. He asks her a number of questions and soon realises that something is wrong. He tells her to answer yes or no. Then asks if there are people standing next to her. She says yes. Have they threatened you? She says yes. He tells her not to worry and puts down the phone. He instructs the auditors to put the tally sheet into the 'contested results' pile for further checking before it is counted. Instructions are given via the ops centre for security forces to get to the counting station and to secure it.

In fact, each counting station should have been properly secured by either police or soldiers. However, due to the late entry of Inkatha there are a number voting stations that have little or no security. Another serious problem is that some voting stations in KwaZulu and Natal have been illegally set up by Inkatha, and these certainly have no security. We call them pirate stations.

The count is moving fast now. I light a cigarette in celebration as Eddie Hendrickx tells me that we have passed the point where the electronic count was frozen. We have agreed to move significantly beyond this figure before we switch on the feed to Gallagher Estate. Hendrickx estimates that to be in about three hours.

We have reached a turning point. Walking out of my office into the counting area, I feel a new energy. Can the country hold on?

I rush upstairs to tell the judge. Both Cyril Ramaphosa and Roelf Meyer are waiting to speak to him. They are there to lodge complaints about irregularities in certain provinces. The ANC feels the national and provincial elections in KwaZulu and Natal have not been conducted freely and fairly. Pirate stations and biased presiding officers head their complaints. There are also allegations against Inkatha for the forced removal of IEC and ANC polling monitors from voting stations, the issuing of voting cards on a widespread basis to children under the age of eighteen, and the 'stacking' of ballot boxes.

On the other hand, there are allegations of the ANC having illegal voting stations in the Transkei as well as polling officials biased in their favour in parts of the Eastern Cape. These are not the only objections, but they are among the most serious. Both the Democratic Party as well as the National Party threaten litigation to stop the IEC from proceeding with the count and also from announcing the results. The African Moderates Congress Party lodges an objection challenging the election on the grounds of the poor distribution of voting materials and the alleged illegal issuing of temporary voting cards. And there are more. Fortunately, dealing with these complaints is the responsibility of the commission. Teams of investigators are sent out.

Downstairs in the counting centre, we keep focused. Our eyes are on the total number of votes counted, which now seems to be moving at speed. Again, I trek upstairs to tell the judge that in a few hours we should be able to reconnect. He looks at me with a distinct 'no incidents' kind of look.

Two hours later Phiroshaw Camay steps into my office. 'Pete, I think we are far enough.'

At Gallagher Estate, there are few journalists as no news has been released here for some days now. Those that are there notice some activity and then the black screen flickers and lights up. They stare at the board, puzzled. Suddenly the black spaces click over, revealing first the names of the parties and then their votes. There is a cheer. The flow of results becomes a stream.

It is past midnight when I get home. Everyone is asleep. I move quietly from room to room, checking the still forms of my family, finally stopping in Luke and Dominic's room. I sit in the small armchair between them, the darkness and quiet cloaking me as I watch their tiny silhouettes in the two cots. Their gentle breathing is in tune, regular and rhythmic, as they breathe in the air of this new country.

EPILOGUE

The count is concluded on the afternoon of Thursday, 5 May 1994 and the verification centre finally shuts down. With the confirmed election results to be announced by the commission the next day at Gallagher Estate and the country quiet, we open a bottle of whisky; in fact, a few. Most of the team who made it happen are present. There is shaking of heads, smiles and laughter. We are too tired and the drink goes to our heads, as whisky does. It is finally over. I go home to Caroline and the children. It is their time now.

Some days later Eddie Hendrickx and Jules Koninckx, together with telecommunications guru Willem Ellis and some of the Telkom team, relax in a game park in the north of the country. After a braai and some beers, they lie on the bushveld grass gazing at the Southern Cross in the immense starry sky. They fall asleep on the veld.

On Tuesday, 10 May 1994, Caroline and I stand in the small amphitheatre of the Union Buildings in Pretoria and watch Nelson Mandela ascend the stairs to the podium where he will be sworn in as our new president. The chief of the South African Defence Force, General George Meiring, marches closely behind him. It is history. It cannot be stopped.

APPENDIX

Piet Koekemoer, the man who built the election bombs, turned out to be a police informer who worked for the police intelligence unit. He gave evidence against the perpetrators in their trials. He was later relocated in terms of the witness protection programme of the TRC.

Clifton Barnard and Koper Myburgh were eventually arrested and convicted for the election bombings. They were not prepared to apply for amnesty to the Truth and Reconciliation Commission, as it represented, in their view, 'the humiliation of the Boerevolk'.

Etienne le Roux and Johan 'Duppie' du Plessis were each sentenced to an effective twenty-nine years in prison for their part in the blasts at Bree Street in Johannesburg, in Germiston and at Jan Smuts Airport. They were released after receiving amnesty from the TRC in December 1999. Abie Fourie was sentenced to an effective twenty-one years in prison for his role in the election bombings. He now lives with one of his children, after receiving amnesty from the TRC in December 1999.

Gert Fourie stayed on the run for three months before being arrested on a farm in Brits. He was given an effective twenty-one-year prison sentence for his part in the Pretoria pipe-bomb attack on Sannie's Café. Together with the other Pretoria pipe-bombers, Jacobus Nel and Peet Steyn, Gert Fourie was released after receiving amnesty from the TRC in December 1999. The Carletonville and Randfontein pipe-bombers received amnesty from the TRC at the same time.

Johan 'Vlokkie' Vlok went on the run after the Germiston bomb. He evaded arrest for two years and three months before being caught in Germiston in 1996. He and Jan de Wet were released after receiving amnesty from the TRC in December 1999.

In 1997, Eugène Terre'Blanche, the AWB leader, was sentenced to a six-year prison sentence for assaulting a black petrol attendant and for the attempted murder of a security guard. After his release in 2004, he claimed that he had moderated his racist views and become a born-again Christian. He was murdered at his farm on Saturday, 3 April 2010. Two young farmworkers in the employ of Terre'Blanche have been charged with his murder.

Thele Moema was appointed to the national team that supervised the restructuring and integration of intelligence services in the new democracy.

Judge Johann Kriegler was appointed to the Constitutional Court of South Africa in 1994.

Chief Mangosuthu Buthelezi was appointed minister of home affairs in the cabinet of President Nelson Mandela in South Africa's first post-apartheid government.

Zac Yacoob and Dikgang Moseneke were appointed to the Constitutional Court of South Africa in 1998 and 2004 respectively.

Two separate detailed investigations failed to identify the hacker or hackers who sabotaged the electronic count and almost stopped South Africa's first democratic election. There were no traces. Gone.